Hands-On Serverless Applications with Kotlin

Develop scalable and cost-effective web applications using
AWS Lambda and Kotlin

Hardik Trivedi
Ameya Kulkarni

BIRMINGHAM - MUMBAI

Hands-On Serverless Applications with Kotlin

Commissioning Editor: Richa Tripathi
Acquisition Editor: Sandeep Mishra
Content Development Editor: Anugraha Arunagiri
Technical Editor: Bharat Patil
Copy Editor: Muktikant Garimella
Project Coordinator: Ulhas Kambali
Proofreader: Safis Editing
Indexer: Priyanka Dhadke
Graphics: Tania Dutta
Production Coordinator: Shantanu Zagade

First published: September 2018

Production reference: 1280918

Published by Packt Publishing Ltd.
Livery Place
35 Livery Street
Birmingham
B3 2PB, UK.

ISBN 978-1-78899-370-8

www.packt.com

mapt.io

Mapt is an online digital library that gives you full access to over 5,000 books and videos, as well as industry leading tools to help you plan your personal development and advance your career. For more information, please visit our website.

Why subscribe?

- Spend less time learning and more time coding with practical eBooks and Videos from over 4,000 industry professionals

- Improve your learning with Skill Plans built especially for you

- Get a free eBook or video every month

- Mapt is fully searchable

- Copy and paste, print, and bookmark content

Packt.com

Did you know that Packt offers eBook versions of every book published, with PDF and ePub files available? You can upgrade to the eBook version at www.packt.com and as a print book customer, you are entitled to a discount on the eBook copy. Get in touch with us at customercare@packtpub.com for more details.

At www.packt.com, you can also read a collection of free technical articles, sign up for a range of free newsletters, and receive exclusive discounts and offers on Packt books and eBooks.

Contributors

About the authors

Hardik Trivedi is a self-taught computer programmer. He has worked on Android and Java since 2010 and has immersed himself in Kotlin and JavaScript. Apart from client projects, he loves contributing back to the development community by spending time on Stack Overflow and writing tech blogs. Hardik also mentors college students, professionals, and companies are interested in mobile app development. He is also an active community speaker.

At Packt, I would like to thank Sandeep Mishra, who believed in me and gave me the opportunity to write this book. I would like to thank Anugraha, Bharat, and the entire copy editing team, who helped me to improve the quality of the book by doing reviews.

Ameya Kulkarni has 8 years of work experience in the IT industry. He is adept with JVM technologies, Golang, designing microservice-based architectures, and DevOps. He has been working with Webonise for the past six years and as a Vice President, Engineering, for the last three years. He has a good grip at agile and lean product development. He likes designing solutions and consulting businesses to augment their core abilities with technology. He has experience of building scalable and distributed systems using JVM technologies.

This book is based on research that I did on serverless architecture using Kotlin as a programming language. I am thankful to my family. They are the ones who kept me and this book going.

I wrote this book while working at Webonise Lab. I would like to thank all my colleagues there, especially Rob Katz, Rich Davis, Saurav Mishra, Vijay Kumbhar, Nayan Deshmukh, Bhuvan Khanna, Sachidanand Kulkarni, Atul Jadhav, Pradeep Patil, Alok Choudhary, Vijayraj Nathe, and Hardik Trivedi, my former-colleague and the co-author of this book, for their unwavering support while I embarked on this literary journey. I could not have done this without you all.

About the reviewer

Peter Sommerhoff is the founder of CodeAlong.tv and teaches more than 40,000 learners from around the globe how to code, combining the foundations of software development with plenty of hands-on practice. He holds a master's degree in Computer Science from RWTH Aachen University in Germany.

Peter is most passionate about Kotlin, and has distilled his knowledge about the language into his book, *Kotlin for Android App Development*—an in-depth and practical introduction to Kotlin that guides you through the language, interoperating with Java, and writing two Android apps purely in Kotlin.

When he's not teaching, he enjoys learning new things, cooking food, playing badminton, and going on biking tours.

Packt is searching for authors like you

If you're interested in becoming an author for Packt, please visit `authors.packtpub.com` and apply today. We have worked with thousands of developers and tech professionals, just like you, to help them share their insights with the global tech community. You can make a general application, apply for a specific hot topic that we are recruiting an author for, or submit your own idea.

Table of Contents

Preface

Introduction

Serverless architecture allows you to build and run applications and services without having to manage the infrastructure. This book will be your companion and guide to designing serverless architectures for your applications with AWS and Kotlin. This book will help you build the client application and the backend functions serving it.

The book will begin with an explanation of the fundamentals of serverless architecture and the working of AWS lambda functions. You will then learn to build, release, and deploy your application to production. You will also learn to log and test your application and build a serverless API. You will then learn to troubleshoot and monitor your app and AWS lambda programming concepts with API references. Moving on, you will learn how to scale up serverless applications and handle distributed serverless systems in production. By the end of the book, you will be equipped with the knowledge needed to build scalable and cost-efficient Kotlin applications with the serverless framework.

Who this book is for

This book is intended for technical practitioners who have some experience in building mobile applications with cloud-based API services using JVM technologies, such as Java, Groovy, and Kotlin. It is desirable that you have some knowledge about how such systems are managed and maintained from an infrastructural point of view. You are also expected to have some experience in developing REST APIs on traditional monolithic architectures.

This book is intended to be an introduction to serverless architecture and its associated tooling. The code accompanying this book was developed on macOS systems using IntelliJ Idea IDE Community Edition Kotlin and Gradle. You should set up the appropriate tools on your machines as per your platform choice (Linux or Windows).

By the end of this book, you will be familiar with the various AWS offerings that are required for building modern applications backed by serverless APIs, as well as the tooling that is required for developing, deploying, monitoring, and supporting such systems.

What this book covers

Chapter 1, *Basics of Serverless*, will enable you to understand serverless architectures, along with how to recognize them. You will gain insights into serverless applications by comparing them with traditional architectures. Lastly, you will have a brief overview of the Serverless ecosystem, consisting of providers and tooling.

Chapter 2, *AWS Serverless Offerings*, will introduce the concepts of AWS lambda and explain the concepts, intuition, and the components involved in the tool. It also explains the nuances involved in security, user controls, and versioning code inside AWS lambda.

Chapter 3, *Designing a Kotlin Serverless Application*, will analyze a case study of a serverless application entirely using Kotlin.

Chapter 4, *Developing Your Serverless Application*, will develop your serverless application using Kotlin and AWS by analyzing a case study.

Chapter 5, *Improve Your App with Firebase Service*, will improve your application using Firebase services.

Chapter 6, *Analyzing Your Application*, will cover how to log the important events of your application and best practices for logging your application behavior using AWS.

Chapter 7, *Secure Your Application*, will cover the hardening of your Kotlin AWS serverless application and best practices for granting secure access to your application.

Chapter 8, *Scale Your Application*, will discuss the practice of scaling up serverless architectures for large workloads using a number of third-party tools.

Chapter 9, Advanced AWS Services, will leverage advanced AWS services to extend the functionality of the application.

To get the most out of this book

This book focuses more on practical aspects than it does on theoretical ones. In each chapter, you will see a perfect blend of theory and practice. This book will explain each and every necessary step and line of code with screen captures, code snippets, and other practical examples. By the end of the book, you will have a deployment-ready application written in Kotlin that uses a serverless approach. You will see how to use architectures and design patterns to write scalable code. You will also see how Firebase works with Kotlin.

You will need to have the following software installed on your local system:

1. Intellij IDEA CE IDE 2018.2
2. Gradle
3. Node.js and NPM
4. Docker
5. JDK1.8

Download the example code files

You can download the example code files for this book from your account at www.packt.com. If you purchased this book elsewhere, you can visit www.packt.com/support and register to have the files emailed directly to you.

You can download the code files by following these steps:

1. Log in or register at www.packt.com.
2. Select the **SUPPORT** tab.
3. Click on **Code Downloads & Errata**.
4. Enter the name of the book in the **Search** box and follow the onscreen instructions.

Once the file is downloaded, please make sure that you unzip or extract the folder using the latest version of:

- WinRAR/7-Zip for Windows
- Zipeg/iZip/UnRarX for Mac
- 7-Zip/PeaZip for Linux

The code bundle for the book is also hosted on GitHub at https://github.com/ PacktPublishing/-Hands-On-Serverless-with-Kotlin. In case there's an update to the code, it will be updated on the existing GitHub repository.

We also have other code bundles from our rich catalog of books and videos available at https://github.com/PacktPublishing/. Check them out!

Conventions used

There are a number of text conventions used throughout this book.

`CodeInText`: Indicates code words in text, database table names, folder names, filenames, file extensions, pathnames, dummy URLs, user input, and Twitter handles. Here is an example: "Mount the downloaded `WebStorm-10*.dmg` disk image file as another disk in your system."

A block of code is set as follows:

```
"x-amazon-apigateway-request-validators": {
"Validate body": {
"validateRequestParameters": false,
"validateRequestBody": true
}
```

When we wish to draw your attention to a particular part of a code block, the relevant lines or items are set in bold:

```
"parameters":[
{
"name":"pollId",
"in":"path",
}
```

Any command-line input or output is written as follows:

```
$ mkdir css
$ cd css
```

Bold: Indicates a new term, an important word, or words that you see on screen. For example, words in menus or dialog boxes appear in the text like this. Here is an example: "Select **System info** from the **Administration** panel."

 Warnings or important notes appear like this.

 Tips and tricks appear like this.

Get in touch

Feedback from our readers is always welcome.

General feedback: If you have questions about any aspect of this book, mention the book title in the subject of your message and email us at customercare@packtpub.com.

Errata: Although we have taken every care to ensure the accuracy of our content, mistakes do happen. If you have found a mistake in this book, we would be grateful if you would report this to us. Please visit www.packt.com/submit-errata, selecting your book, clicking on the Errata Submission Form link, and entering the details.

Piracy: If you come across any illegal copies of our works in any form on the internet, we would be grateful if you would provide us with the location address or website name. Please contact us at copyright@packt.com with a link to the material.

If you are interested in becoming an author: If there is a topic that you have expertise in and you are interested in either writing or contributing to a book, please visit authors.packtpub.com.

Reviews

Please leave a review. Once you have read and used this book, why not leave a review on the site that you purchased it from? Potential readers can then see and use your unbiased opinion to make purchase decisions, we at Packt can understand what you think about our products, and our authors can see your feedback on their book. Thank you!

For more information about Packt, please visit packt.com.

1
Basics of Serverless

Serverless computing is the latest advancement in the ever-changing technical landscape of the internet era. This advancement offers a new perspective on the development and deployment of modern production-grade systems, delivering cutting-edge user experiences. It is a constantly evolving realm, and, true to the nature of the software industry, it is improving its tooling and frameworks. It's worth looking over an introduction to the basics of serverless computing in order to better understand it.

This chapter will cover the following topics:

- Understanding serverless architectures
- Why serverless, and why now?
- Diving into serverless computing with a use case
- The pros and cons of serverless
- The serverless computing ecosystem

What is serverless computing?

The official literature of **Amazon Web Services** (**AWS**), one of the de facto serverless providers, defines serverless computing as follows:

> *Serverless Computing allows you to build and run applications and services without thinking about servers. Serverless applications don't require you to provision, scale, and manage any servers. You can build them for nearly any type of application or backend service, and everything required to run and scale your application with high availability is handled for you.*

> *It's worth exploring the implications of this definition as our first step into the serverless world.*

> *....build and run applications and services without thinking about servers.*

Producing software involves much more than just writing code. The code that the development team writes exists to solve a real-world problem, and needs to be available to the intended audience. For your code to serve the world, it (traditionally) has to exist on a server. The server itself has to be created (provisioned) and made capable of handling the workload that the business demands. The capabilities of a server are defined in many ways, like its processing power, memory capacity, and network throughput, just to name a few. These parameters are so vast and deep that they have spun up a vast market of jobs that businesses require. The jobs go by titles such as infrastructure management associate, operations associate, and, more recently, DevOps engineer.

It's the responsibility of these folks to evaluate and manage the hardware properties. That is what the definition highlights when it states, *thinking about servers.*

> *...Serverless applications don't require you to provision, scale, and manage any servers.*

Serverless computing takes away the aforementioned need to think about the servers and other hardware resources.

> *...nearly any type of application or backend service.*

As a paradigm, serverless computing can be applied to any solution that requires a backend or a piece of architecture and code that is not (or cannot) be exposed to the general public (loosely termed **clients**).

> *...everything required to run and scale your application with high availability is handled for you.*

In the serverless paradigm, there are computational hardware assets, like servers, the management of these computational assets is not the developer's concern.This turnkey management is offered on a pay-as-you-use models keeping the costs as high or as low as the utilisation of the assets necessitate.

So, serverless computing itself is a misleading term, or misnomer. There are computational hardware assets serving your code, but their management is the cloud providers' problem.

This frees the companies adopting this paradigm from the overhead of the mundane, but equally important, tasks of tending and managing systems that behave well in production. It allows them to have a laser-sharp focus on their most valuable task - that is, writing code.

The evolution of serverless computing

To better explain serverless computing, we will take a trip down memory lane and revisit the various paradigms used to host software, and the impact they have had on software design.

On-premise

On-premise servers were one of the earliest paradigms, where the companies producing software had to not only deal with designing, architecting, and writing the code, but also had to execute and create a rainbow of auxiliary activities and elements, as follows:

- Budgeting, purchasing, and arranging for real estate to host servers
- Budgeting and purchasing of bare metal computational and networking hardware
- Installation of computational assets
- Equilibrium of environment
- Authoring code
- Configuration and provisioning of servers
- Deployment strategies
- Designing and implementing strategies for high availability of the applications.
- Backup and restore mechanisms
- Performance and scalability
- Patch management and uptime

The typical makeup of such a company had a less-than-optimal ratio of the development team to the overall headcount, vastly slowing down the delivery of its most valuable proposition, which was designing and shipping software.

It is obvious, looking at the scope of the preceding work, that such a setup and work environment posed a lot of hurdles to the growth of the organizations, and had a direct impact on their bottom-line.

Colocation providers

Next, colocation providers came on the scene, with a business model to take away some of the responsibilities and provide services for a fee. They took away the need for companies to purchase real estate and other peripheral assets, like HVAC, by renting out such services for a fee.

They offered a turnkey solution for customers to house their own computational, networking assets for a charge. The customers still had to budget, purchase assets, and forecast their capacity requirements, even while renting out real estate.

Things got slightly better and the organizations grew leaner, but there were still a lot of activities to be done and elements to be created while supporting software development. These included the following:

- Budgeting and purchasing of bare metal computational and networking hardware
- Configuration and provisioning of servers
- Authoring code
- Deployment strategies
- Designing and implementing strategies for high availability of the applications.
- Backup and restore mechanisms
- Performance and scalability
- Patch management and uptime

Virtualization and IaaS

The colocation model worked well until the early 2000s. Organizations had to deal with managing a bare metal infrastructure, including things like server racks and network switches. Due to the sporadic nature of the internet traffic, most of the assets and bandwidth were not utilized in an optimum fashion.

While all of this was considered business as usual, innovation gifted the world with **platform virtualization**. This enabled the bare metal racks to host more than one server instance in a shared hardware fashion, without compromising security and performance. This was a primary step toward the inception of cloud computing, spawning the **pay-as-you-use** paradigm, which was very attractive to organizations looking to bump up their bottom-lines.

Amazon launched **Elastic Compute Cloud** (**EC2**), which rented out virtualized computational hardware in the cloud, with bare minimum OS configurations and the flexibility to consume as many hardware and network resources as required. This took away the need for organizations to perform approximated capacity planning, and made sure that the infrastructure costs were a function of traction that a business was breaking. This paradigm is called **Infrastructure as a Service (IaaS)**. It was widely adopted, and at a fast pace. The reduction in operational costs was the biggest driver behind its adoption.

At the same time, there were some activities that the company still had to undertake, as follows:

- Authoring code
- Configuration and provisioning of servers
- Deployment strategies
- Design of high availability
- Backup and restore mechanisms
- Performance and scalability
- Patch management and uptime

PaaS

The adoption of IaaS and cloud computing pushed innovation and churned out a paradigm called **PaaS**, or **Platform as a Service**. Leveraging the foundation set by IaaS, cloud providers started to abstract away services like load balancing, continuous integration and deployment, edge and traffic engineering, HA, and failover, into opinionated turnkey offerings. PaaS further reduced the responsibility spectrum of a company producing code to the following responsibilities:

- Architecting and designing systems
- Authoring code
- Maintenance and patch management

BaaS

PaaS enabled companies to focus solely on the backend and client application development. During this phase, applications and systems started to take a common shape. For example, almost every application requires a login, sign up, email, notifications, reporting, and so on.

Cloud providers leveraged this trend and started offering such common services as part of **Backend as a Service, or BaaS**. This enabled the companies to avoid reinventing the wheel, purchasing off-the-shelf products for common components. The management and uptime of such services are guaranteed as a part of **Service Level Agreements (SLAs)** by cloud providers.

Such an approach freed BaaS adopters up so that they could deliver rich and engaging user experiences, contributing to faster growth.

SaaS

Software as a Service (SaaS) is a special type of Software as a Service model, where companies purchase entire systems, whitelist them, and offer them as a part of the solution that they provide. For example, Intercom.io provides an in-app messaging solution that drives up customer support.

Adopters and customers offload parts of their systems to specialized providers, who excel at offering such solutions to build it in-house.

FaaS

For all of the benefits that BaaS and SaaS provide, companies still have to incorporate bespoke feedback into products, and they often feel the need to retain control of some of the business logic that comprises the backend.

This control and flexibility doesn't have to be achieved at the cost of the benefits of BaaS, SaaS, and PaaS. Companies, having tasted the benefits of such big strides in infrastructure management don't want to add costs to managing and maintaining hardware, whether bare metal or in the cloud.

This is where a new paradigm, **Function as a Service (FaaS)**, has evolved to fill the gap.

Function as a Service is a paradigm wherein a function is a computation unit and building block of backend services. Formally, a function is a computation that takes some input and produces some output. At times, it produces side effects and modifies state out of its memory, and at times, it doesn't.

What's true in both of the cases is that a function should be called, its temporal execution boundary should be defined (that is, it should run in a time-boxed manner), and it should produce output that is consumable by downstream components, or available for perusal at a later time.

If one was to architect their backend service code along these lines, they would end up with an ephemeral computational unit that gets called or triggered to do its job by an upstream stimulus, performs the computation/processing, and returns or stores the output. In all of this execution, one is not worried about the environment that the function runs in. All one needs, in such a scenario, is code (or a function) that is guaranteed to perform the desired calculation in a determined time.

The runtime for the code, the upstream stimulus, and the downstream chaining, should be taken care of by the entity that provides such an environment. Such an entity is called a **serverless computing provider,** and the paradigm is called Function as a Service, or Serverless Computing.

The advantages of such an architecture, along with the benefits of BaaS and SaaS, are as follows:

- Flexibility and control
- The ability to deliver the discrete and atomic components of the system
- Faster time to market

Serverless computing

Serverless paradigms started as FaaS, but have grown, and are beginning to encompass BaaS offerings as well. As described previously, this is an ever-changing landscape, and the two concepts of FaaS and BaaS are coalescing into one, called **serverless computing**. As it stands today, the distinction is blurring, and it's difficult to say that serverless is pure FaaS. This is an important point to note.

To create modern serverless apps, FaaS is necessary, but not sufficient.

For example, a production-grade service that can crunch numbers in isolation can be created by using only FaaS. But a system that has user-facing components requires much more than a simple, ephemeral computational component.

Serverless – the time is now

In the past decade or so, investments in hardware and innovations in the tools that optimize hardware have paid off. Hardware has become a commodity. The era of expensive computational assets is long gone. With the advent and adoption of virtualization, renting hardware is a walk in the park, and is often the only option for companies that do not have the resources or inclination to bootstrap an on-premise infrastructure.

With the sky being the limit for current hardware capabilities, the onus is on software to catch up and leverage this. Serverless is the latest checkpoint in this evolution. Commoditized hardware and rapidly commoditizing allied software tooling enables companies to further reduce their operational costs and make a direct impact on their bottom-line. The question is not really whether companies will adopt the serverless paradigm, but when.

This revolution is happening now, and it is here to stay. The time is now for serverless!

Diving into serverless computing with a use case

In this section, we'll how a real-life serverless application looks. First, we will review what we have seen before, and we will then try to slice and dice a traditional system into one that fits the serverless paradigm.

A review of serverless computing

In the previous sections, we touched upon the basics of the serverless paradigm and saw how systems in production evolved to arrive at this point.

To recap, the serverless architecture started as Function as a Service, but has grown to be much more than just ephemeral computational units.

Serverless abstracts away the humdrum but critical (scalability, maintenance, and so on) and functional but standard (email, notifications, logging, and so on) pieces of your system, into a flexible offering that can be consumed on demand. This is like a case of build versus buy, where a decision to buy is made, but at a fraction of the upfront cost.

Comparing and contrasting traditional and serverless paradigms

It's worthwhile to compare and contrast the traditional and serverless paradigms of building systems using a case study.

The case study of an application

Let's assume that we are a services company that builds software for our clients. We get contracted to build an opinion poll system on the current state of technology. Users can only log in to this system using their Facebook credentials. Users can create polls that other users can participate in. They can also invite people to participate in the polls that they have created. Finally, they can see the outcomes of their polls.

This system has to be audited and monitored, and should be readily scalable. The functionality of the system has to be exposed via a mobile app.

The functional requirements are as follows:

- As a user, I should be able to sign in to the application using my Facebook credentials
- As a user, I should be able to create a poll of my choice
- As a user, I should be able to invite people to participate in my polls
- As a user, I should be able to participate in the polls
- As a user, I should be able to check the results of my polls

The non-functional requirements are as follows:

- As a system, I should be able to keep track of all activities performed by all users
- As a system, I should be able to scale horizontally and transparently
- As a system, I should be able to be monitored, and deviations from standard operations should be reported back

The architecture of the system using traditional methods

The following diagram shows how the system would look if it was created and developed in the traditional way:

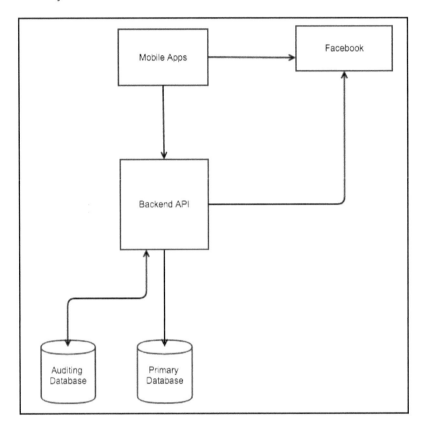

At a high level, the preceding diagram shows the moving parts of the system, as follows:

- Mobile app
- Backend APIs, consisting of the following modules:
    - Social sign-in module
    - Opinion poll module
    - Logging module
    - Notification module
    - Reporting module

- Facebook as an **identity provider** (iDP)
- Primary database
- Auditing database

In this setup, we are responsible for the following:

- Development of all of the backend API modules, like polling, notification, logging, auditing, and so on
- Deployment of all backend API modules
- Design and development of the mobile app
- Management of the databases
- Scalability
- High availability

In production, such a topology would almost definitely require two servers each for high availability for the primary database, auditing database, and backend APIs.

In addition to the preceding topology, we would require the following (or equivalent) toolchain, required for all of the preceding non-functional requirements:

- Nagios, for monitoring
- Pagerduty, for notifications
- Jenkins, for CI
- Puppet, for configuration management

This traditional architecture, though proven, has significant drawbacks, as follows:

- Monolithic structure.
- Single point of failure of backend APIs. For example, if the API layer goes down due to a memory leak in the reporting module, the entire system becomes unavailable. It affects the more business-critical portions of the system, like the polling module.
- The reinvention of the wheel, rewriting standard notification services like email, SMS, and log aggregation.
- Dedicated hardware to cater to the SLAs of HA and uptime.
- Dedicated backup and restore mechanisms.
- The overhead of deploying teams for maintenance.

The architecture of the system using the serverless paradigm

The following diagram shows how the system would look if the serverless paradigm was used:

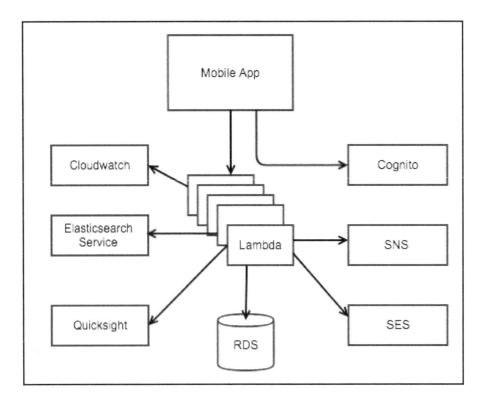

Its salient features are as follows:

- The primary RDBMS has been replaced by an **AWS RDS (AWS Relational Database Service)**. RDS takes care of provisioning, patching, scaling, backing up, and restoring mechanisms for us. All we have to do is design the DB schema.
- The social sign-in module is replaced by AWS Cognito, which helps us to leverage Facebook (or any well-known social network). Using this, we can implement AuthN and AuthZ modules in our system in a matter of minutes.
- The notification modules have been replaced by AWS **Simple Email Service (SES)** and AWS **Simple Notification Service (SNS)**, which offer turnkey solutions to implement the notification functionality in our system.
- The auditing DB has been replaced with the AWS ElasticSearch service and AWS CloudWatch in order to implement a log aggregation solution.

- The reporting and analysis module can be substituted with AWS Quicksight, which offers analysis and data visualization services.
- The core business logic is extracted into AWS Lambda functions, which can be configured to execute various events in the system.
- The maintenance of the system is managed by AWS, and load scaling is handled transparently.
- Monitoring of the system can be implemented by leveraging AWS CloudWatch and AWS SNS.

This architecture also enables us to develop our system in a micro-service based pattern, where there is an inherent failure tolerance due to highly cohesive and less coupled components, unlike with the traditional monolithic approach. The overhead for management is also reduced, and the costs come down drastically, as we are only charged for the resources we consume. Aside from this, we can focus on our core value proposition, that is, to design, develop, and deliver a cutting edge user experience.

Thus, we can clearly observe that serverless doesn't only mean ephemeral Functions as a Service, but includes mechanisms that deal with the implementation of peripheral (auditing and logging) and mission-critical (social identity management) components as turnkey solutions.

Traditional versus serverless, in a nutshell

The following table compares and contrasts the traditional and serverless ways of developing and deploying applications:

Parameter	Traditional	Serverless
Architectural style	Monolithic, SOA	Microservices-based
Time to market	Slower	Quicker time to market
Development velocity	Slow	Fast
Focus on core value proposition	Diffused	Laser focused
Infrastructure management overhead cost	High	Low
Deployment of code	Complex tooling	Simple as an upload of `.zip` or `.tar.gz`
Operational efficiency	Low	High

Pros and cons of serverless

Now that we have defined serverless computing, we will explore its pros and cons.

Advantages of serverless systems

The following sections will cover the advantages of serverless systems.

Reduced operational costs

The reduction in the operational costs of serverless systems is on two dimensions. There are upfront savings on hardware, and cost savings achieved by outsourcing infrastructure management activities.

Optimized resource utilization

For a system with sporadic or seasonal traffic, it doesn't make sense for companies to invest in the upkeep of hardware capacity catering to peak loads. Serverless empowers companies to design applications that scale up and down transparently, as per the demands of the load. This enables optimum resource utilization, saving costs and reducing the impact on the environment.

Faster time to market

The promise of serverless is to empower the developer to focus only on developing business logic and delivering cutting edge user experiences. Serverless stays true to this by abstracting away the infrastructure plumbing and wiring as a turnkey solution. The time to market is therefore greatly reduced.

For example, suppose that an API that you wrote is seeing exceptional traction. To further drive adoption and fuel growth, an Alexa skill seems like the perfect next level. Exposing the feature as an Alexa skill is easy, leveraging the already implemented integration of AWS Lambda and AWS Lex.

High-development velocity and laser-sharp focus on authoring code

As mentioned in the previous section, serverless empowers developers to have a laser-sharp focus on authoring business logic and new user experiences. This greatly accelerates the development velocity and enables a faster time to market.

Promoting a microservices architecture

The serverless paradigm is tailor-made for designing a system based on a microservices architecture. Because of the nature of how serverless computing providers offer their services, one ends up developing serverless systems as a set of loosely coupled and highly-cohesive systems, with separated concerns.

Although traditional architectures can be reimagined in a microservices-based architecture, there is a hidden cost with respect to the maintenance and infrastructural management that is not immediately visible, but becomes acute at scale.

The drawbacks of serverless systems

There are no free lunches in life, and serverless architectures come with their own set of drawbacks that have to be considered by architects creating such systems.

Nascent ecosystem

As discussed previously, the serverless paradigm is a recent advancement. There are teething problems, as is expected. The knowledge base of the serverless paradigm can be significantly smaller than those of its traditional counterparts. This can be attributed to it being a new paradigm, seeing a steady adoption curve. Nonetheless, troubleshooting and clearing blocker issues can be a daunting and time-consuming task, especially if one encounters a hitherto unknown issue.

Yielding of control

As with cloud computing, adopters of the serverless paradigm make a conscious decision to host their artifacts in the cloud provider's infrastructure. This is referred to as **yielding control** to the providers. It is obvious that the production systems are exposed to the vagaries of the environment of the provider. Internal issues affecting the providers indirectly affect your production systems. The big players in the market, like AWS, Google, and Azure, among others, invest heavily in mitigating and reducing such impacts, but there are times when things do go south. Adopters need to take cognizance of this fact and design their serverless systems to be adaptable and fault tolerant.

For example, during the outage in the AWS US-East-1 region in early 2017, adopters that relied solely on the service uptime guarantee of AWS faced significant outage. But adopters that had a backup planned for it, like Netflix, did not face any outage.

For systems requiring stricter compliance, serverless might not be a fair choice to make, as typically, such compliances require on-premise and strictly controlled hardware.

Opinionated offerings

As mentioned previously, Serverless is not only Function as a Service, but encompasses other peripheral and mission-critical components, abstracted away as turnkey offerings. Because they are abstracted away, these offerings are designed in an opinionated manner that the provider deems appropriate. This takes some of the flexibility away from the adopters when they want to support a custom use case for their systems.

Provider limits

Although serverless claims to work on a *share nothing* paradigm, the reality is that providers operate in a multi-tenant fashion. To cater to every customer based on a fair usage policy, providers enforce limits to avoid resource hogging.

Limits are typically enforced on the duration of the execution, the size of the function, network utilization, storage capacity, memory usage, thread count, request and response size, and the number of concurrent executions per customer. These limits will be increased as more and more hardware capacity is added, but there will always be a hard stop. Serverless systems need to be designed with these limits in mind.

Standardized and provider-agnostic offerings

Because the serverless ecosystem is at a nascent state, there is no standardized implementation of services across vendors. This makes an adopter lock in to a vendor. While that is not necessarily a bad thing in the case of established players like AWS or Google, there are business requirements that mandate a provider migration. This exercise is in no way trivial, and can incur significant rewrites.

Tooling

It is early in the days of serverless systems, and the toolchain is still evolving. As compared to their traditional counterparts, who have battle-tested and widely adopted tooling for building, deployment, configuration management, monitoring, and so on, serverless systems don't have a standardized, go-to tooling chain. However, frameworks like serverless are quickly evolving to fill this gap.

Competition from containers

Containers are another exciting paradigm, providing new ways to develop modern systems. They tend to solve some of the issues of serverless, like limitless scaling, flexibility, control, and testability, but at the cost of maintainability. The adoption of Docker and Kubernetes has been on the rise, and has yielded many success stories.

There will be a time when the concepts of serverless and containers will merge and create a hybrid paradigm, leveraging the best of both worlds. It is indeed an exciting time.

Rethinking serverless

There are some concepts in serverless architectures that are not immediately obvious to someone seasoned in developing systems the traditional way. Although these are not necessarily drawbacks of serverless architectures, their ramifications need be examined as well as those that precipitate a change in the well-established mindset of the adopter.

Let's take a look at some of them, in detail.

An absence of local states

In traditional architectures, because the code is guaranteed to execute in a single runtime, it is taken for granted that it is possible to chain or pipe output from one component to another. This is called a **local state**. Because serverless systems are in fact ephemeral computational units, it is impossible to pass the local state created or mutated as a part of the computation to downstream functions or components without storing it in a temporary datastore.

It is important to note that this is not necessarily a drawback, as modern systems are recommended to be stateless, and should share nothing. However, it takes a significant mindset shift, especially for new serverless adopters.

For example, with the AuthN of REST API, created using AWS Lambda, creating sticky sessions (like one would in a traditional web application) is impossible. AuthN is achieved by using bearer authentication. The clients are identified by tokens, which are issued for the first time and are subsequently sent in every request. Such tokens have to be stored in read and write optimized datastores, like Redis. These tokens can then be accessed by the ephemeral functions by performing a simple lookup. This is a simple example to eliminate the need of using local state.

Applying modern software development practices

The nascent nature of serverless architectures makes it difficult to develop them by applying modern development practices, like CI, versioning, deployment, unit testing, and so on. Tooling platforms like serverless are quickly creating mechanisms to enable this, but those might not be very obvious to a new adopter coming from a traditional mindset.

Time-boxed execution

As we explained previously, serverless systems' building blocks are ephemeral functions that execute in a time-boxed manner. The corollary to this is obvious; each function has to have a well-defined execution boundary. So, the ideal candidates to run as Functions as a Service are deterministic computations that are guaranteed to return execution results in a finite amount of time. Adopters have to be careful when architecting long-running, probabilistic jobs in a serverless manner. Running such jobs can incur heavy costs, which defeats the purpose of adopting serverless.

Startup latency

Serverless' building blocks are ephemeral and time-boxed functions that get executed based on specific triggers or events, generated upstream of the execution. The runtime for these functions are configured and provisioned by the providers on demand. In the case of a runtime that requires some startup time, like JVM, the execution time of the function is buffered by the time taken for the startup. This can be a tricky situation for real-time operations, as it presents a lagging user experience. There are, of course, workarounds for such problems, but this has to be taken into account when creating solutions powered by serverless architectures.

Testability

The development of traditional systems has been governed by a well-defined protocol for integration testing. Applying that knowledge to the serverless world is tricky, and often requires jumping through hoops to achieve it. Because serverless systems run in ephemeral environments, with an inability to chain output to downstream components, integration testing is not as straightforward as it is in traditional systems.

Debugging

Because serverless systems run in environments not under the adopters' control, debugging issues in production can be difficult. In traditional systems, one could attach a remote debugger to the production runtime when troubleshooting issues. Such a mechanism is not possible in the serverless world. Previously, the only way to work around this was to instrument the code execution. But providers have taken cognizance of this fact and are shipping tooling to support this. It is not complete and overarching, but the tooling will get there in due time.

It is important to note that even these drawbacks are not really deal breakers; there are workarounds for them, and, as the serverless paradigm evolves and the tooling gets standardized, we will see their impact being mitigated in the near future.

The serverless computing ecosystem

Now that we have explored what the serverless paradigm is in detail – its evolution, and its pros and cons – let's take a look at the current serverless ecosystem and its landscape.

Serverless computers and infrastructure providers

The most important entity in the serverless world is the provider. A **serverless cloud provider** is an entity that takes care of hardware provisioning, runtime configuration and bootstrapping, creating turnkey solutions, and all of the plumbing required to support a serverless system and offer it as a packaged solution.

The following sections will cover the current big players in the ecosystem.

AWS Lambda

AWS Lambda is perhaps the most complete and well-known FaaS provider on the market. Since it's a great contribution to the serverless world, it is often mistakenly considered as the only serverless offering on the market. Although there are other providers, the adoption of AWS and Lambda's deep integration with other AWS offerings often make this the de facto choice of provider, all of the other factors, like budget, notwithstanding.

It only supports 64-bit binaries, and the OS version is the Amazon flavored, Linux-based on CentOS.

It offers the following runtime to code your functions:

- **Node.js**: v8.10, 4.3.2, and 6.10.3

- **Java**: 8

- **Python**: 3.6 and 2.7

- **.NET Core**: 1.0.1 and 2.0

- **Go**: 1.x

IBM OpenWhisk

IBM OpenWhisk is the Apache Incubator open source serverless platform that IBM has adopted, and it offers FaaS as a part of its IBM Cloud offering. The official name of the service is IBM Cloud Functions.

It supports the following runtime environments: JavaScript (Node.js), Swift, Python, PHP, Java, Binary Compatible Executable, and Docker.

Microsoft Azure Cloud Functions

Microsoft's cloud offering, Azure, has its own FaaS offering, called Azure Cloud Functions.

There are two versions of its runtime, as follows:

- Version 1.x is the only one approved for production use, and is **general availability (GA)**
- Version 2.x is experimental, and in preview

Overall, it offers the following runtime: C#, JavaScript, F#, Java, Python, PHP, TypeScript, batch executables, bash executables, and PowerShell executables.

As of the time of writing this book, most of them are in experimental and preview states. The versions 1.x for Javascript, C#, and F#, are GA, and approved for production use. Microsoft has big plans for Azure Cloud Functions. Check the `roadmap` for the current status of the Azure Cloud Functions.

Google Cloud Functions

Google Cloud platform's FaaS offering is called Google Cloud Functions. It is in the beta stage, and the API will change for the better.

At the time of writing this literature, it only supports Node.js as a runtime.

Auth0 Webtasks

Auth0 is a BaaS offering, providing a solution for identity management. Recently, it moved into FaaS by offering Webtask as a serverless platform.

It offers Node.js as a runtime environment, for functions that can be triggered via an HTTP endpoint.

Others

Other serverless providers include the following:

- `Spotinst`: Spotinst is an interesting provider that automates cloud-agnostic FaaS orchestration. It also provides Containers as a Service across multiple cloud providers, like AWS, Azure, Alibaba Cloud, and so on.
- `Kubless`: This is a Kubernetes native FaaS framework that allows ephemeral functions to be developed on top of Kubernetes.
- `Iron.io`: Iron.io is a serverless provider, offering solutions like message queue, caching, functions, and Containers as a Service, at a scale that was recently open sourced.

Serverless toolkits

As discussed earlier in this chapter, the biggest chink in the armor of the serverless promise is the absence of standardization in implementing and tooling. This is not a drawback so much as a work in progress.

The traction that serverless architecture is gaining is spawning a lot of innovation, and startups are coming up with interesting offerings to fill the gaps that the current ecosystem has. The gaps that the tooling platforms have to fill are the deployment, configuration, and monitoring concerns.

Serverless is the biggest player, actively blazing a trail while creating a toolkit that eases up the aforementioned tasks of serverless computing. It enables you to focus on your code, and not on the operations of your FaaS environments.

The other toolkits in this ecosystem are Clay, NodeLambda, Back&, Synk, and so on, each aimed at solving niche and overlapping problems in the serverless ecosystem.

There is so much traction in this space that we will continue to see newer and more powerful tools at a breakneck speed. Cautious evaluation and due diligence are a must while selecting the right platform and toolkit to adopt the serverless paradigm.

Summary

In this chapter, we covered the basics of serverless computing. We went over the evolution of serverless computing, its pros and cons, and the current state of the ecosystem. The last decade's innovation in hardware has given rise to an inventory of very high computational power at commodity hardware prices. Now, the software is catching up with the hardware advancements and churning out different paradigms to deploy modern software systems, like virtualization, cloud computing, PaaS, IaaS, BaaS, FaaS, and so on, presenting developers with a variety of options to design, architect, and deploy their systems.

Serverless computing started as pure FaaS, but it is rapidly converging with BaaS concepts, and the lines will continue to blur. The cost savings that manifest because of the adoption of serverless are so attractive that there is a revolution underway to adopt this paradigm, and for good reason. Teams are getting leaner and more laser focused. Turnkey serverless offerings are speeding up the time to market.

Although there are high praises for serverless, one must proceed cautiously when adopting this paradigm, especially if one is coming from a traditional background. The absence of a local state, potential startup latencies, and so on, are some of the caveats that must be kept in mind while designing a serverless application. Although these are not drawbacks in the real sense of the term, cognizance has to be given in an opinionated manner while developing serverless systems.

The cloud-native nature of the serverless paradigm inherently makes an adopter provider dependent. This might have ramifications for security, compliance, and so on, for companies that have a strict demand for it. This is being rapidly addressed by the big cloud providers, employing a compliance-first strategy while packaging their serverless offerings. The key takeaway here is that the adopters must take due diligence while embarking on this journey.

Some of the biggest and most dependable serverless providers are Amazon Web Services, Microsoft Azure, and Google Cloud Engine, among others. As we explore the serverless landscape in this book, we will dive into the serverless offerings of Amazon Web Services. We will also explore some of the toolkits that can simplify the adoption of serverless systems even further.

AWS Serverless Offerings 2

In Chapter 1, *Basics of Serverless*, we entered the serverless mindset, covering the definition and evolution of serverless computing. We also listed the various serverless providers and their offerings. AWS, with its early adoption of FaaS and BaaS services and their deep integration with each other, is a good choice for developing serverless applications.

In this chapter, we will take a detailed look at the AWS serverless/FaaS offering, Lambda, and will explore its various aspects, as follows:

- Lambda execution environments
- Service limits
- Invocation types and event sources
- Supported Runtime environments
- Error handling and scaling
- Configuration
- Creating a deployment package of Lambda functions via the web console
- Testing Lambda functions
- Exposing a function as an API endpoint using the Amazon API Gateway
- Basic monitoring of Lambda functions
- Versioning of Lambda functions

 The next few chapters assume that the reader has basic knowledge of the AWS console and concepts like IAM roles and policies. It is recommended that the reader sign up *for an account and follow the flow of this book by doing hands on exercises*

AWS Lambda overview

Lambda is the FaaS offering from Amazon Web Services. It provides a platform to package functions as code and run them in an ephemeral environment. Let's explore this in a little more detail in the following sections.

Execution environment

AWS Lambda promises the execution of your code without a need to manage the underlying infrastructure. That doesn't mean that the underlying infrastructure and servers don't exist. They need to exist to provide an execution environment to the Lambda function. AWS manages them for you and abstracts away the nuts and bolts.

AWS maintains a fleet of machines to run the functions via various orchestration mechanisms. The underlying hardware is as follows:

- Public Amazon Linux **Amazon Machine Image** (**AMI**) (`https://docs.aws.amazon.com/AWSEC2/latest/UserGuide/AMIs.html`): More information about the Amazon flavor of Linux can be found here (`https://aws.amazon.com/amazon-linux-ami/`). The AMI name is `amzn-ami-hvm-2017.03.1.20170812-x86_64-gp2`.
- At the time of writing this book, the Linux kernel version used internally is `4.9.93-41.60.amzn1.x86_64`. This is subject to change and is at AWS' discretion. The reader can stay updated with the official documentation on AWS (`https://docs.aws.amazon.com/lambda/latest/dg/current-supported-versions.html`).

Service limits

FaaS, or, for that matter, any cloud offering, works on a shared and multi-tenant architecture. That means that the available inventory is earmarked to serve all of the customers of the provider. Naturally, this implies that the usage of services is capped at a sensible limit.

Lambda is no different. AWS puts a limit on the usage parameters of the service. Some of these limits can be increased by submitting a request to the AWS support center. The service team reviews and grants the approval if it makes business sense to them.

The following list enumerates the limits that are applied to each Lambda function at the time of writing this book. The official page has the latest numbers:

- **Memory allocation range**: 128 MB to 3,008 MB
- **Ephemeral disk capacity (**`/tmp` **space)**: 512 MB
- **Number of file descriptors**: 1,024
- **Total number of processes and threads**: 1,024
- **Maximum execution duration per request**: 300 seconds
- **Synchronous invocation request and response size**: 6 MB
- **Synchronous invocation request and response size**: 128 KB
- **Deployment package size (compressed)**: 50 MB
- **Cumulative size of all deployment packages**: 75 GB
- **Code size (uncompressed)**: 250 MB
- **Size of environment variables**: 4 KB
- **Number of concurrent executions per region**: 1,000

The above are subject to change and the reader can stay updated with the `AWS Lambda Service Limits official documentation` page.

Invocation types

As discussed previously, FaaS requires events as triggers to start the execution of the function. These are called the **invocation types**. Let's take a look at the invocation types in AWS Lambda.

There are two types in which a Lambda executes, as follows:

- **Synchronous**: Also called a `RequestResponse` invocation
- **Asynchronous**: Also called an `Event` invocation

Custom invocation via AWS CLI or embedded AWS SDK in an application

A typical use case would be an application that has its own memory space and custom business logic that decides to offload some of the background jobs to run in Lambda. An example would be a reporting job that runs at a fixed period of time.

Event sources from other AWS Services

Event sources are the upstream components of an FaaS that produce triggers and contexts that are wired to an AWS Lambda execution environment automatically, for the developer to consume. The following AWS Services event sources are supported by Lambda:

- **API Gateway**: The Amazon API Gateway is the turnkey solution to set up a production-grade API service. This can serve as the gatekeeper to Lambda functions. Using this, the developer can expose the function by REST verbs, like GET, PUT, POST, DELETE, and many more, over HTTPS.

- **AWS IoT Button**: The AWS IoT Button is a programmable button based on the Amazon Dash Button hardware, which can be configured to invoke a Lambda function. The developer can expose an IoT backend using this.

- **Alexa Skills Kit**: Developers can expose the existing APIs of their applications via a new user interface called Alexa Skills. Lambda functions configured to respond to an Alexa ask command get the **Natural Language Processing** (**NLP**) context, distilled by Lex, passed to them automatically.
  An example would be a platform for restaurant reservations having its core functionality exposed as a skill via an Alexa device. Lambda functions play a crucial role in piping the user's intent to the corresponding platform API.

- **Alexa Smart Home**: Similar to Alexa Skills, Lambda functions can augment smart home solutions powered by the Alexa Voice Assistant.

- **CloudFront**: CloudFront is AWS' **Content Delivery Network** (**CDN**) offering. Lambda functions configured to run as a response to Cloudfront events can deliver edge engineering at scale. A typical example would be applying interceptors and inspection logic on request headers, redirection, and rolling out an A/B testing scheme, among others.

- **CloudWatch Events**: CloudWatch is the AWS in-house monitoring solution that generates millions of events in response to changes in the state of the infrastructure. Lambda functions can be configured to tap into some of them, based on a rule engine, to augment the infrastructure management capability. A typical example would be a Lambda function that triggers a PagerDuty alert if operational thresholds are breached in order to signal a possible deviation from the norm.

- **CloudWatch Logs**: As mentioned earlier, CloudWatch is the monitoring solution. It generates events to audit the infrastructure state of a system. These events are piped into log files, called CloudWatch Logs. One can configure a Lambda function to consume these log files and roll out a custom log monitoring solution.

- **CodeCommit**: AWS CodeCommit is a hosted version control system from AWS. In this integration, events are generated when a developer pushes code to a branch, when a branch is merged, and so on. These events can be consumed by a Lambda function, which can execute code as a part of a continuous integration pipeline.
- **Cognito Sync Triggers**: AWS Cognito is an AuthN solution from AWS. Using Cognito, developers can get AuthN implemented into their system in a matter of minutes. Cognito Sync helps to synchronize user data, like preferences, tokens, and so on. Lambda functions can be set up to consume such events, and to sync such user data across all user devices. This helps to maintain consistency across all sessions pertaining to a user.
- **DynamoDB**: In a typical RDBMS environment, there is the concept of triggers, which is SQL code executed in response to **Data Modification Language** (**DML**) statement execution. Using Lambda functions, one can simulate such triggers in DynamoDB, which is a NoSQL store. This is a powerful combination. The only caveat is that the Lambda platform needs to poll DynamoDB to monitor for changes.
- **Kinesis Data Streams**: AWS Kinesis is the mechanism to ingest streaming data from a variety of sources into AWS. Lambda functions can be configured to consume these streams and apply a transformation logic to the incoming streaming packet. A typical example would be a pixel tracking mechanism that tracks all user interactions in the frontend and pushes them to AWS for further analysis. A Lambda function can intercept this packet and apply collation logic, like the filtering of duplicates.
- **S3**: The AWS **Simple Storage Service** (**S3**) is an offering that provides scalable and secure storage in the cloud. S3 is used to store files from a variety of sources. The files in S3 are stored in buckets. Lambda functions can be configured to execute in response to S3 bucket events. Typical S3 events that can invoke Lambda functions are file uploads to an S3 bucket or file deletes from an S3 bucket.
- **SNS**: The AWS **Simple Notification Service** (**SNS**) is a mechanism to produce notifications in response to various upstream events. Lambda functions can be configured to consume these events and apply custom business logic to them.

The Lambda functions sourcing events from Kinesis Data Streams and DynamoDB work on a pull model. What this means is that the Lambda function has to be configured to poll these sources in order to decide whether execution should be triggered.

Executions triggered by the other sources work on a push model. Lambda functions execute as a part of a reaction to a published event.

The preconfigured event source mappings are the sets of events that can occur along with the corresponding parameters that are passed to a Lambda function.

AWS Lambda functions require permissions to access allied AWS Services in order to tap into the preconfigured event sources. These permissions are applied by an `IAM (AWS'` `offering for Identity and Access Management) role, called the` **execution role**. `There are various policies associated with an execution role when one creates a lambda function.`

Execution environments/runtimes

Now that we have familiarized ourselves with the invocation types and event sources, let's take a detailed look at the execution runtimes that Lambda supports, as follows:

- Java and other JVM languages: JRE 8
- Node.js: v8.10, v6.10, or v4.3
- Golang: Go 1.x
- Python: v3.6 and v2.7
- .NET Core: 1.0.1 and 2.0

The following sections will provide a brief overview of the components of an AWS Lambda execution environment.

Handler

The **handler** is the entry point to the Lambda function. It encapsulates the outermost boundary of the code that is to be executed. Think of it as the main function of your Lambda. It is the first frame that gets pushed into the execution stack, and the last one that gets popped during unwinding.

The handler gets passed the event data that triggers the execution and the context as parameters. The handler can call other functions as it sees fit.

A typical definition of a handler would look as follows, in a hypothetical programming language:

```
ReturnType FunctionName (InputType input ,Context ctx);
```

Lets have a look at the different components of the function signature -

- The `ReturnType` is the data structure that encapsulates the execution output.
- The `InputType` is the data structure that encapsulates the input to the Lambda function. These can be preconfigured or custom event sources.
- The `Context` is the object that encapsulates the execution environment that the function is executing in.

For Lambda functions written in JavaScript, which supports callbacks, a third parameter is passed to the function, which is exactly what it says on the tin: code that executes after the first function has finished execution. In this scenario, the Lambda signature is as follows:

```
ReturnType FunctionName(InputType input, Context ctx, Callback callback);
```

 The decision for the JSON serializing/deserializing of the `InputType` and `ReturnType` is taken by the Lambda runtime for the particular language. If a custom marshaling is to be adopted, the developer needs to deal with the byte stream representation of these types.

Context

The context is the second parameter passed by the Lambda execution environment to the function. It encapsulates the methods and attributes that enable the code to interact with the environment that it is running in.

A typical example would be accessing the environment variables that are bound in that context and gauging the statistics of the execution, like the execution time.

Logging

Logging is what it says on the tin: statements that get printed out during the execution of the function. They are helpful in instrumenting the code.

In a typical API, these are directed to either `StdOut` or a file using different appenders.

In AWS Lambda, they are piped to a CloudWatch log group, which can be inspected at a later time.

Exceptions and error handling

Depending on the execution environment, a Lambda execution function can have platform-specific constructs for signaling errors and exception handling. For Java, the try/catch semantics can be used. For GoLang, the error paradigm is used.

The Lambda platform takes care of serializing the error's context, like the cause, stacktrace, and so on, should an exception be thrown, and it also makes it available to the caller.

Storing the state

As mentioned previously, Lambda functions have to be designed in a stateless manner.

During the time of execution, the Lambda function has access to the memory and local filesystem, but after it terminates, the contents of that memory location are wiped away. It's impossible to get a handle on the same memory space during the next execution.

As a consequence of this mandate, it becomes incumbent on the developer to store the computational results of an execution in a cloud storage service, like S3 or DynamoDB, should they be required for downstream processing at a later time.

JVM execution environment

Now, let's explore how the preceding concepts apply to a Lambda executing in a JVM runtime environment, as we will be using one in later chapters of this book. The details of the other environments are included in the official documentation.

AWS has created SDKs for simplifying the development of Lambda functions using Java. The library is as follows:

- `aws-lambda-java-events`: This package abstracts away the integration of various AWS services which can be supplied input to trigger Lambda
- `aws-lambda-java-core`: This library provides the basic interfaces and other framework components to `aws-lambda-java-events`

The link redirects to Maven Central, which hosts these libraries, and can be included in the deployment package with a build tool like Gradle or Maven, or just by adding them to the classpath by placing them in the `/lib` directory. This is standard Java packaging.

Handlers in Java

As seen previously, the handler becomes the entry point to the Lambda function. The AWS Lambda functions in Java can have two types of handlers, discussed as follows. Please note that this holds true for any language that runs on the JVM.

Handlers implementing standard interfaces, in this approach, the Lambda function handler implements the standard interfaces that are defined in the `aws-lambda-core` library. There are two standard interfaces, as follows:

1. `RequestHandler`: The following code block shows how a Lambda function is written when implementing the `RequestHandler<I, O>`interface. The `RequestHandler<I, O>` interface has a method definition, as follows:

```
public O handleRequest(I name, Context context);
```

The code with this variant for Lambda function with input as a `String` and output as a `String` is as follows:

```
package example;
import com.amazonaws.services.lambda.runtime.RequestHandler;
import com.amazonaws.services.lambda.runtime.Context;

public class Hello implements RequestHandler<String, String> {
    public String handleRequest(String name, Context context) {
    String greetingString = String.format("Hello %s.", name);
        return greetingString;
    }
}
```

The function takes in a String, and returns a greeting with `Hello` prefixed. `RequestHandler` is the preferred interface to implement when there are POJOs or primitives as input or output.

2. `RequestStreamHandler`: The following code block shows how a Lambda function is written when implementing the `RequestStreamHandler` interface.

The `RequestStreamHandler` has a method definition, as follows:

```
public void handleRequest(InputStream inputStream, OutputStream
outputStream, Context context)throws IOException;
```

The code for such a variant is as follows:

```
package example;

import java.io.IOException;
import java.io.InputStream;
import java.io.OutputStream;

import
com.amazonaws.services.lambda.runtime.RequestStreamHandler;
```

```
import com.amazonaws.services.lambda.runtime.Context;

public class Hello implements RequestStreamHandler {
    public void handleRequest(InputStream inputStream,
OutputStream outputStream, Context context)
            throws IOException {
        int letter;
        while((letter = inputStream.read()) != -1)
        {
            outputStream.write(Character.toUpperCase(letter));
        }
    }
}
```

The preceding code is taken from the official AWS Lambda
documentation. RequestStreamHandler is the preferred interface to
implement when the input and output are best handled as streams.

3. **Custom Handler**: If the developer chooses not to use the AWS SDKs provided as
standard building blocks for Lambda, they can create a handler function without
having the enclosing class implement an interface.

The following code block shows a Lambda function ingesting a name and
returning a greeting that is created without implementing the predefined
interfaces, as shown in the previous section:

```
package example;

import com.amazonaws.services.lambda.runtime.Context;
import com.amazonaws.services.lambda.runtime.LambdaLogger;

public class Hello {
    public String myHandler(String name, Context context) {
        LambdaLogger logger = context.getLogger();
        logger.log("Going to greet : " + name);
        return String.format("Hello %s ",name);
    }
}
```

There are slight differences between the two approaches, which we will explore when we
create the deployment package.

Context object

The context object provides methods to interact with the Lambda execution environment. The context object provides access to the following properties (by using a getter, of course):

- Logger
- MemoryLimitInMB
- FunctionName
- FunctionVersion
- InvokedFunctionArn
- AwsRequestId
- LogStreamName
- LogGroupName
- ClientContext
- Identity
- RemainingTimeInMillis

Logging

Logging for an AWS Lambda Java function can easily be set up with it. Logging helps to trace execution paths and troubleshoot issues, and generally, it provides insight on how the code is behaving.

Each statement to log creates an AWS CloudWatch event. You can find the logs in the console. Also, for the synchronous execution of functions via the Lambda console, one can find the logs right there.

There are two methods for having a logging solution set up in your AWS Lambda code, as follows:

- **Using Log4j2**: Log4j2 is a widely used logging library, used in the JVM world. To configure logging for the Lambda function using Log4j2, the following settings are required.

    It will require the following artifacts on the classpath of the deployment package:

    ```
    com.amazonaws:aws-lambda-java-log4j2:1.0.0
    org.apache.logging.log4j:log4j-core:2.8.2
    org.apache.logging.log4j:log4j-api:2.8.2
    ```

You will have to configure the handler as follows:

```
package example;
import com.amazonaws.services.lambda.runtime.Context;
import org.apache.logging.log4j.LogManager;
import org.apache.logging.log4j.Logger;

public class Hello {
    // Initialize the Log4j logger
    static final Logger logger =
LogManager.getLogger(Hello.class);
    logger.info("info event");
    logger.debug("debug event");
}
```

Log4j requires a log4j2.xml with the logging configuration as a part of the classpath in the package as well. A sample configuration, taken from the official AWS literature, is as follows:

```
<?xml version="1.0" encoding="UTF-8"?>
  <Configuration
packages="com.amazonaws.services.lambda.runtime.log4j2.LambdaAp
pender">
    <Appenders>
      <Lambda name="Lambda">
        <PatternLayout>
            <pattern>%d{yyyy-MM-dd HH:mm:ss} %X{AWSRequestId}
%-5p %c{1}:%L - %m%n</pattern>
        </PatternLayout>
      </Lambda>
    </Appenders>
    <Loggers>
      <Root level="debug">
        <AppenderRef ref="Lambda" />
      </Root>
    </Loggers>
  </Configuration>
```

- Using LambdaLogger(): LambdaLogger is a property of the context object, passed to the Lambda handler function as the second argument.

    A developer can choose to use this turnkey solution without configuring a Log4j2 setup, as described in the previous example.

An example of using the solution is as follows:

```
package example;

import com.amazonaws.services.lambda.runtime.Context;
import com.amazonaws.services.lambda.runtime.LambdaLogger;

public class Hello {
    public String myHandler(String name, Context context) {
        LambdaLogger logger = context.getLogger();
        logger.log("Logged from the LambdaLogger);
    }
}
```

Log Generator: Code statements that generate log entries in the CloudWatch repository or in the console are as follows:

```
//Standard output
System.out.Println()

//Standard error
System.err.Println()

//Lambda Logger
Logger.log()

//Log4j2 info
log.info()

//log4j2 debug
log.debug()

//log4j2 errir
log.error()
```

Error handling

In an AWS Lambda function written in Java, error handling can be done by using the usual try/catch semantics.

If one requires the exception context to be propogated back to the caller (only in the case of a synchronous execution), the following code shows how Lambda returns the exception context in a JSON format. Notice how the stack trace elements are a part of the JSON array:

```
{
    "errorMessage": "An invalid input was supplied",
    "errorType": "java.lang.Exception",
```

```
    "stackTrace": [
      "example.Hello.handler(Hello.java:9)",
      "sun.reflect.NativeMethodAccessorImpl.invoke0(Native Method)",
  "sun.reflect.NativeMethodAccessorImpl.invoke(NativeMethodAccessorImpl.java:
  62)",
  "sun.reflect.DelegatingMethodAccessorImpl.invoke(DelegatingMethodAccessorIm
  pl.java:43)",
      "java.lang.reflect.Method.invoke(Method.java:497)"
    ]
  }
```

During synchronous execution, if an error condition is signaled, the preceding error is shown in the console logs.

In the case of asynchronous execution, these are stored in CloudWatch. There are ways to allow for advanced error handling by using AWS state machines, which are out of the scope of this book.

Now that we have provided an overview of the basic concepts of AWS Lambda, let's create and configure a simple Lambda function.

A case study of a simple Java Lambda function

In this section, we'll look at how we can create a basic Lambda function end-to-end, using the Java programming model. The Java programming model for Lambda functions can be extended to any language that runs on JVM. In the later sections of this book, we will explore Kotlin, but for the sake of focusing on AWS Lambda basics, we'll perform this exercise in Java. This section will aim at providing a starting point for the reader for creating, configuring, deploying, and testing Lambda functions. We will apply all of the concepts that we have seen in a practical example.

We will be creating a very basic Lambda function. It will be a greeter service. The input will be a String parameter, and it will return a greeting composed by prefixing `Hello` to the passed parameter.

 We will be using Java 8 as the programming language, Gradle as the dependency management and packaging tool, and IntelliJ Idea CE as the IDE in this exercise. A basic knowledge of these technologies is recommended. In addition, there will be screenshots for the user to follow. It is recommended that the reader sign up for an AWS account and follow the steps in a hands-on fashion.

Creating the Lambda function

In this section, we'll create a Lambda function from the AWS console.

Lambda dashboard

After you select **Lambda** from the AWS Console landing page, you will see the Lambda dashboard, as shown in the following screenshot:

Basics of creation

After clicking on **Create function**, you will see the screen where the Lambda function can be created.

There are various options for creating a Lambda function, as follows:

1. **Author from scratch**: Write the function from the ground up, with all of the configuration and code done by the developer.

2. **Blueprints**: There are multiple templates that AWS has created to abstract away the boilerplate code and configuration when creating a Lambda function, allowing for a quick start.

3. **Serverless Application Repository**: The Serverless Application Repository has the turnkey Lambda functions that can be deployed to production in one click. These are created by the community, AWS developers, and other companies.

For the purpose of this exercise, we will author a Lambda function from scratch. The following screenshot shows the details:

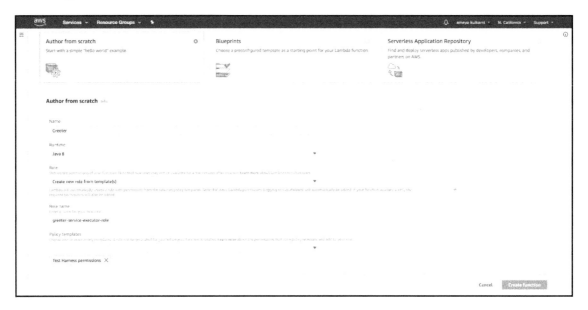

Note the following steps from the preceding screenshot:

1. Choose to author a Lambda function **Author from scratch**.
2. Choose the runtime as **Java 8.**
3. Create a new execution IAM role: `greeter-service-executor-role`.
4. Select **Test Harness permissions** as the policy to attach to the `greeter-service-executor-role`.

These are sensible defaults, provided by AWS. One has to be careful with the nomenclature. Clicking on **Create function** provides the basic skeletal structure for further configurations.

Configuring the Lambda function

Having created the function, the next steps are as follows:

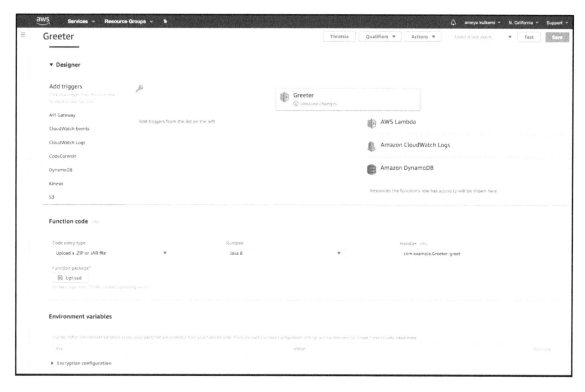

Note the following about the preceding screenshot:

- In the **Designer** section, we can wire up the preconfigured event sources from other AWS offerings as an upstream trigger to the function. In addition, we can configure access to downstream and allied components, like other Lambda functions, DynamoDB, and CloudWatch logs.
- The important section is the **Function code** section, which allows for choosing to upload the deployment package as a .zip or .jar. It also allows us to configure the handler name in the following format:

  ```
  packageName.ClassName::methodName
  ```

- As you will see in the subsequent sections, for this exercise, we will choose the package/group name as com.example, the class as Greeter, and the method as handleRequest.

The next part of the configuration is shown in the following screenshot:

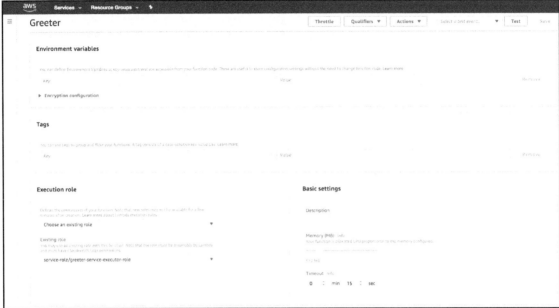

As you can see, the developer can set the environment variables, tag the Lambda function for easier lookup, supply the basic settings (like memory and limit out duration), and set the execution role.

We chose the sensible defaults for the settings, and you can see that the execution role **greeter-service-executor-role** is already selected.

Writing a Lambda function

In this section, we will get down to coding our first Lambda function, as follows:

1. In your IDE and build tool of choice (in this literature, we prefer to use IntelliJ and Gradle), create a simple Java project with the package name `com.example`.

2. Add the following dependencies to your dependency management file (or, place them in the classpath). The Gradle code looks as follows (comments are removed for conciseness):

```
apply plugin: 'java'
apply plugin: 'idea'

repositories {
```

```
        jcenter()
    }
    dependencies {
        compile group: 'com.amazonaws', name: 'aws-lambda-java-core',
    version: '1.2.0'
        compile group: 'com.amazonaws', name: 'aws-lambda-java-events',
    version: '2.1.0'
    }
```

3. In the package com.example, create a class, Greeter (which will be our LambdaHandler), implementing the RequestHandler interface. Keeping it simple, we will state that the input type is a string and the output type is also a string. Also, let's write a piece of code that takes in the greetee variable, logs it using the LambdaLogger instance, appends it to the predefined string Hello, and returns the result. The first iteration of the code will look as follows:

```
package com.example;

import com.amazonaws.services.lambda.runtime.Context;
import com.amazonaws.services.lambda.runtime.LambdaLogger;
import com.amazonaws.services.lambda.runtime.RequestHandler;

public class Greeter implements RequestHandler<String,String> {
    @Override
    public String handleRequest(String greetee, Context context){
        LambdaLogger logger = context.getLogger();
        logger.log("Lets greet "+ greetee);
        return "Hello, " + greetee;
    }
}
```

This very simplistic function is ready to be used. For that, we need to upload it to the AWS environment.

Deploying the Lambda function

We will package the application as a .jar file and upload it to the AWS web console. To do so, we use the following command:

```
./gradlew clean jar
```

Note that there are more sophisticated methods for deploying a Lambda function to the AWS environment. We will explore using tools like SAM and aws-cli later on. This section is just to familiarize the reader with the basics of the web console.

This will yield a greeter-service.jar in the build/libs directory. Depending on the choice of build tool, the location and artifact name may vary. The crux is that this is the package that can be deployed to the AWS environment.

 The preceding command is for executing the Gradle build on a Unix machine. It is a different command on the Windows machine. The reader should be familiar with Gradle or follow the equivalent steps in Maven.

Next, perform the following steps:

1. Select the .jar file that was built as a part of the build process. Navigate to the file and select it from the file uploader, as follows:

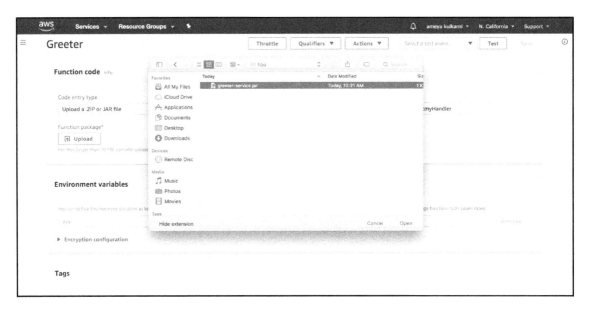

The following screenshot shows that the `.jar` was uploaded:

2. Change the handler from `example.Hello::myHandler` to `com.example.greeter::handleRequest`, and click on **Save**:

The end state of the UI when the Lambda function is uploaded

At this point, we have our Lambda function written, deployed, and ready to be tested.

Testing a Lambda function

To test the Lambda function that we wrote and uploaded in the preceding sections, we have to create a test harness via the **Configure Test Event** drop-down menu in the header. This test will happen in isolation (think of it as a sandbox mode). We have not wired it up to any of the event sources just yet.

The following screenshots show the process, which can be described as follows:

1. Select the drop-down menu to configure a new test event:

Initial step

2. Configure the test events. First, let's configure a positive scenario, where a valid input is given, as follows:

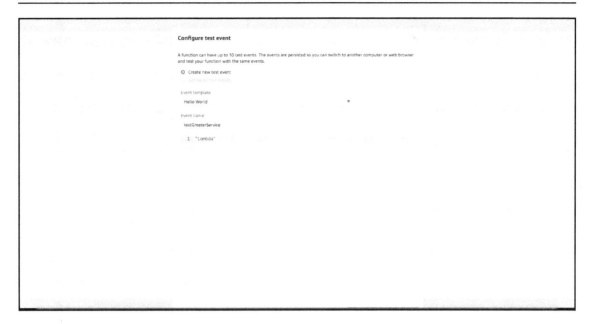

Test event for positive flow is created

A few points should be noted, as follows:

1. Create a new test event from a template.
2. Name the event `testGreeterService`.
3. Add the value for this invocation. This is an important part of setting up a test harness. As described earlier, this maps to the `InputType` parameter that is passed to the function. This harness accepts a JSON object, and it's incumbent on the developer to specify the value properly, so that it gets marshaled to the `InputType`.

In our example, we have assumed that the input type is a `java.lang.String`, and hence, we specify one. For more complex and nested types, one has to add the value accordingly.

Let's create a test event for the negative scenario of the preceding template where in we provide an input which will break the function. The following screenshot shows how to configure the test event for a negative flow:

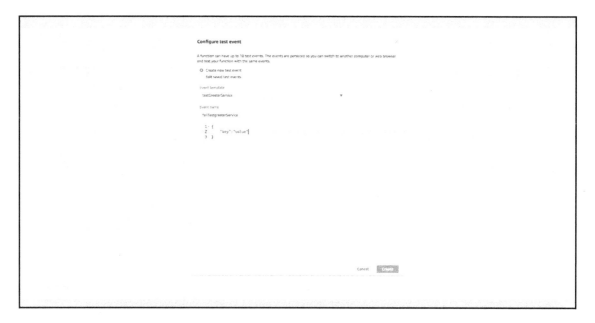

Note that instead of giving a string value, we have used a simple JSON string, which can't be parsed, because our handler just accepts the string.

4. Click on **Create** and then the **Save** button and invoke the function with the test events that were created by clicking on **Test**. The output is shown in the following screenshot:

 Note the output, `Hello, Lambda`, which is as per our expectations.

The following screenshot shows the negative test event execution:

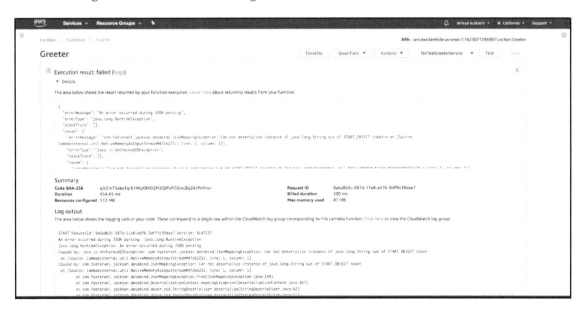

Note that the JSON deserialization fails. In a production-grade Lambda function, this error has to be handled gracefully, and appropriate actions need to be taken. In this book, it is left out for simplicity's sake.

This concludes the basics of creating, configuring, and testing a Lambda function via the console. In the following sections, we'll take a look at wiring it up to an upstream component, like an API Gateway, so that we will have an end-to-end working example of a simple (but production-grade) Lambda function.

Case study of a simple Kotlin Lambda function

In the previous section, we had a look at a simple Lambda function written in Java. Java is much more than a language. It includes the JVM, which is the execution environment that executes the compiled bytecode. It includes libraries that can be compiled into bytecode and run on the JVM.

The Lambda Java 8 runtime also executes functions written in Kotlin and Groovy among other languages, which get compiled to bytecode. So, a Lambda function can be authored in any of the languages that run on the JVM. In this section of the book, you'll take a look at Lambda functions created in Kotlin.

Tooling

- In this section, we'll be using the following tools:
  - Gradle 4.3 to build
  - JDK8
  - Kotlin
  - IntelliJ Idea IDE CE 2018.2

Anatomy of a Kotlin Lambda function

This section takes a look at the basic structure, build configuration, handlers, and packaging of a Lambda function written in Kotlin.

Project structure

The following code block shows the schematic of a Kotlin Lambda function.
In the following code block, the handler function is
`com.packt.serverles.kotlin.greeter.Handler.kt`:

```
greeter-service/
 -build.gradle
 -src/
     -main/
       -kotlin/
           -com.packt.serverless.kotlin.greeter/
               - Handler.kt
 -gradle/
     -wrapper/
         -gradle-wrapper.jar
          -gradle-wrapper.properties
  -build/
      -libs
         -greeter-1.0.jar
```

build.gradle

The `build.gradle` for a typical Kotlin Lambda function is as shown in the following code
block:

```
apply plugin: 'java'
apply plugin: 'maven'
apply plugin: 'idea'
apply plugin: 'kotlin'
apply plugin: 'com.github.johnrengelman.shadow'


group = 'com.packt.serverless.kotlin'
version = '1.0.0'

description = """Simple Greeter lambda function"""


sourceCompatibility = 1.8
targetCompatibility = 1.8
tasks.withType(JavaCompile) {
  options.encoding = 'UTF-8'
}

buildscript {
  repositories {
```

```
      mavenCentral()
      maven { url "https://plugins.gradle.org/m2/" }
    }
    dependencies {
      classpath "org.jetbrains.kotlin:kotlin-gradle-plugin:1.1.51"
      classpath "com.github.jengelman.gradle.plugins:shadow:2.0.1"
    }
  }



repositories {
  maven { url "http://repo.maven.apache.org/maven2" }
}

dependencies {
  compile group: 'org.jetbrains.kotlin', name: 'kotlin-stdlib', version:
'1.1.51'

  compile group: 'com.amazonaws', name: 'aws-lambda-java-core',
version:'1.1.0'
  compile group: 'com.amazonaws', name: 'aws-lambda-java-log4j2',
version:'1.0.0'
  compile group: 'com.amazonaws', name: 'aws-lambda-java-events',
version:'2.0.1'

  compile group: 'com.fasterxml.jackson.core', name: 'jackson-core',
version:'2.8.5'
  compile group: 'com.fasterxml.jackson.core', name: 'jackson-databind',
version:'2.8.5'
  compile group: 'com.fasterxml.jackson.core', name: 'jackson-annotations',
version:'2.8.5'
}

shadowJar{
  mergeServiceFiles('META-INF/spring.*')
  exclude "META-INF/*.SF"
  exclude "META-INF/*.DSA"
  exclude "META-INF/*.RSA"
  exclude "META-INF/LICENSE"
  archiveName = "greeter-${version}.${extension}"
}
```

Here are a few points to know about the preceding code:

- We use the Gradle Shadow plugin to get a `.jar` deployment package with all its dependencies
- We change the configuration of the `shadow` task to yield a better-named uber jar, for example, `greeter-1.0.0.jar`

Handler

A typical `RequestHandler` looks like below:

```
package com.packt.serverless.kotlin.greeter

import com.amazonaws.services.lambda.runtime.Context
import com.amazonaws.services.lambda.runtime.RequestHandler

class Handler:RequestHandler<String,String> {
  override fun handleRequest(input:String, context:Context):String {
      return "Hello, $input from Kotlin"
  }

}
```

Few points to note about the preceding code:

- With the above structure the handler that should be configured becomes `com.packt,serverless.kotlin.greeter.Handler::handleRequest`
- The handler is configured so that it receives a string object and returns a string object

Packaging and deploying

To package a Kotlin Lambda function using Gradle on Unix-based systems, use the following command:

```
./gradlew clean shadow
```

This yields `/build/libs/ greeter-1.0.0.jar`, which can be uploaded as a deployment package in the console, like we did for the Java Lambda function.

Testing the Kotlin function

Now that we have seen the basic anatomy of the Kotlin Lambda function after building it, we can go ahead and replace the Lambda function that was authored in Java previously from the console with the `build/libs/greeter-1.0.0.jar` package.

The following screenshot shows the test run:

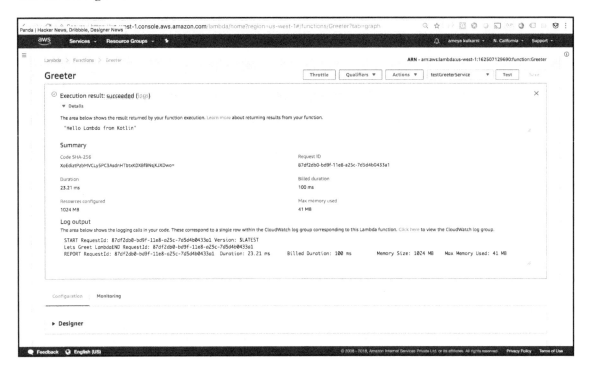

Integrating a Lambda function with an upstream component

In the previous sections, we went over the basics of Lambda functions and the programming model, and we created, configured, deployed, and tested a very simple Lambda function, which greeted the caller.

In this section, with the goal of having an end-to-end working example of a Lambda function, let's hook our greeter to an API Gateway that allows the Lambda function to be exposed as an API.

In a production-grade application, none of the following have to be done via the console. The API Gateway provides extensive Swagger extensions, which can be leveraged to eradicate the boilerplate steps.

> Some working knowledge of REST APIs is required to properly understand this section. Knowledge of the AWS API Gateway is desirable but not mandatory. This section assumes that the reader at least knows what the AWS API Gateway is, its integration types, its configuration settings, and what benefits it offers. Details about configuring the Gateway are beyond the scope of this section.

Types API Gateway and Lambda integrations

There are two choices for integrating an API Gateway with a downstream Lambda function:

- Lambda integration
- Lambda proxy integration

There are a few differences that the readers need to be aware of. So let's look at each in brief.

Lambda integration/ Lambda custom integration

In Lambda integration, there is flexibility to process the payload received by the API Gateway to be passed to the downstream Lambda function.

This approach is highly customizable at the API Gateway level using a Velocity Templating Language (VTL), which can be used to process the input payload before passing to the Lambda. This way, the Lambda function handler can be expected to receive any types as its input, as long as it can parse it properly.

The return value from the Lambda function also doesn't need to conform to any particular type as long as the API Gateway can translate this output into a type that is understandable by the upstream client. There is also an option for processing the response received from the Lambda before sending it back to the client. The responses to the HTTP client are also set by the API Gateway.

This way, the Lambda function is completely decoupled from a REST API's HTTP semantics.

We will see in brief the Lambda integration of our greeter-service with an API Gateway in the later sections.

 Please note that this is a legacy integration and AWS recommends the use of Lambda proxy integration as the way to integrate API Gateway with Lambda.

Lambda proxy integration

AWS recommends that Lambda proxy integration is the way to integrate the API Gateway with Lambda.

The request that is received by the API Gateway is passed through to the Lambda function in a specific format. The Lambda function is expected to parse this payload into an appropriate type that it requires to perform the action.

The following code block shows the input passed to the Lambda function from the API Gateway in the case of a Lambda proxy integration:

```
{
    "resource":"Resource path",
    "path":"Path parameter",
    "httpMethod":"Incoming request's method name",
    "headers":{
        "key":"value"
    },
    "queryStringParameters":{
        "key":"value"
    },
    "pathParameters":{
        "key":"value"
    },
    "stageVariables":{
        "key":"value"
    },
    "requestContext":{
        "accountId":"12345678912",
        "resourceId":"roq9wj",
        "stage":"testStage",
        "requestId":"deef4878-7910-11e6-8f14-25afc3e9ae33",
        "identity":{
            "cognitoIdentityPoolId":null,
            "accountId":null,
            "cognitoIdentityId":null,
            "caller":null,
```

```
            "apiKey":null,
            "sourceIp":"192.168.196.186",
            "cognitoAuthenticationType":null,
            "cognitoAuthenticationProvider":null,
            "userArn":null,
            "userAgent":"PostmanRuntime/2.4.5",
            "user":null
        },
        "body":"A JSON string of the request payload.",
        "isBase64Encoded":"A boolean flag to indicate if the applicable
    request payload is Base64-encode"
    }
}
```

The Lambda function is also expected to set the HTTP error codes and return the response object in a particular format:

```
{
    "isBase64Encoded": false,
    "statusCode": 200,
    "headers": { "headerName": "headerValue"},
    "body": "{\"key\":\"value\"}"
}
```

For more information on the Lambda proxy integration, please refer to the official documentation: API gateway documentation for Lambda Proxy integration.

Anatomy of the Lambda function when used in Lambda proxy integration

In Lambda integration, because the Lambda function and the API are decoupled, the Lambda function handler can implement the RequestHandler<INPUT, OUTPUT> interface with INPUT and OUTPUT being any types that are transformed and sent by the API Gateway. In fact, the Lambda function that we saw in the previous section is a valid candidate as a Lambda function for Lambda integration.

For Lambda proxy integration, since INPUT and OUTPUT conform to a particular format, the handler function needs to respect that.

In the case of Lambda proxy integration, the handler function is as follows:

```
.class Handler : RequestHandler<Map<String, Any>, ApiGatewayResponse> {
    override  fun handleRequest(input: Map<String, Any>, context: Context):
ApiGatewayResponse {
        //Do the work
        return ApiGatewayResponse.build {
            statusCode = 200
            objectBody = Response()
        }

    }
}
```

Such a handler takes in a map of `String` keys and `Any` values, and returns the output in the form of `ApiGatewayResponse`.

`API gatewayResponse` is a type that helps build out an integration response from the Lambda function, which can be processed by the API Gateway. We saw the sample payload in the previous section.

The definition of this class is as follows:

```
import com.fasterxml.jackson.core.JsonProcessingException
import com.fasterxml.jackson.databind.ObjectMapper
import org.apache.logging.log4j.LogManager
import org.apache.logging.log4j.Logger
import java.nio.charset.StandardCharsets
import java.util.*

class ApiGatewayResponse(
  val statusCode: Int = 200,
  var body: String? = null,
  val headers: Map<String, String>? = Collections.emptyMap(),
  val isBase64Encoded: Boolean = false
) {

  companion object {
    inline fun build(block: Builder.() -> Unit) =
Builder().apply(block).build()
  }

  class Builder {
    var LOG: Logger = LogManager.getLogger(Builder::class.java)
    var objectMapper: ObjectMapper = ObjectMapper()


    var statusCode: Int = 200
```

```kotlin
    var rawBody: String? = null
    var headers: Map<String, String>? = Collections.emptyMap()
    var objectBody: Response? = null
    var binaryBody: ByteArray? = null
    var base64Encoded: Boolean = false

    fun build(): ApiGatewayResponse {
      var body: String? = null

      if (rawBody != null) {
        body = rawBody as String
      }
      else if (objectBody != null) {
        try {
          body = objectMapper.writeValueAsString(objectBody)
        } catch (e: JsonProcessingException) {
          LOG.error("failed to serialize object", e)
          throw RuntimeException(e)
        }
      } else if (binaryBody != null) {
        body = String(Base64.getEncoder().encode(binaryBody),
StandardCharsets.UTF_8)
      }
      return ApiGatewayResponse(statusCode, body, headers, base64Encoded)
    }
  }
}
```

 In the subsequent sections, we will be using the lambda functions and API Gateway integration of the Lambda proxy type.

Now that we have seen the types of integrations of Lambda with API Gateway, let's proceed with integrating the Lambda function that we created with an API Gateway. Please note that this is of the type Lambda integration and not Lambda proxy integration.

Creating an API Gateway

The following screenshots depict the creation, configuration and integration of an API Gateway.

From the dashboard of the API Gateway, create an API named `Greeter`, as follows:

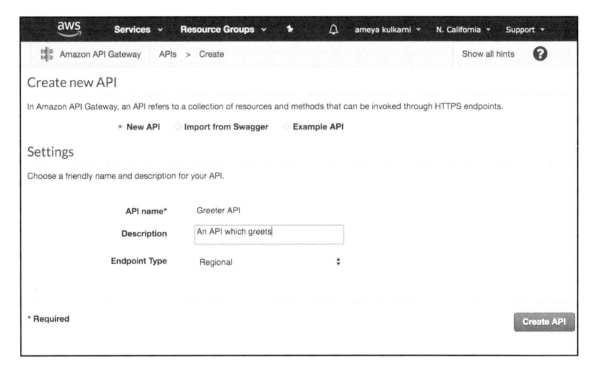

Create a resource named `greeter`, as follows:

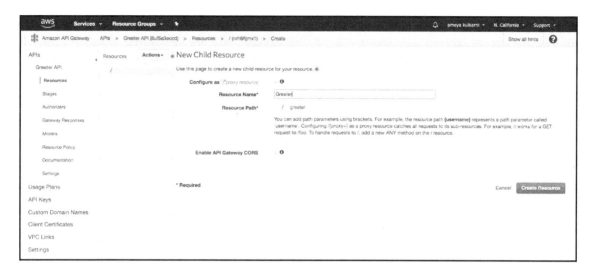

Create a resource, /, to handle the HTTP POST request. Notice that we specify the integration type to the Lambda function, and select Greeter, the function that we created in the previous sections, to be invoked. Also, notice that we leave the Use **Lambda Proxy integration** box unchecked. This means that we are choosing this integration to be of the Lambda type:

Once the POST resource is created, you will see a pictorial representation of how the integration of the API Gateway and AWS Lambda works. Since we have chosen the Lambda integration type, we can see four configuration stages in the flow that can be configured separately, as follows:

- **Method Request**: This is the configuration that deals with the requests received by the API Gateway from the client. One can configure request validations, URL param validations, and the request body to models mapping in this stage.

- **Integration Request**: This is the configuration that deals with the request that is passed to the Lambda from the API Gateway. One can configure the mapping of the URL params, request body, and header transformation to an appropriate structure that your Lambda function expects.

- **Integration Response**: This is the configuration that deals with responses from the Lambda returned to the API Gateway. One can transform the Lambda output to appropriate HTTP error codes that are relayed back to the API Gateway.

- **Method Response**: This is the configuration that deals with the response from the API Gateway to the client. One can attach HTTP error codes to their respective response bodies and modify the response headers that are to be returned to the client:

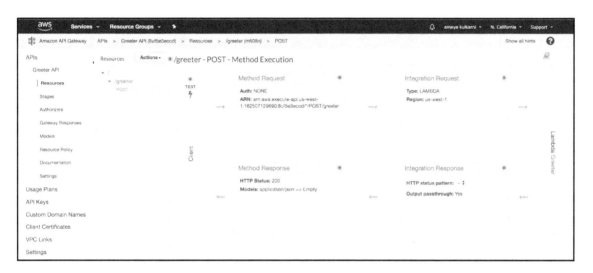

Integration testing

Once the API Gateway is configured and integrated with Lambda, one can test it in sandbox mode.

 Note that the function is not currently deployed or configured to receive triggers from the outside world. To expose the API to the outside world, it has to be deployed on something called the API Gateway Stage. We will explore that in future sections.

To test in the sandbox mode, you have to click on the Test link, as shown in the following screenshot:

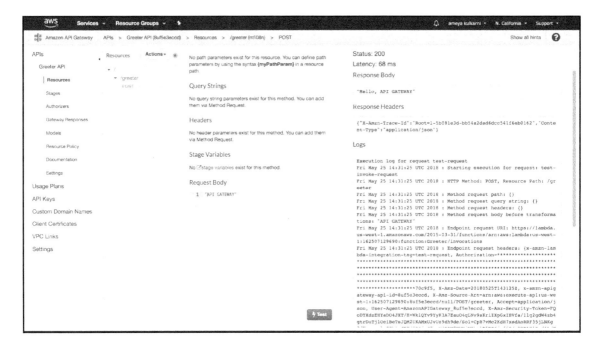

The preceding screenshot shows the test of the positive flow of the API, invoking the Gateway with a request that has a string in the body with the value `API GATEWAY`. The response is as expected: `Hello, API GATEWAY`. The following screenshot shows the test of the negative flow via the API Gateway, sending an unparseable response body. As expected, it throws a `JSONMappingException`:

> The preceding screenshot shows that the invalid input error is not handled correctly. This is not the best practice for a production-grade app. A production-grade app has to validate its input parameters and return an appropriate error code.

To configure request validation with API Gateway, one can go to the **Method Request** configuration stage of the integration and apply a proper request validation so that incorrect requests are not passed to the backend Lambda function.

To do so, define a model using the JSON schema, which models the input to the API. Then, attach this model to the method request for the API.

Define a model named `GreetingInput`. This definition takes in a model schema in `JSON Schema - Draft 04 format`.

Because our input is a simple string, the JSON schema definition is as follows:

```
{
 "$schema": "http://json-schema.org/draft-04/schema#",
 "type": "string"
}
```

The following screenshot shows the steps taken to create the model in the console:

Once the model is created, it has to be attached to the request body via the **Method Request** configuration section. The content type is `application/json`.

The following screenshot shows the details for attaching the model `GreeterInput` as the request body to the `/greeter` API.

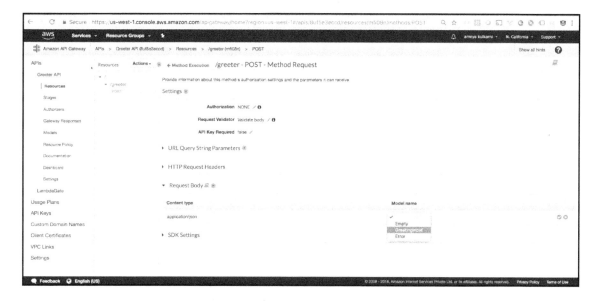

Once this is done, you can test the integration by clicking on **Test**. As expected, the error code for an invalid input (which is not a simple string) is **400**:

Deploying the API Gateway

Now that the API Gateway has been tested, let's deploy it to an environment. The environment, in API Gateway terms, is called the **stage**.

To create a stage click on the **Actions** drop down and selecting **Deploy API**. Select the **New Stage** option in the **Deployment Stage** dropdown and name it beta by supplying the value for **Stage Name**. Leave every thing to defaults and click on **Deploy**.

We land up on the following screen:

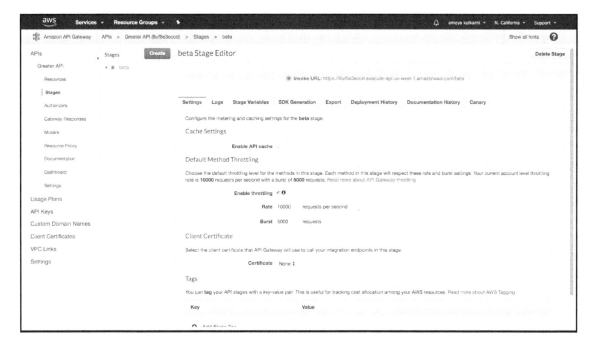

Creating the stage beta

A few things to note are as follows:

- An HTTPS-enabled URL came with our application, out of the box. The base URL is `https://8uf5e3eccd.execute-api.us-west-1.amazonaws.com`.
- We created a stage name, `beta`, so the URL has now become `https://8uf5e3eccd.execute-api.us-west-1.amazonaws.com/beta/`.
- We created a resource name, `/greeter`, so the URI to invoke it has become `https://8uf5e3eccd.execute-api.us-west-1.amazonaws.com/beta/greeter/`.

Up to this point, we have not enabled authentication on our API, so it is open to the world. Even though this API is not doing much, it is possible that it could be hit with a lot of requests in an attempt to break the API. Authenticating it is always a good idea in order to protect the APIs that you create.

End-to-end test

Once the API has been deployed to the `beta` stage, let's try to consume the API via a third-party REST client, like `Postman`, as shown in the following screenshot:

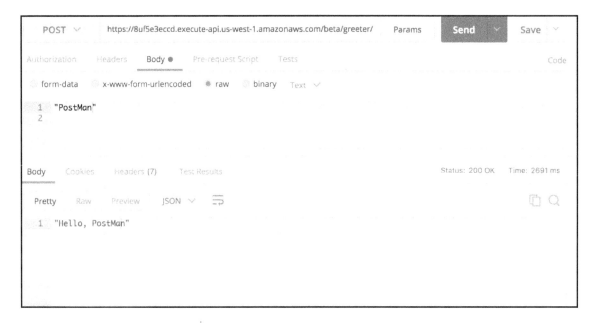

This completes our end-to-end exercise to integrate a Lambda function with an API and expose it to the world.

Basic monitoring of lambda functions

Lambda functions are monitored implicitly by the AWS CloudWatch service. The following metrics are monitored:

- **Invocation Count**: The count of times that the Lambda function is invoked.
- **Invocation Errors**: The count of times that the Lambda function is invoked, but results in an error.
- **Invocation Duration**: The time, in milliseconds, that the Lambda function took to execute.

- **Throttled Invocation**: The count of times that the Lambda function was throttled and prevented execution, because of a breach of the service limit thresholds.
- **Iterator Age**: A special metric, only for stream-based execution triggers like Kinesis. Represents the time difference, in milliseconds, between the time when Lambda received a batch of stream data to process and the time the last record in the batch was written to.
- **DLQ Errors**: The count of times when the Lambda function did not execute, due to a variety of reasons. DLQ stands for **Dead Letter Queues**.

Versioning Lambda functions

Suppose that we want to push a change to the function that we just created. Let's assume that the change is as simple as adding the time that the greeting took place. To version your Lambda function, go to the **Actions** drop-down menu on the Lambda configuration screen and click on **Publish New Version**.

You will be presented with a screen that looks like the following:

Once you click on **Publish,** a new version of your Lambda function will be created:

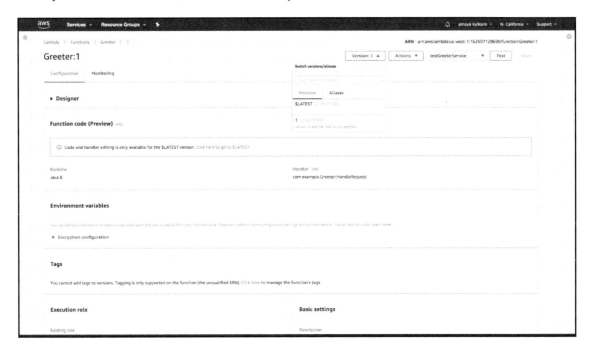

 When you create a version, a copy of the current code and its configuration is made from the $LATEST version and tagged in a numerically incremental manner. Changes to code or configurations can only be done on the $LATEST version.

Switching to Version 1 and executing the code via the test harness, we can see that Version 1 provides the intended output, with the date of the greeting attached to the response:

Summary

In this chapter, we covered the nuts and bolts of how AWS Lambda (FaaS) works. We took a look at the Java programming model, which can be extended to other JVM-based languages. We provided a brief overview of all preconfigured AWS events that can be used as trigger points in Lambda.

You saw how Lambda functions can be created, packaged, deployed, and tested, via the console. In this process, we created a simple Lambda function that greets its callers, and then tested it. We then created an API Gateway to integrate with this Lambda function. We deployed this API Gateway and invoked the Lambda function via Postman.

In short, we executed an end-to-end exercise with Lambda functions.

In the next chapter, we will dive into AWS offerings and look at how they can be integrated with Lambda. In the process, we will create a modern serverless application using Kotlin.

Designing a Kotlin Serverless Application

3

In the last chapter, we covered how Lambda functions are developed and deployed. Lambda functions are amazing, aren't they? They work so beautifully for our requirements.

In this chapter, we will go over our requirements and look at how various services can be applied to fulfill those requirements, using serverless paradigms. This chapter will mostly be an exercise, covering what every developer, leader, and architect has to do every time they start to develop an app.

In this chapter, we will cover the following steps:

- Analyzing a problem statement
- Designing a client app (an android app) requirements
- Identifying API endpoint requirements
- Designing events to be used by Lambda functions
- Designing the persistence layer and storing the data

Our goal is to make this chapter as interesting as possible, using figures and diagrams to help you understand the content.

The problem statement

"I want a product which can help me to conduct a poll, where a user can reply with Yes or No."

- A typical client

The preceding quote can relate to your project – you will always have an initial requirement when creating an app. Your next step should be analyzing that requirement and breaking it down into possible features that will make your product ready for the market, creating the **Minimum Viable Product** (**MVP**).

So, let's poll. Oh! Doesn't that make a nice app name? Let's name our app Let's Poll.

Analyzing the problem statement

The **problem statement** that was conveyed in the preceding section can be broken down into the following developmental requirements:

- As a user, I should be able to log in to the app using my Facebook credentials.
- As a user, I should be able to create a poll. The poll should have a title, a question, and a list of responses. The responses to the poll should be singular and objective.
- As a user, I should be ablc to delete a poll that I created.
- As a user, I should be able to respond to a particular poll.
- As a user, I should be able to see the poll responses for the poll that I created.

Functional specifications of the app

To fulfill the preceding requirements from your client, you will have to develop the following features:

- A welcome, or splash, screen
- A screen from which the user can log in to the app using Facebook
- A screen upon which the user can create poll and enter poll details and options
- A screen upon which the user can see all of the polls created by others
- A screen upon which the user can respond to the poll by selecting one of the poll responses
- The ability to delete previously created polls
- A screen to display responses to the poll that the user created

The preceding features can be represented in a use case diagram, as follows:

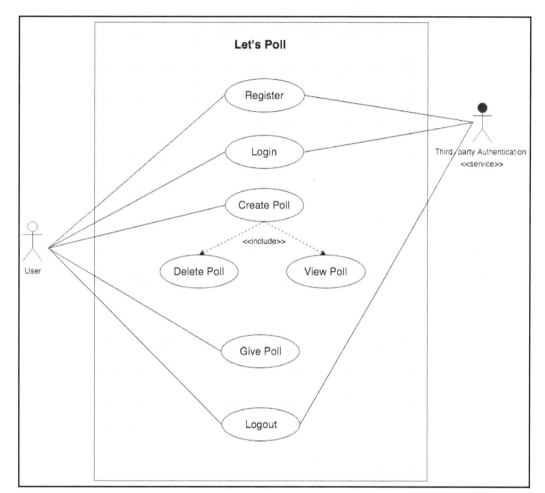

Designing the serverless API

Let's jump to the server side – I mean, the serverless side. Now, we have to list our API requirements. These will mainly be REST APIs, over an HTTP connection. The request and response format will be in JSON. We already listed our UI requirement in the previous section. Keeping these requirements in mind, as we will jot the APIs down one by one, along with their structures.

You may recall having used AWS Lambda with the help of the API Gateway service in the previous chapter. In this lesson, the same concept will be our weapon. With it, we can develop RESTful web services. Let's delve a bit deeper into the API design.

Architectural and design decisions

Every system requires some architectural decisions before implementation begins. The following sections will highlight some of these decisions.

AWS Cognito for login and registration

No application is possible without a user registration journey. This is where the magic of the serverless ecosystem starts.

Suppose that I want my user to sign up for the app using Facebook, Gmail, SAML providers, or a traditional proprietary sign up. Painful, right? All we know is that this is monotonous work. You need user management so that you can identify unique users and serve them the correct data.

What if I told you that you do not need to build a traditional registration API that validates the user, insert it into the database, and generate a token against it? AWS (along with many other providers, such as Firebase) provides its own user management services.

Typically, AWS Cognito provides a **user pool**. User pools include the following:

- Sign-up and sign-in services
- A built-in, customizable web UI to sign in users
- Social sign in, with Facebook, Google, and login with Amazon, as well as sign in with SAML identity providers from your user pool
- User directory management and user profiles
- Security features, such as **multi-factor authentication (MFA)**, checks for compromised credentials, account takeover protection, and phone and email verification
- Customized workflows and user migration through AWS Lambda triggers

The following diagram will help you to visualize these elements; it was taken from AWS Cognito User Pools, at `https://docs.aws.amazon.com/cognito/latest/developerguide/cognito-user-identity-pools.html`:

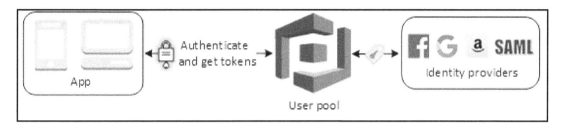

As you can see in the preceding diagram, the **User pool** service is available, and it can be consumed by mobile apps or from browsers. We will be using AWS Cognito Auth SDK. You can find the detailed code in `Chapter 4`, Developing Your Serverless Application.

 When using Amazon Cognito events, you can only use the credentials obtained from Amazon Cognito Identity. If you have an associated Lambda function, but you call `UpdateRecords` with AWS account credentials (developer credentials), your Lambda function will not be invoked.

We will use AWS Cognito to create a user pool to manage the following:

- User identity pools
- Getting credentials

The Kotlin language

In any system's design, the programming language plays a vital role. You cannot write a modern day requirement in COBOL or FORTRAN. Modern requirements need smart languages. Nowadays, programming languages do not just focus on creating machine-understandable code. Although creating binary instructions is their core role, they also focus on how things can be done easily. How simply they can take input (a set of instructions can be considered input for the programming language to process) from developers also counts. Kotlin is not just another programming language. It is maintained by industry giants like JetBrains (creator of the language) and Google (officially, Kotlin is a language for Android app development).

You can see Kotlin as an easy, safe, statically typed, open source language. But it comes with a great vision to be everywhere. Such a programming language is a developer's fantasy. Every developer desires to learn only one language that allows them to do everything, like creating the frontend and backend, scripting, mobile app development, embedded system programming, and so on. Kotlin is that dream come true.

With the aim of converting that dream to reality, we are writing this book. All of the code that we have written is thanks to Kotlin.

PostgresSQL 10 on Amazon RDS

Every system in the world requires a persistent datastore as a backing service. This datastore not only stores the data that is required by the system, but also stores the changes that are made to the system by its users.

The datastore can be anything, ranging from a flat file or an RDBMS (like MySQL, PostgreSQL, and Oracle) to a NoSQL database (like Cassandra, Aerospike, and DynamoDB).

For this project, we have decided to use an RDBMS system to create our persistent datastore. This datastore will be used to store polls, respondents, and responses.

We chose PostgreSQL 10 as our RDBMS choice. Its advantages are as follows:

- Fully open source
- Vibrant and big community
- ACID compliance
- Smart indexing techniques
- An extensive list of features

To host our database, we can either provision a VM and manage the infrastructure ourselves, or, being in the serverless mindset, opt for a turnkey solution that gets us up and running in a matter of minutes.

Amazon AWS has just the solution for us: the `Amazon Relational Database Service (RDS)`.

Amazon RDS provides a fully-managed relational database service for the following engines:

- Amazon Aurora
- PostgresSQL
- MySQL
- Oracle
- MS SQL Server
- MariaDB

Implementing the RDS provides the following benefits:

- Fully monitored and managed
- Secure (supports encryption)
- Scalable
- Highly available
- Turnkey operations, like backup and restore

API Gateway for proxy and edge engineering

API Gateway is a fully-managed AWS offering that sets up a system interface for the outside world (over the internet). It provides seamless integration with AWS Lambda, which is the FaaS solution we have chosen to write our business logic with. With API Gateway, we can create, publish, maintain, and version production-grade API systems, without much effort.

In *Chapter 2*, *AWS Serverless Offerings*, you saw how easy it is to set up an API Gateway to proxy the calls to a simple Lambda function.

In this section, we'll walk through some of the advanced and necessary configurations of the API Gateway for a production grade system. We will build upon the Greeter API that we created in *Chapter 1*, *Basics of Serverless*. These are critical configurations that need to be completed. At the end of this section, you will see how you can export the configuration as a Swagger 2.0 JSON file, which is a great starting point for designing the Let's Poll APIs.

 This section will not cover the entire API Gateway and its advanced configurations in detail. It will just provide a brief overview of an advanced configuration that we will use while developing the Let's Poll app.

API keys and usage plans

API keys are a well-known concept. They are like gate passes for accessing a particular realm. They comprise the first level of access control that APIs impose.

Let's look at a real-world example. Suppose that Harry is a traveler that wants to travel to a particular location by plane. Harry needs to catch a flight from an airport.

For security reasons, the airport is a strictly access-controlled location. Only folks that have a valid ID card or passport and a plane ticket for that day are allowed to enter. There are further authentications and authorizations that the passenger has to undergo before boarding the flight, but none of them will occur if the passenger is not let on due to invalidity of his/her ID card or ticket.

One can think of the ID card and the ticket as the **API keys**. They are necessary for the passenger (a client) to access the airport (the resources/locations), but are not sufficient to fully use the service.

The Amazon API Gateway uses the concept of API keys. One can choose to have an API key associated with a resource method by following these steps:

- Issue an API key
- Create a usage plan
- Associate the key with the usage plan
- Associate the usage plan with an API stage

The following screenshots illustrate the process of configuring the API key for the Greeter API:

1. In the details for a method, specify that an API key is required, as follows:

2. The **API key** details should be as follows:

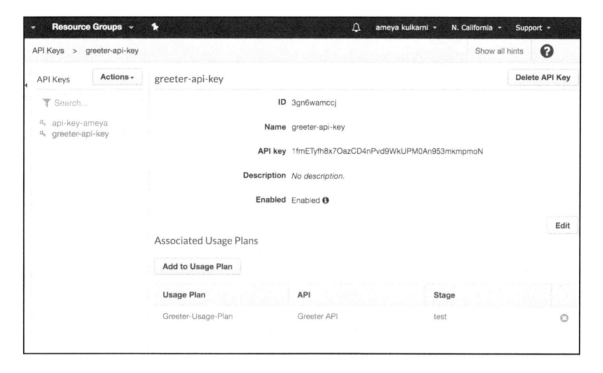

Note the API key
value, **1fmETyfh8x7OazCD4nPvd9WkUPM0An953mkmpmoN**. This is the value
that the client will have to pass.

3. Create a **Usage Plan**, as follows:

4. Associate the **greeter-api-key** with the usage plan that was just created, as follows:

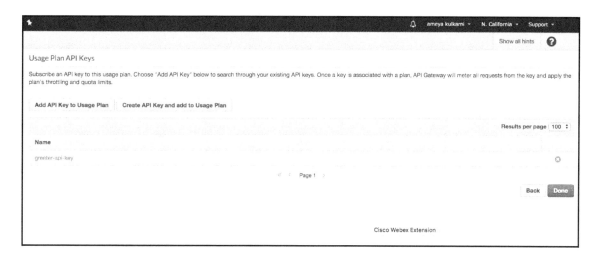

5. Associate the usage plan with the `test` stage of the Greeter API, as follows:

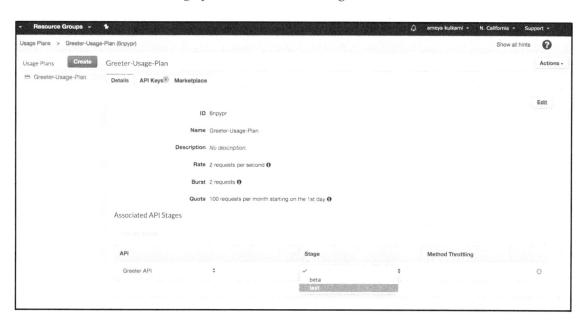

Now that we have created an API key and a usage plan and have associated them, it's time to test the setup.

Let's invoke the Greeter API on `test`, without passing in the auth key. As the output shows, the client can't access the API, and gets a 403 error code:

```
Ameyas-MacBook-Pro:~ Webonise$ curl -X POST
https://8uf5e3eccd.execute-api.us-west-1.amazonaws.com/test/greeter -d
'"ameya"'
{"message":"Forbidden"}
```

Let's invoke the Greeter API on the `test` stage by passing in the API key as a header (`x-api-key`):

```
Ameyas-MacBook-Pro:~ Webonise$ curl -X POST -H 'x-api-
key:1fmETyfh8x7OazCD4nPvd9WkUPM0An953mkmpmoN'
https://8uf5e3eccd.execute-api.us-west-1.amazonaws.com/test/greeter -d
'"ameya"'
"Hello, ameya on Fri Jul 20 14:55:07 UTC 2018"
```

 Amazon API Gateway's convention is to pass in the API key value against a header, `x-api-key`.

Authorization

An API Gateway in production endures traffic. It would be naive to assume that all of the traffic sources have benevolent intentions. APIs have to be protected through various mechanisms.

API keys impart the first line of defense, but they don't provide any authentication or authorization functionality:

- **Authentication:** It is the process of verifying identity. For example, you can authenticate that a client of an API is actually who they claim they are
- **Authorization:** It is the process of applying access controls to an authenticated client. Both of these are critical pillars of a production-grade API system. In this section, we will look at how API Gateway can be protected/authorized

- **Using Cognito pools:** As seen previously, AWS Cognito is the identity and access management offering of AWS. One can create a user pool that can be considered an **Identity Provider (iDP)**

Applications that leverage this setup have to sign in (authenticate) users against a user pool and obtain an identity (ID) token, access token, and refresh token. This is the standard **OpenID Connect** (**OIDC**) specification. The identity token is used to authorize API calls based on the user's identity, and the access token is used to authorize API calls. This is a turnkey solution for most apps that drive their user identity management with Cognito, and it is often a great choice. If the user pool is set up and consumed by an application properly, the only configuration that has to be done is choosing the header name in the request that the app sends for authorization, the API Gateway and Cognito integration does the magic.

The official documentation outlines this approach elegantly.

- **Using Lambda authorizers:** Using Cognito pools as **authorizers** to the API Gateway is elegant, but it requires that the resources be modeled properly; otherwise, it might not work as expected. For a more flexible approach, one can roll up their own custom authorization mechanism, using Lambda functions

In this approach, the client (or app) sends a bearer token, which has the necessary information to verify the claims of the owner. This token can be passed via a header, request parameters, the stage `env` variables, and more.

Whenever the API Gateway that is configured to authorize via Lambda authorizers receives an API call, a Lambda function is triggered and the authorizer verifies the claim and returns a principal (the user) and AWS policy, dictating whether the API call should be passed through (allowed) or not (unauthorized).

Essentially, one is rolling up their own authorization scheme. This requires in-depth knowledge of standard specifications, like JWT, OpenID Connect, OAuth2.0, and the AWS concept of policies.

The following diagram depicts this functionality on a high level:

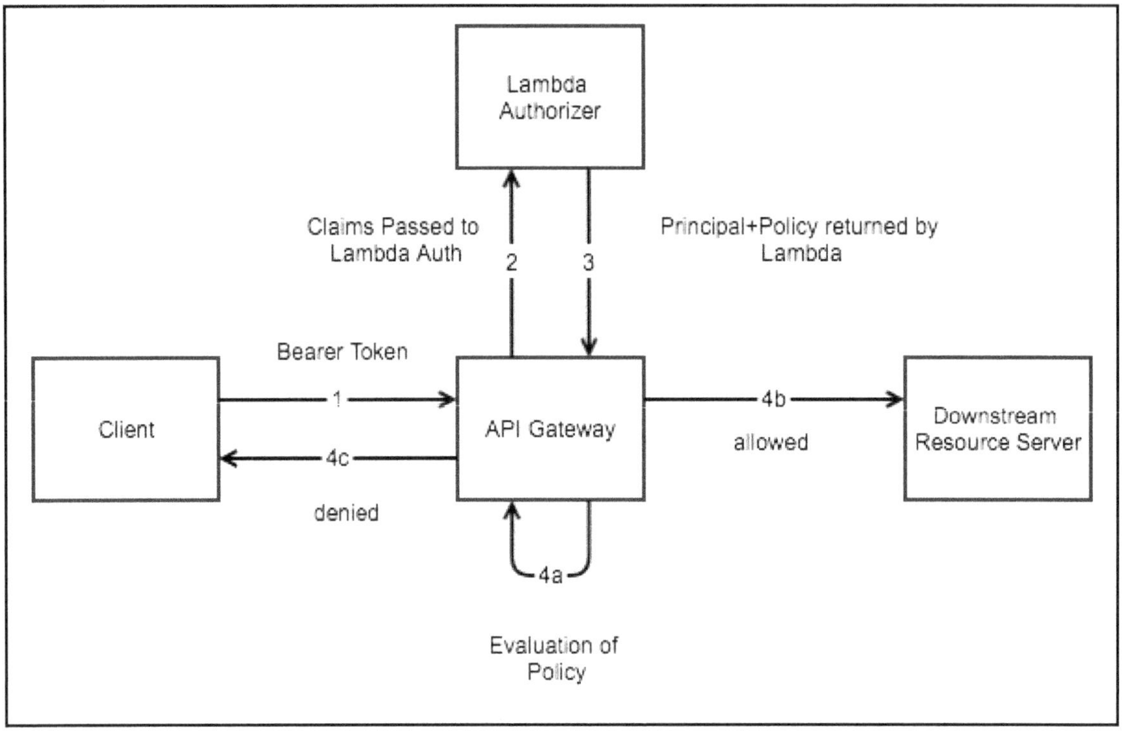

Defining request and response models

API Gateway provides a mechanism to model the incoming requests and outgoing responses and apply basic request validations.

It also provides a mechanism to transform these payloads into the integration requests/responses that are passed and returned from the downstream Lambda functions.

The models are defined using JSON Schema.

For example, for our Greeter API, the request that the API Gateway takes in is only a string. The JSON schema definition for such an entity is as follows. We have named it GreetingInput:

```
{
  "$schema": "http://json-schema.org/draft-04/schema#",
  "type": "string"
}
```

API Gateway extensions to Swagger

As you have seen, API Gateway has various configuration options. Once the configurations are complete, they can be exported as a part of the Swagger 2.0 JSON/YAML documentation.

This is a broad topic, and interested readers can refer to the `official literature` for more information.

Swagger 2.0 JSON documentation with API Gateway extensions

After deploying the API on a stage, there is the option to export the documentation from the console.

The following code block shows the documentation of the Greeter API. We will use this as a boilerplate to create the `LetsPoll` APIs in `Chapter 4`, *Developing Your Serverless Application*:

```
{
  "swagger": "2.0",
  "info": {
    "version": "2018-07-29T11:09:39Z",
    "title": "Greeter API"
  },
  "schemes": [
    "https"
  ],
  "paths": {
    "/greeter": {
      "post": {
        "consumes": [
          "application/json"
        ],
        "produces": [
          "application/json"
        ],
        "parameters": [
          {
            "in": "body",
            "name": "GreetingInput",
            "required": true,
            "schema": {
              "$ref": "#/definitions/GreetingInput"
            }
          }
        ],
        "responses": {
          "200": {
```

```
              "description": "200 response",
              "schema": {
                "$ref": "#/definitions/GreetingResponse"
              }
            },
            "400": {
              "description": "400 response",
              "schema": {
                "$ref": "#/definitions/Error"
              }
            }
          },
          "security": [
            {
              "Greeter-Authorizer": []
            },
            {
              "api_key": []
            }
          ],
          "x-amazon-apigateway-request-validator": "Validate body",
          "x-amazon-apigateway-integration": {
            "uri": "arn:aws:apigateway:us-
west-1:lambda:path/2015-03-31/functions/arn:aws:lambda:us-
west-1:162507129690:function:Greeter/invocations",
            "responses": {
              "default": {
                "statusCode": "200"
              },
              ".*Exception*": {
                "statusCode": "400"
              }
            },
            "passthroughBehavior": "when_no_templates",
            "httpMethod": "POST",
            "contentHandling": "CONVERT_TO_TEXT",
            "type": "aws"
          }
        }
      }
    },
    "securityDefinitions": {
      "api_key": {
        "type": "apiKey",
        "name": "x-api-key",
        "in": "header"
      },
      "Greeter-Authorizer": {
```

```
      "type": "apiKey",
      "name": "x-authz-key",
      "in": "header",
      "x-amazon-apigateway-authtype": "custom",
      "x-amazon-apigateway-authorizer": {
        "authorizerUri": "arn:aws:apigateway:us-
west-1:lambda:path/2015-03-31/functions/arn:aws:lambda:us-
west-1:162507129690:function:GreeterAuthorizer/invocations",
        "authorizerResultTtlInSeconds": 300,
        "type": "token"
      }
    }
  },
  "definitions": {
    "Error": {
      "type": "object",
      "properties": {
        "message": {
          "type": "string"
        }
      },
      "title": "Error Schema"
    },
    "GreetingResponse": {
      "type": "string"
    },
    "GreetingInput": {
      "type": "string"
    }
  },
  "x-amazon-apigateway-request-validators": {
    "Validate body": {
      "validateRequestParameters": false,
      "validateRequestBody": true
    }
  }
}
```

The fragments that are API Gateway extensions to Swagger are as follows:

- x-amazon-apigateway-request-validator
- x-amazon-apigateway-integration
- x-amazon-apigateway-request-validators
- securityDefintions

AWS Lambda as an FaaS platform

In the previous chapters, you learned about the advantages of running business logic in ephemeral functions, or FaaS. AWS Lambda is the FaaS solution that we have chosen. It has seamless and turnkey integration with API Gateway, which is our system's interface to the outside world. As you will see in the upcoming chapters, Lambda and API Gateway can be integrated together in a turnkey, without writing boilerplate code to perform request validations and response transformations, keeping the edge and business layers separate.

System design

In the next section, we'll take a look at the domain model of our app, as well as its required API structure.

Domain models

In this section let us explore the domain model of our system. We will be defining them in the JSON Schema Specification,Draft 4.
The code for these domain models can be found in the code for the book.

APIErrorResponseWithMessage

This is the response object when the API needs to send a message when the API succeeds:

```
{"type":"object","properties":{"message":{"type":"string"}}}
```

APISuccessResponseWithMessage

This is the response object when the API needs to send a message when the API fails:

```
{"type":"object","properties":{"message":{"type":"string"}}}
```

Poll

Poll is a domain object which encapsulates the poll details in the `PollDetails` object:

```
{
    "type":"object",
    "required":[
        "pollOptions",
        "pollQuestion",
        "pollTitle"
```

```
        ],
        "properties":{
            "pollId":{
                "type":"string"
            },
            "pollTitle":{
                "type":"string"
            },
            "pollQuestion":{
                "type":"string"
            },
            "pollOptions":{
                "type":"array",
                "items":{
                    "type":"string"
                }
            }
        }
    }
```

PollCreationRequest

`PollCreationRequest` models the request body for the poll creation API:

```
    {
        "type":"object",
        "required":[
            "createdBy",
            "pollQuestion",
            "pollTitle"
        ],
        "properties":{
            "createdBy":{
                "type":"string"
            },
            "pollTitle":{
                "type":"string"
            },
            "pollQuestion":{
                "type":"string"
            }
        }
    }
```

RespondentDetails

`RespondentDetails` is a domain object which encapsulates the Respondent object and is embedded in the `PollDetails` object:

```
{
    "type":"object",
    "properties":{
        "respondentEmail":{
            "type":"string"
        },
        "respondentDisplayName":{
            "type":"string"
        }
    }
}
```

PollResponseStatistics

`PollResponseStatistic` is a domain model which encapsulates the statistics of the responses to a poll. It will be embedded in the `PollDetails`:

```
{
    "type":"object",
    "properties":{
        "response":{
            "type":"string"
        },
        "percentage":{
            "type":"number"
        },
        "count":{
            "type":"integer"
        }
    }
}
```

PollDetails

`PollDetails` is a composite object which has Poll, `RespondentDetails`, and `PollResponseStatistics` embedded. This models the API response for fetching the details of the polls:

```
{
    "type":"object",
    "properties":{
```

```
      "createdBy":{
         "type":"object",
         "$ref":"/#definitions/RespondentDetails"
      },
      "poll":{
         "type":"object",
         "$ref":"/#definitions/Poll"
      },
      "statistics":{
         "type":"array",
         "$ref":"/#definitions/PollResponseStatistics"
      }
   }
}
```

API model

The following is a conceptual list of APIs that will be required to service the app:

- For registering a respondent
- For creating a poll
- For getting a list of all of the polls
- For submitting a poll
- For deleting a poll
- For retrieving a poll
- For Database Migrations
- For Fixing Database Migrations

We will create a Lambda function for each of these endpoints in the upcoming chapters. First, let's take a look at the design of these APIs.

For each API, we will take a look at the following:

- HTTP method
- Relative URL
- Headers (if any)
- Sample request body
- Responses

The preceding details will be encapsulated in the fragments of the Swagger 2.0 documentation of the API. The full copy of the API documentation can be found in the repository of the code for this book on `Github`.

Registering a respondent

This is the API to register a respondent. The backend needs to have a mapping of the user signed up in the Cognito pool. The API expects an object of type `RespondentRegistrationRequest` as the request body and receives a response object of type `RespondentRegistrationResponse` if the respondent is successfully registered. The following code block shows the fragment from the swagger documentation:

```
"/respondent": {
    "post": {
      "summary": "Registers a respondent",
      "consumes": [
        "application/json"
      ],
      "produces": [
        "application/json"
      ],
      "parameters": [
        {
          "in": "body",
          "name": "RespondentRegistrationRequest",
          "description": "Request body description",
          "required": true,
          "schema": {
            "$ref": "#/definitions/RespondentRegistrationRequest"
          }
        }
      ],
      "responses": {
        "200": {
          "description": "200 response",
          "schema": {
            "$ref": "#/definitions/RespondentRegistrationResponse"
          }
        }
      }
    }
}
```

Fetching all Polls

This is an API to fetch all `Polls` from the database. The app receives an object of type `Polls` as a response. The following code block shows the fragment from the swagger documentation:

```
"/polls": {
 "get": {
 "tags": [
 "Tag1"
 ],
 "summary": "Gets all Polls",
 "description": "Gets a List of All polls\n",
 "produces": [
 "application/json"
 ],
 "responses": {
 "200": {
 "description": "200 response",
 "schema": {
 "$ref": "#/definitions/Polls"
 }
 },
 "404": {
 "description": "404 response",
 "schema": {
 "$ref": "#/definitions/APIErrorResponseWithMessage"
 }
 }
 }
 }
```

Creating a Poll

This is the API definition for creating a Poll. The app needs to send a object of type `PollCreationRequest` as the request body and gets a list of `Polls` as the response on successful creation of the poll. The following code block shows the fragment from the swagger documentation:

```
"/polls/": "post": {
        "tags": [
          "Name"
        ],
        "summary": "Creates a Poll",
        "description": "Creates a Poll\n",
        "consumes": [
          "application/json"
```

```
      ],
      "produces": [
        "application/json"
      ],
      "parameters": [
        {
          "in": "body",
          "name": "PollCreationRequest",
          "description": "Request body description",
          "required": true,
          "schema": {
            "$ref": "#/definitions/PollCreationRequest"
          }
        }
      ],
      "responses": {
        "200": {
          "description": "200 response",
          "schema": {
            "$ref": "#/definitions/Polls"
          }
        },
        "409": {
          "description": "409 response",
          "schema": {
            "$ref": "#/definitions/APIErrorResponseWithMessage"
          }
        }
      }
    }
  }
```

Fetching a Poll

This is the API definition for fetching a single Poll by its `pollId`. The app sends a path parameter `pollId` which is the `pollId` that is generated by the backend as a unique handle on a particular poll. The response is of the type `PollDetails`:

```
"/polls/{pollId}": {
    "get": {
      "tags": [
        "Name"
      ],
      "summary": "Gets a single poll by Id",
      "description": "Gets a Poll\n",
      "produces": [
        "application/json"
```

```
    ],
    "parameters": [
      {
        "name": "pollId",
        "in": "path",
        "required": true,
        "type": "string"
      }
    ],
    "responses": {
      "200": {
        "description": "200 response",
        "schema": {
          "$ref": "#/definitions/PollDetails"
        }
      },
      "404": {
        "description": "404 response",
        "schema": {
          "$ref": "#/definitions/APIErrorResponseWithMessage"
        }
      },
      "409": {
        "description": "409 response",
        "schema": {
          "$ref": "#/definitions/APIErrorResponseWithMessage"
        }
      }
    }
  }
}
```

Deleting a Poll

This is an API to delete the poll. The app sends a `pollId` to be deleted and receives a generic success message on successful deletion of the poll. This API needs to take care of the fact that the user who is deleting the poll should be the one who created it in the first place. The following code block shows the fragment from the swagger documentation:

```
"/polls/{pollId}":{
  "delete":{
    "tags":[
      "Name"
    ],
    "summary":"Gets a single poll by Id",
    "description":"Deletes a Poll\n",
    "produces":[
      "application/json"
```

```
        ],
        "parameters":[
            {
                "name":"pollId",
                "in":"path",
                "required":true,
                "type":"string"
            }
        ],
        "responses":{
            "200":{
                "description":"200 response",
                "schema":{
                    "$ref":"#/definitions/APISuccessResponseWithMessage"
                }
            },
            "409":{
                "description":"409 response",
                "schema":{
                    "$ref":"#/definitions/APIErrorResponseWithMessage"
                }
            }
        }
    }
}
```

Responding to a Poll

This is the API to respond to the poll. The app sends a object of type
`PollResponseRequest` as the request body and receives a generic success message
response on successful response registration. The following code block shows the fragment
from the swagger documentation:

```
"/response": {
    "post": {
        "tags": [
            "Name"
        ],
        "summary": "Responds to the poll",
        "description": "Records the response for a poll\n",
        "consumes": [
            "application/json"
        ],
        "produces": [
            "application/json"
        ],
        "parameters": [
```

```
        {
          "in": "body",
          "name": "PollResponseRequest",
          "description": "Request body description",
          "required": true,
          "schema": {
            "$ref": "#/definitions/PollResponseRequest"
          }
        }
      ],
      "responses": {
        "200": {
          "description": "200 response",
          "schema": {
            "$ref": "#/definitions/APISuccessResponseWithMessage"
          }
        }
      }
    }
}
```

Persistence layer design

In this section, we will take a look at the persistence layer (in other words, the database). As mentioned previously, we will be using Amazon RDS with the PostgreSQL engine.

In this section, you will learn about the following:

- Creating a database using RDS
- Connecting to the database using a command-line SQL tool
- Creating the schema in the database

First, let's create a database instance from the console.

 The following screenshots and configurations are for creating a free-tier database. The configurations are done for a dev/test use case. For production use, there are other recommended settings.

1. Select **PostgreSQL** as the engine on the **RDS** landing page, as follows:

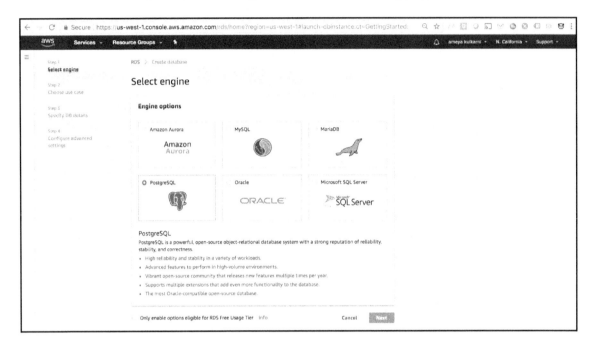

2. Specify the instance details, as follows:

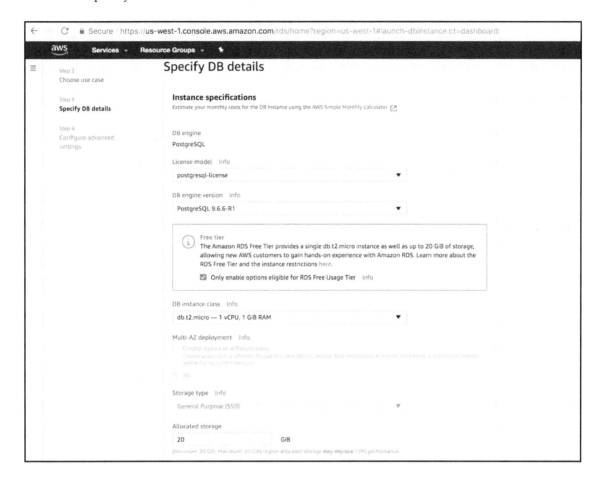

3. Name the database `letsPollDB` and create a master user for it. The username for the master user is `letsPollDB_master`. Choose a strong password. These credentials are used to log in to the instance for the first time. It is highly recommended that you create an application-specific user, and do not use the master user credentials in the client:

4. Configure the advanced settings as follows:

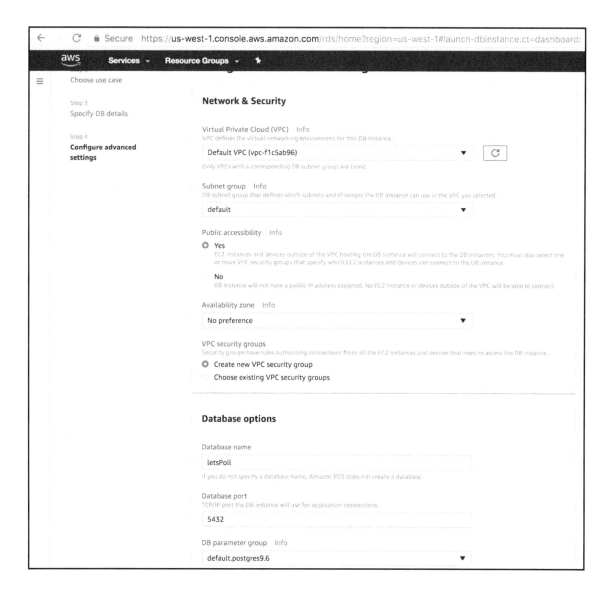

5. Build the advanced settings as follows:

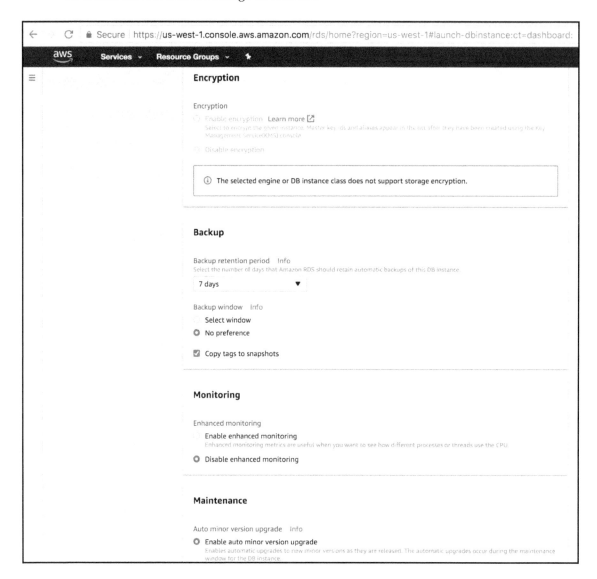

6. The database instance listing is as follows:

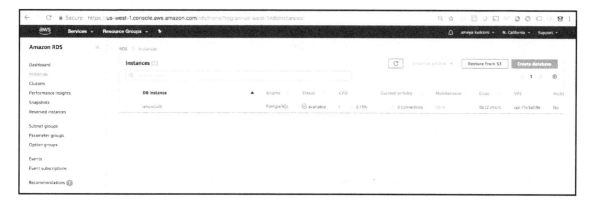

7. The database instance details are as follows:

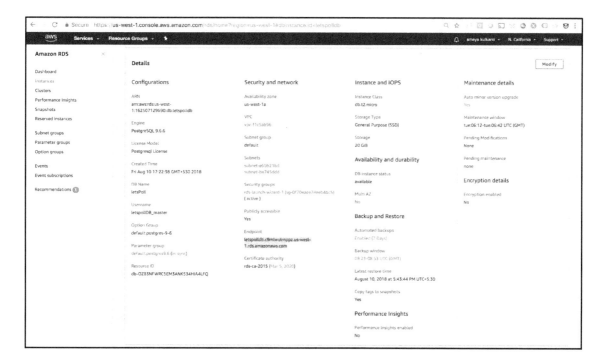

As can be seen in the details, the endpoint to connect to this is `letspolldb.c9mlwulrnppz.us-west-1.rds.amazonaws.com`. You can use an SQL tool, like psql or SQL Developer, to connect to this instance.

Connecting to the instance

Now that we have created the database instance, let's connect to it using psql, which is a command-line utility. The parameters are as follows:

- The database host.
- The port.
- The database master user that was supplied during instance creation.
- The database that was requested during instance creation:

```
Ameyas-MacBook-Pro:~ Webonise$ psql -h letspolldb.c9mlwulrnppz.us-
west-1.rds.amazonaws.com -p 5432 -U letspollDB_master -W letsPoll

Password for user letspollDB_master:

psql (9.6.1, server 9.6.6)
SSL connection (protocol: TLSv1.2, cipher: ECDHE-RSA-AES256-GCM-SHA384,
bits: 256, compression: off)
Type "help" for help.

letsPoll=>
```

Configuring an application user

Once the master user has logged in to the database via the psql command-line utility, create a user named LetsPoll, as follows:

```
letsPoll=> CREATE USER letsPoll WITH PASSWORD '........';
```

Once the LetsPoll user has been created, grant all privileges to that user, as follows:

```
letsPoll=> GRANT ALL PRIVILEGES ON ALL TABLES IN SCHEMA public TO letsPoll;
GRANT
```

Granting all privileges to a user is not desirable in production environments very often. This step has to be exhaustively reviewed by a database administrator. For the purpose and scope of this chapter, we'll go ahead with this configuration.

Schema definition

Now that we have configured the RDS properly, let's take a look at the schema of our `letsPoll` database. After analyzing the requirements, we can design the database to have three tables/relations, as follows:

1. `RESPONDENT`: The respondent/user store is the AWS Cognito user pool. It dictates the authorization and authentication. It will serve us well if we maintain the minimum required data of the respondent in our backend database, as a tie-in to the user pool. It will have the following elements:

   - `A_RESPONDENT_ID`: The auto-incremented primary key
   - `RESPONDENT_ID`: A randomly generated public respondent ID
   - `RESPONDENT_EMAIL_ID`: The respondent's email ID from the Cognito user pool
   - `RESPONDENT_DISPLAY_NAME`: The display name of the respondent
   - `RESPONDENT_TOKEN`: The token that represents the respondent in the Cognito user pool

   The DDL is as follows. Those queries can be run by hand by logging in to the PostgreSQL database in the same order that they occur:

   ```
   CREATE TABLE RESPONDENT (
    A_RESPONDENT_ID SERIAL NOT NULL,
    RESPONDENT_ID VARCHAR(200) UNIQUE NOT NULL,
    RESPONDENT_EMAIL_ID VARCHAR(255) NOT NULL UNIQUE,
    RESPONDENT_DISPLAY_NAME VARCHAR(255) NOT NULL UNIQUE,
    RESPONDENT_TOKEN VARCHAR(255) NOT NULL,
    PRIMARY KEY (A_RESPONDENT_ID)
   );
   ```

2. `POLL`: This table will hold the information of all the polls. It will have the following fields:

   - `A_POLL_ID`: The auto-incremented primary key.
   - `POLL_ID`: The randomly generated string to denote a `pollID`.
   - `POLL_TITLE`: The title of the poll that is created by a user.
   - `POLL_QUESTION`: The question that is being polled.
   - `CREATED_BY`: The foreign key that references the respondent's table. We require this to trace the poll's creation.

The DDL is as follows:

```
CREATE TABLE POLL (
A_POLL_ID SERIAL NOT NULL,
POLL_ID VARCHAR(200) NOT NULL,
POLL_TITLE VARCHAR(500),
POLL_QUESTION VARCHAR(2000),
CREATED_BY integer REFERENCES RESPONDENT (A_RESPONDENT_ID),
PRIMARY KEY (A_POLL_ID)
);
```

3. `RESPONDENT_POLL_RESPONSE`: This table will hold the records of responses to the poll by the respondents. It will have the following fields:

4. `A_RESPONDENT_POLL_RESPONSE_ID`: The auto-incremented primary key

- `A_RESPONDENT_ID`: The foreign key that references the `RESPONDENT` table
- `A_POLL_ID`: The foreign key that references the `POLL` table
- `RESPONSE`: A string that stores the response given by a respondent to a particular poll

The DDL is as follows:

```
CREATE TABLE RESPONDENT_POLL_RESPONSE (
A_RESPONDENT_POLL_RESPONSE_ID SERIAL NOT NULL,
A_RESPONDENT_ID integer REFERENCES RESPONDENT
(A_RESPONDENT_ID),
A_POLL_ID integer REFERENCES POLL (A_POLL_ID),
RESPONSE VARCHAR(255),
PRIMARY KEY(A_RESPONDENT_POLL_RESPONSE_ID)
);
```

Security and access control to the API

In this section, we'll have a look at the Authentication and access control to the API.We will be using two mechanisms:

- API key
- Cognito User Pool Authorization

API key

As seen in the previous section, we will set up an API Key and a usage plan to control access to the API. After this setup, there has to be header that has to be set by the app. It takes the following form:

```
x-api-key:YOUR_API_KEY_VALUE
```

The `YOUR_API_KEY_VALUE` will be sourced from the console or the output of the orchestration framework like serverless.

Cognito authorizer for API

We will use the Cognito User Pool authorizer for controlling access to the endpoints that have to be accessed by registered users only. All the APIs have to be consumed by the users who sign up using the Cognito pool that we created.

The app has to set the ID Token sourced from Cognito in the `Authorization` header of the request. It is of the following format:

```
Authorization:ID_TOKEN
```

This approach is called Cognito Authorization. This ensures that only the registered users can access the API.

Note on the local development environment

Now that we have seen the conceptual model of the API, we will go through a brief walkthrough of the local development environment. This is necessary as the APIs that we will develop in the next chapter assume knowledge about AWS, Liquibase data migration, and JOOQ code generation.

Setting up

Now let us set up the local development environment.

AWS Account

The reader should `sign up for an AWS Account` which has got a free tier usage.

Installing IntellIj Idea CE

As mentioned previously, we will be using IntelliJ Idea CE as the IDE. The installation steps for IntelliJ Idea are listed on their `website`. Please follow the appropriate links for your respective platforms.

PostgreSQL

PostgresSQL 9+ has to be installed on the local development machine. You can choose to `download` and set up or if `Docker is installed`, the cleanest way of getting a Postgres Database running is by running the `official image` as follows:

```
docker run --name lets-poll-db -p 5432:5432 -e
POSTGRES_PASSWORD=mysecretpassword -d postgres:9.6
```

This will run a local instance of the database with the username `postgres` and the database name `postgres`, which can be used for development and build creation.

Third-party libraries

In this section we'll take a look at some of the third-party libraries that we will use while developing our app – Liquibase and JOOQ.

Liquibase

`Liquibase` is a tool required for database schema migration. The Data Defintion Queries that we saw need to be run on the database. But in a production database, it is not scalable to migrate the database by running the queries on the database by hand. They need to be centrally sourced controlled for manageable changes to the database.

As we will see in `Chapter 6`, *Analyzing Your Application* we will not have access to the database as it will be running in a virtual private cloud with no public accessibility. To get around this, we will create a Lambda function which migrates the database programmatically.

Liquibase is the tool that solves the aforementioned problems in a programmatic way. It can be used as a dependency in the `build.gradle` file during build time by using the `Liquibase Gradle Plugin`.

Liquibase can also be invoked programmatically, which we will see in `chapter 6`, *Analyzing Your Application.*

The database changes are encapsulated in a file called changelog. The previous queries that we saw are modelled in a file called `letspoll.changelog.xml`, whose contents are as follows:

```xml
<?xml version="1.0" encoding="UTF-8" standalone="no"?>
<databaseChangeLog
xmlns="http://www.liquibase.org/xml/ns/dbchangelog"
xmlns:ext="http://www.liquibase.org/xml/ns/dbchangelog-ext"
xmlns:xsi="http://www.w3.org/2001/XMLSchema-instance"
xsi:schemaLocation="http://www.liquibase.org/xml/ns/dbchangelog-ext
http://www.liquibase.org/xml/ns/dbchangelog/dbchangelog-ext.xsd
http://www.liquibase.org/xml/ns/dbchangelog
http://www.liquibase.org/xml/ns/dbchangelog/dbchangelog-3.4.xsd">
    <changeSet author="Ameya (generated)" id="1536936215590-1">
        <createSequence sequenceName="poll_a_poll_id_seq"/>
    </changeSet>
    <changeSet author="Ameya (generated)" id="1536936215590-2">
        <createSequence
sequenceName="respondent_a_respondent_id_seq"/>
    </changeSet>
    <changeSet author="Ameya (generated)" id="1536936215590-3">
        <createSequence
sequenceName="respondent_poll_response_a_respondent_poll_response_i
d_seq"/>
    </changeSet>
    <changeSet author="Ameya (generated)" id="1536936215590-4">
        <createTable tableName="poll">
            <column autoIncrement="true" name="a_poll_id"
type="SERIAL">
                <constraints primaryKey="true"
primaryKeyName="poll_pkey"/>
            </column>
            <column name="poll_id" type="VARCHAR(200)">
                <constraints nullable="false"/>
            </column>
            <column name="poll_title" type="VARCHAR(500)"/>
            <column name="poll_question" type="VARCHAR(2000)"/>
            <column name="created_by" type="INT"/>
        </createTable>
    </changeSet>
    <changeSet author="Ameya (generated)" id="1536936215590-5">
        <createTable tableName="respondent">
            <column autoIncrement="true" name="a_respondent_id"
type="SERIAL">
                <constraints primaryKey="true"
primaryKeyName="respondent_pkey"/>
            </column>
            <column name="respondent_id" type="VARCHAR(200)">
```

```
                <constraints nullable="false"/>
            </column>
            <column name="respondent_email_id" type="VARCHAR(255)">
                <constraints nullable="false"/>
            </column>
            <column name="respondent_display_name"
type="VARCHAR(255)">
                <constraints nullable="false"/>
            </column>
            <column name="respondent_token" type="VARCHAR(255)">
                <constraints nullable="false"/>
            </column>
        </createTable>
    </changeSet>
    <changeSet author="Ameya (generated)" id="1536936215590-6">
        <createTable tableName="respondent_poll_response">
            <column autoIncrement="true"
name="a_respondent_poll_response_id" type="SERIAL">
                <constraints primaryKey="true"
primaryKeyName="respondent_poll_response_pkey"/>
            </column>
            <column name="a_respondent_id" type="INT"/>
            <column name="a_poll_id" type="INT"/>
            <column name="response" type="VARCHAR(255)"/>
        </createTable>
    </changeSet>
    <changeSet author="Ameya (generated)" id="1536936215590-7">
        <addUniqueConstraint columnNames="respondent_display_name"
constraintName="respondent_respondent_display_name_key"
tableName="respondent"/>
    </changeSet>
    <changeSet author="Ameya (generated)" id="1536936215590-8">
        <addUniqueConstraint columnNames="respondent_email_id"
constraintName="respondent_respondent_email_id_key"
tableName="respondent"/>
    </changeSet>
    <changeSet author="Ameya (generated)" id="1536936215590-9">
        <addUniqueConstraint columnNames="respondent_id"
constraintName="respondent_respondent_id_key"
tableName="respondent"/>
    </changeSet>
    <changeSet author="Ameya (generated)" id="1536936215590-10">
        <addUniqueConstraint columnNames="a_respondent_id,
a_poll_id" constraintName="unique_respondent_response"
tableName="respondent_poll_response"/>
    </changeSet>
    <changeSet author="Ameya (generated)" id="1536936215590-11">
        <addForeignKeyConstraint baseColumnNames="created_by"
```

```
baseTableName="poll" constraintName="poll_created_by_fkey"
deferrable="false" initiallyDeferred="false" onDelete="NO ACTION"
onUpdate="NO ACTION" referencedColumnNames="a_respondent_id"
referencedTableName="respondent"/>
    </changeSet>
    <changeSet author="Ameya (generated)" id="1536936215590-12">
        <addForeignKeyConstraint baseColumnNames="a_poll_id"
baseTableName="respondent_poll_response"
constraintName="respondent_poll_response_a_poll_id_fkey"
deferrable="false" initiallyDeferred="false" onDelete="NO ACTION"
onUpdate="NO ACTION" referencedColumnNames="a_poll_id"
referencedTableName="poll"/>
    </changeSet>
    <changeSet author="Ameya (generated)" id="1536936215590-13">
        <addForeignKeyConstraint baseColumnNames="a_respondent_id"
baseTableName="respondent_poll_response"
constraintName="respondent_poll_response_a_respondent_id_fkey"
deferrable="false" initiallyDeferred="false" onDelete="NO ACTION"
onUpdate="NO ACTION" referencedColumnNames="a_respondent_id"
referencedTableName="respondent"/>
    </changeSet>
</databaseChangeLog>
```

JOOQ

JOOQ is a Java library that is used for database access. The best part about JOOQ is its code generator, which reflects on a given database and generates database access models, this can be used from the code using a fluent API. JOOQ also is available as a dependency that can be included in the `build.gradle` file.

JOOQ generates .java objects during build time, which are then jointly compiled with our Kotlin code, as we will see in the following chapters. We will be using the `Gradle JOOQ Plugin` to generate the `.java` classes in the `src/main/java directory` of the project.

The database to reflect on generally lies in the build environment. Build environments can be powered by any CI tool like Jenkins, Travis CI, AWS CodePipeline, and so on, but for the scope of this book, we will build and deploy our functions locally.

Build life cycle

In this section, we'll take a look at the basic build life cycle.

The basic goals of the build cycle are as follows:

- Migrate/Instrument the local database using Liquibase
- Reflect and generate the .java JOOQ database objects in the /src/main/java folder
- Joint compilation of Kotlin and the generated Java file
- To yielding a uber jar with dependencies which can be deployed

The `build.gradle` file is as follows:

```
apply plugin: 'java'
apply plugin: 'maven'
apply plugin: 'idea'
group = 'com.packt.serverless.kotlin.letspoll'
version = '1.0.0'

description = """Lets Poll API"""


sourceCompatibility = 1.8
targetCompatibility = 1.8
tasks.withType(JavaCompile) {
  options.encoding = 'UTF-8'
}

buildscript {
  repositories {
    mavenCentral()
    maven { url "https://plugins.gradle.org/m2/" }
  }
  dependencies {
    classpath "org.jetbrains.kotlin:kotlin-gradle-plugin:1.1.51"
    classpath "io.spring.gradle:dependency-management-
plugin:1.0.3.RELEASE"
    classpath "com.github.jengelman.gradle.plugins:shadow:2.0.1"
    classpath "de.sebastianboegl.gradle.plugins:shadow-log4j-
transformer:2.1.1"
  }
}

apply plugin: 'kotlin'
apply plugin: "io.spring.dependency-management"
apply plugin: 'com.github.johnrengelman.shadow'
```

```
apply plugin: "de.sebastianboegl.shadow.transformer.log4j"

repositories {
  maven { url "http://repo.maven.apache.org/maven2" }
}

dependencies {
  compile group: 'org.jetbrains.kotlin', name: 'kotlin-stdlib',
version: '1.1.51'

  compile group: 'com.amazonaws', name: 'aws-lambda-java-core',
version:'1.1.0'
  compile group: 'com.amazonaws', name: 'aws-lambda-java-log4j2',
version:'1.0.0'
  compile group: 'com.amazonaws', name: 'aws-lambda-java-events',
version:'2.0.1'

  compile group: 'com.fasterxml.jackson.core', name: 'jackson-
core', version:'2.8.5'
  compile group: 'com.fasterxml.jackson.core', name: 'jackson-
databind', version:'2.8.5'
  compile group: 'com.fasterxml.jackson.core', name: 'jackson-
annotations', version:'2.8.5'
  compile group: 'com.fasterxml.jackson.module', name:'jackson-
module-kotlin',version :'2.9.+'

  compile group: 'org.jooq', name: 'jooq', version:'3.11.4'
  compile group: 'org.jooq', name: 'jooq-meta', version:'3.11.4'
  compile group: 'org.liquibase', name: 'liquibase-core',
version:'3.4.1'
  runtime group:
'org.postgresql',name:'postgresql',version:'9.4-1201-jdbc41'

}

shadowJar{
    mergeServiceFiles('META-INF/spring.*')
    exclude "META-INF/*.SF"
    exclude "META-INF/*.DSA"
    exclude "META-INF/*.RSA"
    exclude "META-INF/LICENSE"
    archiveName = "lets-poll-${version}.${extension}"
}
```

To build the package, you can use the following command:

```
./gradlew clean shadow
```

Summary

In this chapter, we continued on our serverless journey. We analyzed a problem statement, created a task list for the following chapters, and made a few architectural and design decisions. We dove into some of the advanced configurations for serverless services, like API Gateway, Lambda, and Amazon RDS. We also designed the domain model, the API structure, and the persistence layer of our application.

In the following chapters, we will build on top of this architecture and see our application coming to life, fulfilling functional and non-functional requirements that we analyzed earlier in this chapter.

4
Developing Your Serverless Application

In Chapter 3, *Designing a Kotlin Serverless Application*, we analyzed our app requirements and jotted down all the APIs that we need for app development. Also, we described the UI part. In this chapter, we are going to design an app that has end-to-end integration with the AWS instance. We will demonstrate how using Kotlin, both on the client side and on the AWS infrastructure side, will benefit you. We will learn a lot of cool tricks in Kotlin, which save time and reduce the amount of code.

In this chapter, we will learn about the following:

- Configuring the AWS Cognito pool, which we will use for user authentication
- Code lambda functions, which will keep all our business logic
- Making lambda talk with our persistence layer to store the data on the cloud
- Our companion app, which is in Android, and we will learn a bit of Android as well

Preparing the serverless environment

It's very important that we set up each AWS service correctly. In this section, we will tell you how you can configure each and every required service on AWS.

Configuring a Cognito pool

Let's start with configuring a Cognito pool. We use the Cognito service to seamlessly authenticate and verify the user:

1. Got to your AWS console
2. Select **Mobile Hub**. Mobile hub lets you create a Cognito pool very easily and quickly (you could use a normal Cognito pool as well). It will display a list of any apps you have already created. Select Add new app/Create.
3. Create a project is the first option. Enter your project name. It could be `ServerlessWithKotlin`.
4. Select the platform on which you want to integrate. We have chosen Android for this book:

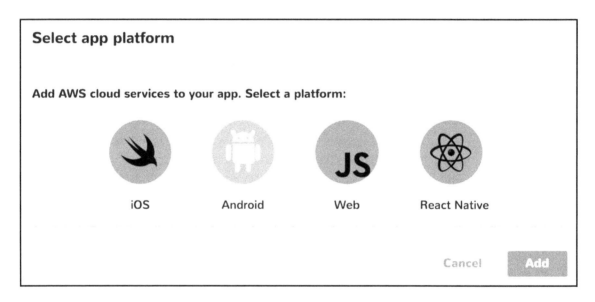

5. Download the configuration file and keep somewhere you can easily locate it. You will need it for app integration. Also you can get the file from the console if you want.

6. The configuration file contains important information, such as pool ID:

Update your backend

Update the cloud configuration file in your app

Mobile Hub generates a cloud configuration file that connects your app to your AWS backend. Download the updated cloud configuration file and place it in *<my-awesome-app>/app/src/main/res/raw/*

    Download Cloud Config

                                                    Cancel   Next

---

7. You should be able to see the final screen with the **Done** option. There is an option to add the AWS mobile SDK as well. There, you can read the entire documentation to integrate the SDK in a step-by-step manner. Go back to your app's landing page and you should find your android app created. Let's integrate it by pressing on the integrate option, which will take you back to step 6.

8. With each app, two services will come by default: User sign-in and Messaging and Analytics. Amazon believes analytics is a very important part of any product, and messaging is important to keep your user engaged with your app. There are other services that you have to configure. From the application's landing page, if you scroll down a bit, you should see the following options:

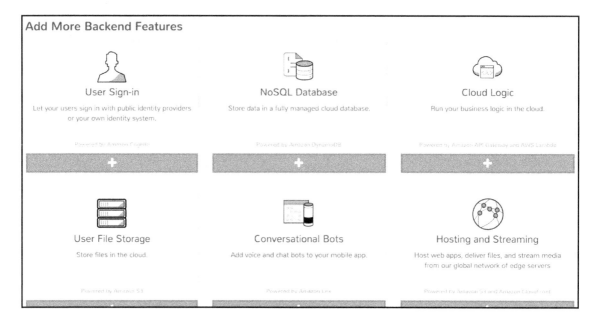

9. Select **User sign-in** from your application's mobile hub page, and it will take you to the page where you will have the choice to select the authentication service. We will proceed using email and password:

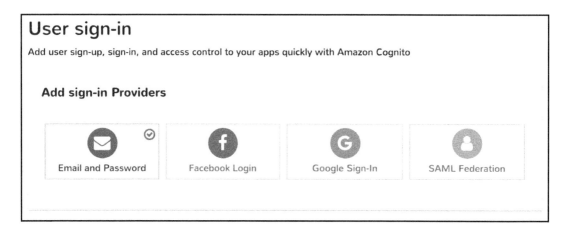

10. You will be presented with a page where you can select the preference for how your signup page will work. You can select how you want your user to sign-up. For example, using email and password or using the phone. AWS allows all the possible ways to sign-up. You can also have options to sign up using third-party services, such as Facebook or Google+. Choose as per your need. We have chosen the normal proprietary sign up using username and password. To follow along, you should choose the same one. Keep it simple for now. Whenever it asks you to create an existing user pool or to create a new one, choose any one. It doesn't matter which user pool creation options you choose. We recommend choosing a new one so that your existing systems will not be affected:

How do you want your end users to sign in?

You can choose to have users sign in with an email address, phone number, username or preferred username plus their password. Learn more ☐

○ **Username:** (Users can sign-in/up with a username and optionally multiple alternatives)

   ☐ **Email**
   ☐ **Username**
   ☐ **Phone**

○ **Email address or phone number:** (Users can sign-in/up with an email or phone # as their "username")

   ☐ Email
   ☐ Phone

Multi-factor authentication

○ **Disabled**

○ **Optional**

○ **Required**

Password minimum length

┌─────────┐
│ 8   │
└─────────┘

Password character requirements

☑ **Uppercase letters**
☑ **Lowercase letters**
☑ **Numbers**

You can also customize the field in your sign-up form. It has also the options like address, photo, gender etc.. Again you are free to choose as per your need. We will stick to the default options for now.

Give the validation criteria for your password. You can set the length and valid combination of the valid charset.

11. There is a **Require user sign-in?** option. Always select **Yes** here since, as a security purpose, we would like to make sure each AWS resource is only accessible if the user is logged in:

Require user sign-in?

Select whether or not you would like to allow users who have not signed in to access AWS resources. You can change this setting at any time.

 YES - Users must sign in to access AWS resources

Amazon will take you through a lot of other user pool settings and configuration, such as **multifactor authentication** (**MFA**), and templates for emails and text messages. If you wish to set them up, you can. Otherwise, keep pressing **Next**.

Swagger for the API

Following the preceding steps, the entire `swagger.json` file can be found at `https://github.com/PacktPublishing/-Hands-On-Serverless-with-Kotlin/blob/master/swagger.json`. Import `swagger.json` into your AWS project and you are good to proceed with the API development and integration.

To import the swagger, you need to have the AWS command-line interface set up on the machine and execute the following command:

```
/aws-api-import.sh --create <path-to-local-swagger-json>
```

Implementing lambda functions

Lambda functions will hold our business logic. They will be executed when an API request is made. We have already shown you how lambda function needs to be bound with an API gateway. You will also see in Chapter 6, *Analyzing your Application*, how the lambda function will sit between the API gateway and CloudWatch. It will serve as a bridge.

Writing your first lambda function in Kotlin

You may have already written a lambda function in your project. AWS supports multiple languages for lambda functions. We will write our lambda function in Kotlin. The Kotlin code will be compiled and converted into a fat `.jar` file. Kotlin code can also be transpiled into JavaScript, and we will target Node.js in `Chapter 5`, *Improve Your App with Firebase Service*.

Choosing an IDE

As you know, Kotlin is a language from JetBrains, a giant famous for their wonderful IDEs. Kotlin works very well with all their IDEs. We have to take the IntelliJ IDEA community edition as an IDE. The community edition is free for personal use. You can download the latest version of the community edition from `https://www.jetbrains.com/idea/download`.

Setting up a project

We will create a single project that contains all the various Kotlin files. Each Kotlin file will contain one lambda function.

Once you have the IDE downloaded and installed, perform the following steps:

1. Launch it and create a project. We will use **Gradle** as a build system.
2. Select **Kotlin (Java)** as an option and deselect all other options:

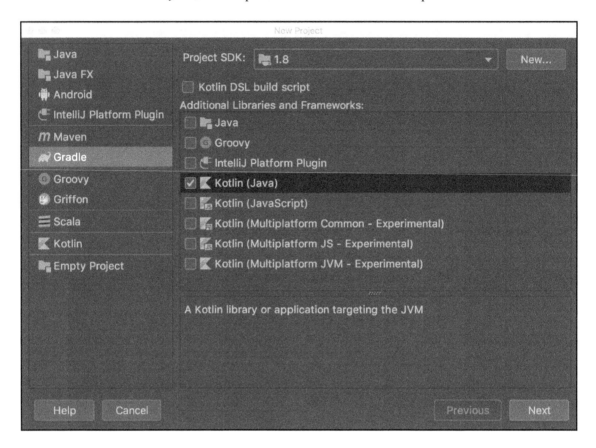

3. Set up **GroupId** and **ArtifactId**. Put ServerlessWithKotlinAWS as the name. I avoid having white spaces and special characters as values.

4. Press **Next**:

5. Uncheck the **Create separate module per source set** option. Select the **Use default Gradle wrapper (recommended)** option, and click **Next**.

6. We are selecting the default Gradle wrapper so that when someone wants to use your project, it will run even if that machine does not have Gradle installed.

7. We unchecked the source set options because that is something we do not want right now. It's for targeting different code bases based on product flavors. It's a logical grouping of your code:

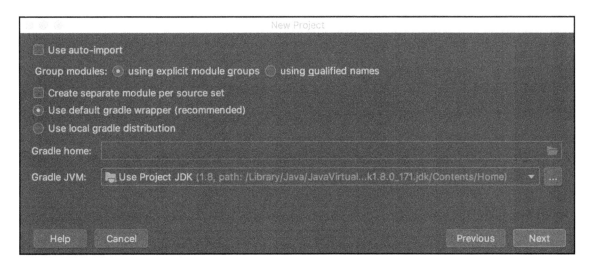

Perform the final steps. Do nothing in this window. All fields will be shown as pre-populated. Simply click on the **Finish** option. IDEA will create a project with the required Gradle files. Check your directory; it will have `build.gradle`, the `settings.gradle` files, and the `gradle` folder generated. The `build.gradle` file is the key file that has all the information that is required to build a project, as shown in the following screenshot:

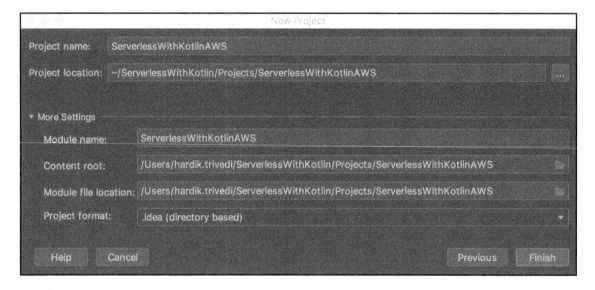

Your directory structure should look like the following. Note that we got the `kotlin` directory inside our `src` directory:

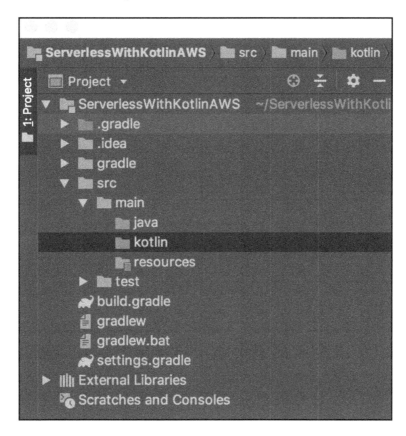

Now we need to add a few things inside our `build.gradle` file. Your `build.gradle` should look like the following:

```
buildscript {
    ext.kotlin_version = '1.2.51'

    repositories {
        mavenCentral()
        jcenter()
    }
    dependencies {
        classpath "org.jetbrains.kotlin:kotlin-gradle-
plugin:$kotlin_version"
        classpath
"com.github.jengelman.gradle.plugins:shadow:1.2.3"
```

```
        }
    }
plugins {
    id 'org.jetbrains.kotlin.jvm' version '1.2.51'
}

version '1.0-SNAPSHOT'
apply plugin: 'com.github.johnrengelman.shadow'

repositories {
    mavenCentral()
    jcenter()
}

dependencies {
    compile "org.jetbrains.kotlin:kotlin-stdlib:$kotlin_version"
    compile "com.fasterxml.jackson.module:jackson-module-
kotlin:2.8.2"
    compile group: 'com.amazonaws', name: 'aws-lambda-java-core',
version: '1.2.0'
}

compileKotlin {
    kotlinOptions.jvmTarget = "1.8"
}
compileTestKotlin {
    kotlinOptions.jvmTarget = "1.8"
}
```

I have highlighted a few lines in the preceding code snippet. You will not see them in your
`gradle` file. You need to add them as an additional setup requirement. The Gradle shadow
plugin is important, and you must have the plugin for this.

The plugin basically generates the kotlin code into fat JAR. It handles a lot of complexity,
which you may need to deal with if not used. With this plugin, your fat JAR file is just one
command away.

Once this is done, we are ready to write our code in Kotlin.

Writing a function that returns dummy static data

Let's write a function that returns the dummy poll response. There are two approaches to writing lambda functions and handlers in Java:

- Loading the handler method directly without having to implement an interface. This section describes this approach.

- Implementing the provided standard interfaces as part of the `aws-lambda-java-core` library (interface approach).

Read more about them at `https://docs.aws.amazon.com/lambda/latest/dg/java-programming-model-handler-types.html`.

Create a file called `Mapper.kt` and include the following line. Here, we simply created a mapper property, which will help us to map all models to JSON and vice versa:

```
val mapper = jacksonObjectMapper().apply {
setSerializationInclusion(JsonInclude.Include.NON_NULL) }
```

Create a file called `PollsGetter.kt` inside the `com.serverless.kotlin` package, and add the following code inside it:

```
package com.serverless.kotlin

import com.serverless.kotlin.model.Poll
import com.serverless.kotlin.model.Polls
import java.io.InputStream
import java.io.OutputStream


class PollsGetter {
  fun handleRequest(input: InputStream, output: OutputStream) {
  val pollList = mutableListOf<Poll>().apply {
  add(Poll("1", "ABC", listOf("Yes", "No")))
  add(Poll("2", "PQR", listOf("Yes", "No")))
  add(Poll("3", "XYZ", listOf("Yes", "No")))
 }
   return mapper.writeValue(output, Polls(polls = pollList))
    }
}
```

To compile the preceding code, you need two classes: `Poll` and `Polls`. Perform the following steps:

1. Create a package inside `com.serverless.kotlin` and name it `model`.
2. Inside `model`, create the `Models.kt` file and have the following classes inside it. Unlike Java, Kotlin has top-level files. You can put functions, property, and data classes all in one file. It doesn't necessarily match the class name and file name:

```kotlin
data class User(val userId: String,
                val userName: String,
                val fullName: String,
                val emailAddress: String,
                val imgUrl: String?)

data class Poll(val pollId: String,
                val pollQuestion: String,
                val pollOptions: List<String>,
                val pollBy: User? = null,
                val result: PollResult? = null,
                val yourReply: YourReply? = null)

data class Polls(val polls: List<Poll>)
data class PollResult(val participant: Int)
data class YourReply(val optionPosition: Int)
```

The code looks so simple. But there are multiple things to learn from this tiny code snippet.

Let's read about all of them. We will break down the preceding code and understand each of the lines that we have written.

Data classes

We are maintaining `Polls` and `Poll`, which is our model. For this purpose, we have data classes in Kotlin. All the pain that we used to endure to create and maintain `POJO` classes in Java is gone. No need to have those dedicated packages to hold your model class. Any Kotlin file can hold your data class. By default, it provides methods such as `toString()`, `equals()`, and `copy()`, as well as the `hashCode()` method implementation. In Android, we mostly use these types of classes to hold our JSON responses in the form of model classes. You can check out the data classes we created in `Models.kt`.

Some points to consider when using data classes:

- The primary constructor needs to have at least one parameter.
- All primary constructor parameters need to be marked as val or var. Data classes cannot be abstract, open, sealed, or inner. Read more about types of classes in Kotlin at `https://kotlinlang.org/docs/reference/classes.html`.

Default parameters

Also, if you observe, each data class has tried to assign some default values to the objects, such as `val pollBy : User?=null`.

Often we end up writing a lot of overloaded methods and method chaining because we want to perform something extra with different values.

For example, say we need to call an API where I want to retrieve either 200 records or whatever value the user has passed, you can only achieve this by writing two function calls.

But Kotlin has a feature where if no parameter is passed, Kotlin picks up the default value if specified, thus overloaded methods can be drastically reduced. The following is the code where you can see how we used default parameters and it's one of the common use cases that is faced by every developer:

```
@GET("/1.1/statuses/home_timeline.json")
fun showHomeTimeline(@Query("count") count: Int = 200):
Call<List<Tweet>>
```

If you see and try to understand the preceding code, the function is expecting a `count` parameter, and `count: Int = 200` says that if the parameter is not passed, the value of the count will be `200` and if the value is passed, `200` will be replaced with a new given value.

Now, the previous function is easily called in two ways:

- If you pass nothing, it will consider the default count size of `200`:

```
timelineService.showHomeTimeline() // This will return 200
records
```

- If you pass any value, that value will override the default value:

```
timelineService.showHomeTimeline(500) // If user wants more
record user will pass desired value
```

Mutable list

Unlike Java, Kotlin has a standard set of collection class. But this `kotlin.collections` package is way more powerful than Java.

The `mutableListOf()` function is one of the functions of this package. It returns the new mutable list of the given object type. You can easily iterate over them. Since it's mutable, it's not thread-safe.

Converting JSON into models using Jackson

There are many efficient and accurate libraries that serve as an ORM and bind your JSON response to a model. Jackson is one of them. Google's GSON and Square.io's Moshi are some popular libraries.

In a static lambda function, there is the `mapper.writeValue` line. A mapper object is defined in a separate file named `Mapper.kt`. And the file has the following source code:

```
val mapper = jacksonObjectMapper().apply {
setSerializationInclusion(JsonInclude.Include.NON_NULL) }
```

The apply() function

The `apply()` function simply executes the function or given block with its own reference as the receiver, and returns the same updated object.

The `apply()` function is defined something like this. The block function always has a reference to the object for which `apply()` is called:

```
inline fun <T> T.apply(block: T.() -> Unit): T (source)
```

If we break the prototype of the preceding function, this means it takes this (its own reference as a parameter and executes all the functions and property calls over it and returns the updated object).

The following two lines demonstrate how android activity can be started and destroyed:

```
activity.startActivity(intent)
activity.finish()
```

It can be written as follows using `apply()`. Not a typical use case, but good enough to understand the usage:

```
activity.apply {
    startActivity(intent)
    finish()
}
```

A typical case of using `apply()` is as follows:

```
val pollList = mutableListOf<Poll>().apply {
    add(Poll("1", "ABC", listOf("Yes", "No")))
    add(Poll("2", "PQR", listOf("Yes", "No")))
    add(Poll("3", "XYZ", listOf("Yes", "No")))
}
```

Which is as good as writing:

```
val pollList = mutableListOf<Poll>()
pollList.add(Poll("1", "ABC", listOf("Yes", "No")))
pollList.add(Poll("2", "PQR", listOf("Yes", "No")))
pollList.add(Poll("3", "XYZ", listOf("Yes", "No")))
```

Having fun with Kotlin code? Our next step is building a fat JAR.

Building a fat JAR

AWS has yet is not provided support to write a code in Kotlin. But being a JVM language, we can convert Kotlin into a JAR file. And we will upload the JAR file to AWS. And once the code is compiled, JVM should not worry about which language it was originally. JVM will only care about byte code, which Kotlin has already generated and bundled into the JAR file.

We have already configured a super-easy way to create a JAR file. In our `gradle` file, we have added a plugin:

```
apply plugin: 'com.github.johnrengelman.shadow'
```

It's a plugin that uses classes and resources used by it, wraps them in a single dependency, and converts them into a `.jar` file. It's often called fat JAR or uber JAR. The documentation says it uses the `JarInputStream` and `JarOutputStream` classes to efficiently process a dependent library and outputs them into JAR.

This has two key benefits:

- Easily bundles dependencies in a library to avoid class-path conflicts
- Creates an executable jar distribution

Open the terminal and go to the root directory of the application. There, execute the following command. (If working on a Windows machine, you can skip the `./` from the following command. We assume the Gradle home path is set, if not please make sure Gradle home is set in `PATH`):

```
./gradlew shadowjar
```

Boom! You will see a Gradle script running on the terminal, and if everything goes right, you will see a **Build Successful** message and a JAR will be generated at `/your_porject_location/build/libs`. The next step is to upload it on AWS.

Deploying a JAR

Go to the Lambda function configuration page. You will find an option to upload the function:

Inside the **Handler** input field, make sure you enter the correct package name, class name, and function name. After this, simply upload it. And you are done. We have deployed our first Kotlin lambda function on AWS. It's time to test it now.

Testing and executing

Go to your API gateway and select the **PollsGetter** API. Remember we imported `swagger.json` early in this chapter. If that step was a success, you should be able to see the following screen:

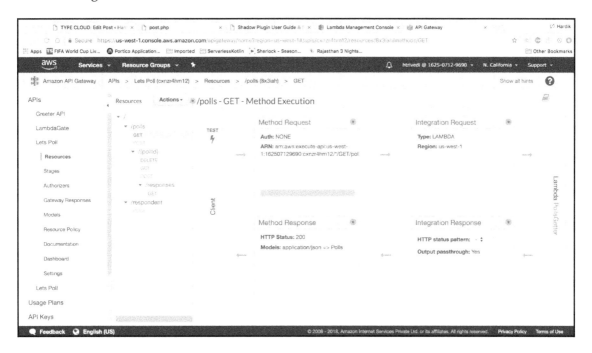

From here, you can navigate to the test console by selecting the **Test** button. You can also test the endpoint from any REST console, such as Postman, the REST API client, or even with Curl.

Your test call should return the JSON result, which is as follows:

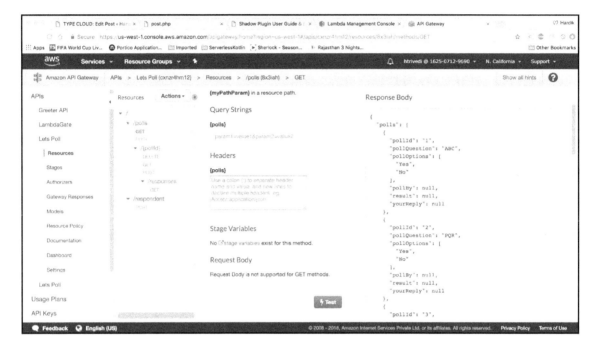

Implementing other lambda functions in Kotlin

I am sure testing the sample lambda function works for you. Once this is done, we can move ahead and complete other lambda functions one by one. Since the preceding one was the dummy one, in this section we will modify it and add other functions. We will cover the following functions in this section:

- Registering respondent
- PollsCreator
- PollGetter

Preparing the data classes

We already discussed the importance of data classes and how they work. Since now we are doing the actual implementation, it's time to restructure it and modify some of them.

In the source code, you will see mainly three files: `requests/RequestModels.kt`, `responses/ResponseModel.kt`, and `Models.kt`:

If I say it's plenty of classes, but still part of only these three files, it's a wonder. Data classes say so much in just one line. Here are those new classes:

- The code for `requests/RequestModels.kt` is as follows:

```
data class PollCreationRequest(val pollTitle: String, val
pollQuestion: String, val createdBy: String)

data class PollResponseRequest(val pollResponse: String, val
respondentId: String, val pollId: String)

data class RespondentRegisterationRequest(val token: String, val
emailId: String, val displayName: String)
```

- The code for `responses/ResponseModel.kt` is as follows:

```
data class PollDetailsResponse(val poll: Poll, val createdBy:
RespondentDetails, val statistics: List<PollResponseStatistics>)

data class PollResponseResponse(val message: String)

data class PollResponseStatistics(val response: String, val count:
Int)

data class RespondentDetails(val respondentDisplayName: String, val
respondentEmail: String)

data class RespondentRegistrationResponse(val letsPollRespondentId:
String)
```

- The code for `Models.kt` is as follows:

```
data class Poll(val pollId: String,
                val pollTitle: String,
                val pollQuestion: String,
                val pollOptions: List<PollResponseOptions> =
listOf(PollResponseOptions.YES, PollResponseOptions.NO))

enum class PollResponseOptions(val response: String) {
    YES("YES"), NO("NO")
}

data class PollResponses(val pollId: String, val response:
PollResponseOptions, val respondentId: String)

data class PollResults(val pollId: String,
                       val pollTitle: String,
                       val pollQuestion: String,
                       val responses:
MutableMap<PollResponseOptions, Int>)

data class Respodent(val respondentId: String, val email: String,
val username: String)
```

That's it. No more talking about the data classes now.

Registering respondents

We are managing the user through Cognito pool. But we will still keep track of the user token, which they get after successfully logging into AWS Cognito pool. We will map this token to one more ID, which is treated as an RID (Respondent ID). It's simple random characters prefixed by RID.

A simple top-level function is written to generate the random ID, which looks like the following code:

```
fun getRandomString(prefix: String): String {
    val mixedBag = "ABCDEFGHIJKLMNOPQRSTUVWXYZ1234567890"
    val salt = StringBuilder()
    val rnd = Random()
    while (salt.length < 18) { // length of the random string.
        val index = (rnd.nextFloat() * mixedBag.length).toInt()
        salt.append(mixedBag[index])
    }
    val sb = StringBuilder().apply {
        append(prefix)
```

```
        append("-")
        append(salt.toString())
    }

    return sb.toString()

}
```

A main code in the handler is a type-safe query written in jOOQ. It stores the random ID along with the token, email address, and the name in the database.

It goes something like this:

```
dslContext?.let {
    try {
        it.insertInto<RespondentRecord, String, String, String,
String>(Tables.RESPONDENT, Tables.RESPONDENT.RESPONDENT_ID,
                Tables.RESPONDENT.RESPONDENT_EMAIL_ID,
Tables.RESPONDENT.RESPONDENT_TOKEN,
                Tables.RESPONDENT.RESPONDENT_DISPLAY_NAME)
                .values(respondentId,
respondentRegisterationRequest.emailId,
                        respondentRegisterationRequest.token,
respondentRegisterationRequest.displayName).execute()
        return
ApiGatewayResponse.builder().setStatusCode(200).setObjectBody(Respo
ndentRegistrationResponse(respondentId))
                .setHeaders(Collections.singletonMap("X-Powered-
By", "AWS Lambda & serverless"))
                .build()
    } catch (e: Exception) {
        e.printStackTrace()
        return ApiGatewayResponse.builder().setStatusCode(409)
                .setObjectBody("Could not create the respondent")
                .setHeaders(Collections.singletonMap("X-Powered-
By", "AWS Lambda & serverless"))
                .build()
    }
} ?: kotlin.run {
    return ApiGatewayResponse.builder().setStatusCode(409)
            .setObjectBody("Could not create the respondent")
            .setHeaders(Collections.singletonMap("X-Powered-By",
"AWS Lambda & serverless"))
            .build()
}
```

We are just being extra safe here and catching all possible exceptions and returning ApiGatewayResponse from the catch block as well and in the run function.

You can see `kotlin.run` is behaving like an else part for the let function.

A very interesting way to write `if else` for null and non-null cases is as follows:

```
someObject?.let {
    // If not null
}?: kotlin.run {
    // If null
}
```

Using an Elvis operator followed by a run function, we can execute the else part if the object is null.

By the way, the Elvis operator is actually named after Elvis Presley. Think of his iconic hairstyle.

Creating a poll

Let's now save all the poll-related information.

We will read the entire raw JSON body and map it to the `PollCreationRequest` class.

jOOQ's `TransactionalRunnable` is a functional interface that has the **Single Abstract Method (SAM)** as its run function:

```
void run(Configuration configuration) throws Exception;
```

This makes `TransactionalRunnable` written in the lambda style.

We verify whether the user is a valid user with a jOOQ transaction:

```
it.transaction { configuration ->
    val respondentRecord = DSL.using(configuration)
            .fetchOne(Respondent.RESPONDENT,
    Respondent.RESPONDENT.RESPONDENT_ID.eq(pollToCreate.createdBy))
    }
```

Note that `respondentRecord` is non-null. And this ensures it's a valid ID.

Rest is a simple db transaction that dumps the data in the database:

```
DSL.using(configuration)
        .insertInto<PollRecord, String, String, String, Int>(POLL,
                POLL.POLL_ID,
                POLL.POLL_TITLE,
                POLL.POLL_QUESTION,
```

```
               POLL.CREATED_BY)
          .values(getRandomString("PID"), pollToCreate.pollTitle,
                  pollToCreate.pollQuestion,
respondentRecord.aRespondentId)
          .execute()
```

You must be loving the way jOOQ is giving you confidence in writing queries. And Kotlin is the cherry on top. Sweet, isn't it?

Getting a poll

Let's write a function to fetch the poll details by poll ID. It's another simple query that returns the `Poll` object along with its result.

The heart of the function is as follows:

```
return if (pollRecord != null) {
    val poll = Poll(pollRecord.pollId, pollRecord.pollTitle,
pollRecord.pollQuestion)

    val respondentDetails = RespondentDetails(respondentDisplayName
= respondentRecord.respondentDisplayName,
            respondentEmail = respondentRecord.respondentEmailId)

    val stateOne = PollResponseStatistics("NO", 10)

    val stateTwo = PollResponseStatistics("YES", 90)

    val pollDetailsResponse = PollDetailsResponse(poll,
respondentDetails, listOf(stateOne, stateTwo))

ApiGatewayResponse.builder().setStatusCode(200).setObjectBody(pollD
etailsResponse)
            .setHeaders(Collections.singletonMap("X-Powered-By",
"AWS Lambda & serverless"))
            .build()
} else {
    ApiGatewayResponse.builder().setStatusCode(404)
            .setObjectBody("The requested Poll with id doesnt
exist")
            .setHeaders(Collections.singletonMap("X-Powered-By",
"AWS Lambda & serverless"))
            .build()
}
```

Nothing much to say here. You just instantiate the model classes and you're done.

One thing to share is how return is written.

In Kotlin, `if else` can be written as an expression. So we just put a return statement outside `if else` and it will be applicable to both. Amazing, isn't it?

Kotlin allows you to write functions as well as if they are expressions. A simple example is as follows:

```
fun add(num1: Int, num2: Int) = num1 + num2
```

Kotlin and the builder pattern

Whenever it comes to builder patterns in Kotlin, it's worth taking a pause to think about whether we really need the builder pattern. In this chapter, the builder pattern is used to create the `ApiGatewayResponse` object.

Now why we strongly feel that Kotlin kind of removes the need for `Builder` classes in most of the cases. The builder pattern says we have all the mandatory parameters as constructors, and the remaining non-mandatory parameters as the `Builder` class, within your main class.

Kotlin has a very powerful yet easy-to-understand feature called named arguments and default parameters. Like we saw earlier in the chapter, the default parameter provides the default value to any function parameter when they are missing at the time of calling.

That you can bind the objects to the function's parameter and not follow the sequence are possible due to named argument/parameter.

So a simple solution to this would be to have all the non-mandatory parameters as the default parameter. Use named arguments extensively and save yourself from using a builder pattern in such cases.

Implementation of the app

Let's see whether everything we have implemented so far is running well. We will set up an Android client app that will consume all the endpoints and services we have written.

Setting up AWS Authentication using Cognito pool

We saw how Cognito pool works in previous chapters. We will implement simple sign-up and sign-in screens, and configure them in an app in 10 minutes. Remember, we created and configured Cognito pool in the *Configuring Cognito pool* section. And we downloaded one file named `awsconfiguration.json`. It's time to use that file. Locate the file and perform the following steps:

1. The `awsconfiguration.json` file contains the configuration of backend resources that Mobile Hub enabled in your project. This contains the pool and details about the backend services your app will need. Analytics cloud services are enabled for your app by default. This sounds cool, doesn't it?
2. Create an Android project using Android Studio. If you are novice in Android, follow this tutorial: `https://developer.android.com/training/basics/firstapp/`. By following this tutorial, you can create an app named `LetsPoll`.
3. When creating a project, on the first screen of the project-creation wizard, select **Kotlin support** as well, because we are also creating the project in Kotlin.
4. In Project Navigator, right-click your app's `res` folder, and then choose **New** | **Directory**.
5. Type `raw` as the directory name and then select **OK**.
6. From the location where the `awsconfiguration.json` configuration file was downloaded in a previous step, drag it into the `res/raw` folder. Android gives a resource ID to any arbitrary file placed in this folder, making it easy to reference in the app.

Connecting to your backend

After following the steps, your app has all the required elements to connect to the server. We will write code to connect the client app to the server now. You will see the concise, well-written Kotlin code doing its magic.

`AndroidManifest.xml` must contain the following two permissions:

```
<uses-permission android:name="android.permission.INTERNET" />
<uses-permission
android:name="android.permission.ACCESS_NETWORK_STATE" />
```

Your `build.gradle` app-level should contain the following dependencies. You might see some library versions not matching exactly. It depends on the SDK level that you have selected. It's advised to select the latest API level:

```
dependencies {
    // Mobile Client for initialising the SDK
    implementation('com.amazonaws:aws-android-sdk-mobile-
client:2.6.+@aar') { transitive = true }

    // Cognito UserPools libs for SignIn
    implementation 'com.android.support:support-v4:27.1.1'
    implementation('com.amazonaws:aws-android-sdk-auth-
userpools:2.6.+@aar') { transitive = true }

    // Sign in UI libs
    implementation 'com.android.support:appcompat-v7:27.1.1'
    implementation('com.amazonaws:aws-android-sdk-auth-
ui:2.6.+@aar') { transitive = true }
}
```

You must create a simple class with a singleton pattern, to access the AWS configuration object whenever needed.

Object declaration

You know writing a singleton is easy, but it requires extra care if you want your singleton class to be thread-safe. Kotlin knows this and offers an elegant keyword, `object`, to solve this. With the use of this keyword, it creates an object, and this is known as object declaration. It is not an expression, so it cannot be assigned to a property. It's a declaration and used by its name directly.

 Objects cannot have a constructor.

The object is also memory-efficient. An object will be only be created when the first invocation happens. And if the invocation never happens throughout the app session, then obviously the object will not be created and no memory allocation will take place.

So let's create a `kotlin` class, `AWSProvider`, in your app, and put the following code as a class body. Remember, the object type declaration is nothing but statically defined functions or properties:

```
import android.content.Context
import com.amazonaws.mobile.auth.core.IdentityManager
import
com.amazonaws.mobile.auth.userpools.CognitoUserPoolsSignInProvider
import com.amazonaws.mobile.config.AWSConfiguration
import
com.amazonaws.mobileconnectors.Cognitoidentityprovider.CognitoUser
import
com.amazonaws.mobileconnectors.Cognitoidentityprovider.CognitoUserP
ool
import com.amazonaws.regions.Regions

object AWSProvider {
    private lateinit var awsConfig: AWSConfiguration

    fun init(context: Context) {
        awsConfig = AWSConfiguration(context)
        val identityManager = IdentityManager(context, awsConfig)
        IdentityManager.setDefaultIdentityManager(identityManager)
identityManager.addSignInProvider(CognitoUserPoolsSignInProvider::c
lass.java)
    }

    fun getIdentityManager(): IdentityManager {
        return IdentityManager.getDefaultIdentityManager()
    }
}
```

Initialize your AWS configuration in your application class. Make sure you add your `Application` class in the `AndroidManifest.xml` file. The `Application` class can be created in your main package, which is as follows:

```
package com.serverlesskotlin.letspoll
```

And in `AndroidManifest.xml`, we specify the name. See the full implementation in the source code:

```
<application
    android:name=".PollApplication">
<!-- Other declarations -->
</application>
```

We have created `PollApplication` as our application class. Any application category class must extend the `Application` class:

```
class PollApplication : Application() {
    override fun onCreate() {
        super.onCreate()
        AWSProvider.init(applicationContext)
    }
}
```

Create `LoginActivity`. `LoginActivity`, which is responsible for launching the AWS signup form and triggering a login event. As with every Android, `Activity` has to be mentioned in the `AndroidManifest.xml` file. We have also added its detail in the `AndroidManifest.xml` file. The intent filter will have action as MAIN and the category will be LAUNCHER:

```
<activity android:name=".LoginActivity">
    <intent-filter>
        <action android:name="android.intent.action.MAIN" />

        <category android:name="android.intent.category.LAUNCHER"
/>
    </intent-filter>
</activity>
<activity android:name=".PollListActivity" />
```

In our `onCreate` function of `LoginActivity`, we will write a code to trigger login flow that will call to the Cognito user pool's authentication module.
The `identityManager.login()` function will take context and return the `success()` or `cancel()` result as the callback. The following code should go right after the `setContentView` function inside the `onCreate()` function. Furthermore, `onSuccess()` will be executed when the user is successfully logged in, and `onCancel()` will be executed whenever the user presses the back button on the login screen. `False` inside `onCancel()` says the activity should not be `finished()` when the back button is pressed. You also need to create one more activity, `PollListActivity`. Mention it inside the `AndroidManifest.xml` file. This activity will be visible after the user is logged in. It can be a simple activity displaying a static text for now:

```
val identityManager = AWSProvider.getIdentityManager()
// Setting up the callbacks to handle the authentication response
identityManager.login(this, object : DefaultSignInResultHandler() {
    override fun onSuccess(activity: Activity, identityProvider:
IdentityProvider) {
        Toast.makeText(this@LoginActivity,
                String.format("You have logged in as %s",
```

```
identityManager.getCachedUserID()),Toast.LENGTH_LONG).show()
        // Go to the main activity
        val intent = Intent(activity, PollListActivity::class.java)
                .setFlags(Intent.FLAG_ACTIVITY_CLEAR_TOP)
        activity.apply{
            startActivity(intent)
            activity.finish()
        }
    }

    override fun onCancel(activity: Activity): Boolean {
        return false
    }
})
```

In the preceding code snippet, observe how we have used the `apply` function. The apply{} function is defined something like this:

```
inline fun <T> T.apply(block: T.() -> Unit): T (source)
```

If we break the prototype of the preceding function, this means it takes this (its own reference as a parameter and executes all the function and property calls over it and returns the updated object).

The following two lines demonstrate how the activity can be started and finished in consecutive calls:

```
activity.startActivity(intent)
activity.finish()
```

With `apply`, it can be written as:

```
activity.apply {
    startActivity(intent)
    finish()
}
```

Now it's time to load the screen that will authenticate you as a user. The following code will launch the login screen. This code should go under the `identityManager.login()` function and as a part of `onCreate()`:

```
// Load the authentication screen
val config = AuthUIConfiguration.Builder()
        .userPools(true)
        .build()
SignInActivity.startSignInActivity(this, config)
finish()
```

While setting up the project or downloading and configuring the dependencies, you may see some errors. Your Gradle may not be able to build the project well. There might be an SDK version mismatch. Check `minSdkVersion` and the library version it's using, correct the version, try cleaning up the project, and build again.

Your registration and login may look as follows:

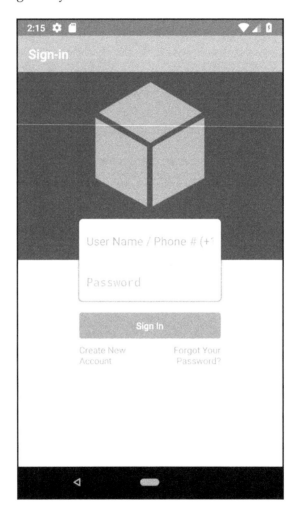

And once you have registered in your app, you can see your user-related information on the AWS console.

Go to **Cognito** | **Manage user pools** | **<Your Pool>** | **General settings** | **Users and groups**:

Integrating the API

Our Android app is written in Kotlin and has a lot of learning's. We will be skipping the other code part where we have created activities, layouts, and so on. We have kept the presenter layer in between for testability purposes. The presenter will have all the business logic. We will keep our views as dumb as possible. It should not have any business logic. The view will not decide anything. It will simply initiate the presenter and let the presenter deal with all delegations.

We need to add the following dependencies in our app-level `build.gradle`:

```
implementation 'io.reactivex.rxjava2:rxandroid:2.0.1'
implementation 'io.reactivex.rxjava2:rxjava:2.1.0'
implementation 'com.squareup.retrofit2:retrofit:2.3.0'
implementation 'com.squareup.retrofit2:adapter-rxjava2:2.3.0'
implementation 'com.squareup.retrofit2:converter-gson:2.3.0'
```

Configuring the API client

RetrofitAPIClient.kt is the file that will initialize the API client. We have used the retrofit library to perform HTTP calls. You will always want your API client to be a singleton (initialized only once and gives access to the same object throughout the application life cycle).

Singleton

Singletons are part of many architecture designs. We like to create the object once and use it multiple times with easy access. Developers like to make the DBHelpers and SharedPreferences manager classes singletons. But not all developers know how to create the best singleton class. The best singleton class is one that supports every scenario of multithreading. A singleton class has various object-creation and initialization methods, such as eager initialization, lazy initialization, and double check.

A widely-used Java code to achieve the singleton design pattern and object initialization will look as follows:

```java
public class Singleton {

    private static Singleton instance = null;

    private Singleton(){

    }

    private synchronized static void createInstance() {
        if (instance == null) {
            instance = new Singleton();
        }
    }

    public static Singleton getInstance() {
        if (instance == null) createInstance();
        return instance;
    }
}
```

In a final class (for example, a class with no open annotation), open members are prohibited. And a member-marked override is itself open, that is, it may be overridden in subclasses. If you want to prohibit re-overriding, use final keyword.

Kotlin creates a singleton with one keyword – `object`:

```
object Singleton {

    init {
        println("init complete")
    }

    fun doSomeThing() {
        // Body of function goes here
    }
}
```

 Objects never have a constructor. You cannot pass any parameter if you want to create a singleton object with an initial value, it's not possible the preceding way.

The format for our API endpoint can look like as follows. It has a URL. The URL is from the project that we configured in AWS. You will see your URL on the configuration page where you map API Gateway with your lambda function. Select **API Gateway** and scroll down, you should be able to see your project's URL.

The AWS base URL is constructed in the following format:

```
https://<apigatewayid>.execute-api.<region>.amazonaws.com/
```

Find both in the following screenshot and a similar one on your AWS console. The highlighted text is what you need to look for on your console and to create your own URL:

The following code will create a singleton object of your API client:

```
object RetrofitAPIClient {
    private val baseURL =
"https://cxnzr4hm12.execute-api.us-west-1.amazonaws.com/"

    private val retrofit: Retrofit by lazy {
        Retrofit.Builder()
                .addConverterFactory(GsonConverterFactory.create())
.addCallAdapterFactory(RxJava2CallAdapterFactory.create())
                .baseUrl(baseURL)
                .build()
    }

    fun getClient() = retrofit

}
```

Another singleton you might have came across in the source code is `DatabaseAccessUtils`. This is the class from the `letsPollApi` project. And this class is giving you another thread-safe singleton to access your `db` object:

```
object DatabaseAccessUtils {
    private var dslContext: DSLContext? = null

    fun getDatabaseConnection(): DSLContext? {
        dslContext?.let {
            return dslContext
        } ?: kotlin.run {
            // Some business logic
        }
    }
}
```

Lateinit versus lazy initialization

While programming, there is always a situation where we debate whether to initialize an object now or when it's required. Well, with Kotlin's lateinit and lazy, there's no need to worry. Often lateinit and lazy confuse developers, let's understand them better here.

Lateinit

As the word says, it indicates that you will initialize before the first usage. We cannot use this property for primitive classes, such as `int` or `float`. Because for every lateinit object, Kotlin uses null to mark that object and throws an exception when trying to access them, and for primitive types, there is no such value. And it always makes sense to initialize them with their default values, such as `0` and `true`/`false`.

You can initialize this type of object in any place where it's accessible. Every non-null object should be initialized at the time of declaration. But often it's not possible. What if the objects are getting initialized using **Dependency Injection** (**DI**). Test setup functions are another place where you want to initialize the object later:

```
class YourClassUnderTest {

    lateinit var mock: SomeClass

    @SetUp
    fun setup() {

        mock = // Initialize mock

    }

    @Test
    fun test() {

// Perform mock test
    }
}
```

 Lateinit cannot be used with nullable and Java primitive types. If you want your property to be initialized from outside in a way probably unknown beforehand, use lateinit. Lateinit will always use `var` and not `val`.

The lazy property

The lazy is a very handy feature in Kotlin. We don't initialize any object unless we require it. This is quite an optimized approach. A typical case can be binding on a view with an object when required. We initialized our API client lazily:

```
private val retrofit: Retrofit by lazy {
        Retrofit.Builder()
                .addConverterFactory(GsonConverterFactory.create())
```

```
.addCallAdapterFactory(RxJava2CallAdapterFactory.create())
                .baseUrl(baseURL)
                .build()
    }
```

A lazy delegated property can only be used with `val`. Whatever you define inside the block will get executed only once.

 Use it carefully, initializing a heavy object when it is required can affect the application's response time. Do not execute functions that are doing too much inside the lazy block.

The following interface will be converted into an implementation by the retrofit library itself. We don't need to write code for the `http` connection:

```
interface PollService {
    @GET("test/polls")
    fun getPolls(): Observable<Polls>
}
```

Interfaces

Interfaces are used to decouple the code. Kotlin interfaces are very much like Java 8 interfaces. That means they can have both abstract methods as well as method implementation.

You can declare properties in interfaces. A property declared in an interface can either be abstract or it can provide implementations for accessors. Properties declared in interfaces can't have backing fields and therefore accessors declared in interfaces can't reference them.

Rxify the API call

Reactive programming has already become very popular among developers. In most android apps, RxJava/Android is used in obvious ways. API calls are one of those use cases. We have attempted to make an API call using RxJava. With Kotlin, you will hardly see any verbosity and the code is so readable.

You might be wondering how the magic is happening here. Lambda functions are the answer. All those curly brackets you see here are lambda functions. I have highlighted them in bold:

```
override fun getPolls() {
    RetrofitAPIClient.getClient().create(PollService::class.java)
        .getPolls()
        .subscribeOn(Schedulers.io())
        .observeOn(AndroidSchedulers.mainThread())
        .doOnSubscribe {
            view.showLoader()
        }
        .doFinally {
            view.hideLoader()
        }
        .subscribe({ polls ->
            view.showPolls(polls)
        }, { error ->
            view.onError()
        })
}
```

Lambda functions

One of the top-selling points of Kotlin is that it supports a function as a type. This means functions can be saved/held as an object or can be passed as a parameter, just like an object. You can think of lambda functions as functions without a name. We used to call them anonymous functions. Kotlin's lambda functions are similar to Java's lambda functions.

They are very useful. They save us a lot of time by not writing specific functions in an abstract class or an interface.

For example, a button's onClick event is one of the boring and stereotype works in Android. But Kotlin does it using lambdas:

```
createPollButton.setOnClickListener {
    presenter.createPoll(pollTitle.text.toString(),
pollQuestion.text.toString(),
getSharedPreferences(getString(R.string.app_name),
Context.MODE_PRIVATE).getString("userId", ""))
}
```

Let's say you want to write a function that adds two numbers but in a lambda style. The code can be written as follows:

```
val sum = { num1: Int, num2: Int -> num1 + num2 }
```

And we can call the preceding function using the following code:

```
val sumAns=sum(10,20)
```

The `val sum` just looks like a property, but it's actually a function. Many developers also use invoke functions, which trigger the lambda function. Using invoke, the same code can be rewritten like:

```
val sumAns=sum.invoke(10,20)
```

Some interesting implementations

Not only we love writing the good code for backend, but we have also like to have our android app written with best coding standards. as well, and that's why there are also a lot of nice implementations of Kotlin features on the client side, and we would like to discuss them.

Returning data from a function

Well this is actually not possible in Kotlin. But it's possible in Android. He he, I just confused you.

Often, we want to return multiple values from a function, since there is no direct way we can use `Pair` and `Triple`.

`Pair` looks as follows:

```
Pair(100, "Hello")
```

`Triple` looks as follows:

```
Triple("Hello", 100, listOf(String))
```

The value within this parameter never holds a true meaning of member data. They can be used for any purpose, and it's perfectly fine if they do not relate to each other at all.

The first statement in this section will not confuse you; by the way, don't look for classes with name `Fourth` or `Fifth`. There are no such classes that map four or five different objects. Use some proper wrapper class, that's what you need.

The destructuring declaration

The destructuring declaration is nothing but a stylish way to extract the data from the model classes at the time of creation. Often, we wrap the data in a model and return it via a function. And on the caller end, we simply access its objects one by one. We actually never wanted an entire class here.

From the statistics object, we want to read the value and the count. Our `getPollStatistics` function cannot return multiple data, so we thought of returning a pair and we are destructuring the pair on the left hand side of assignment operator and use the unpacked data directly.

The signature of the function is as follows:

```
fun getPollStatistics(statistics: List<Statistics>): Pair<Int, Int>
```

And destructuring it and using those values is as follows:

```
val (resultYes, resultNo) = getPollStatistics(pollDetail.statistics)
view.showPollStatistics(resultYes, resultNo)
```

Kotlin's approach to anonymous classes

Sometimes we only need the object to modify some of the member data or to perform a small action. Java was doing this using anonymous inner classes. Kotlin has slightly modified and generalized the approach, and came up with object expressions.

Let's have a look at the following code:

```
CognitoUser?.getDetailsInBackground(object : GetDetailsHandler {
    override fun onSuccess(details: CognitoUserDetails) {
        // Successfully retrieved user details
    }

    override fun onFailure(exception: Exception) {
        // Failed to retrieve the user details, probe exception for the
cause
    }
})
```

`GetDetailsHandler` is an anonymous class used as an object expression.

 Keep in mind that anonymous objects can be used as types only in local and private declarations.

Summary

Wow! I am sure, like me, you are amazed to see how Kotlin can easily do the job. Writing lambda functions has never been so much fun. Kotlin's features greatly help to reduce the code. Not only does it reduce the code, it also gives a great readability to the code.

We saw how we can write lambda functions in Kotlin. We also deployed them in the form of fat JAR onto the console.

Using a jOOQ plugin was fun too. It reduced a lot of boilerplate code.

In the next chapter, we are going to take a deep dive into a service provider called Firebase. Let's see what Firebase is all about!

5
Improving Your App with Firebase Service

Since you're here, I'm sure you've enjoyed the ride with us so far. I can tell that going serverless with Kotlin is giving you a thrill. With AWS, we saw how easy is to develop and deploy the code for Lambda functions. We also saw how we can integrate the database with our code. We performed basic operations, but that should give you a good idea about what we can do in the database with Kotlin. Now, it's time to explore more providers. This time, we will enhance our app using Firebase. Firebase is the mobile and web application development platform by Google.

This chapter will cover the following topics:

- Integrating Firebase authentication
- Writing Firebase cloud functions in Kotlin
- Saving data into the real-time database
- Monitoring crashes
- Monitoring the application's performance

About Firebase

Firebase focuses much on mobile app development, but a good and complete mobile app cannot be developed without the web. This is why Firebase has a lot of services that focus on the backend. To give you an idea, here are a few services that are widely used:

- **Real-time database**: Just like its name, the data is stored and synced in real-time. This can happen on any devices using cloud-hosted NoSQL databases. It takes milliseconds to sync and reflect the data across multiple connected devices. It also supports offline mode and works well. This provides a great user experience, even in flaky or no-network conditions.

- **Cloud storage**: A server is all about processing and serving the data. Not all data is of the String type. We sometimes need to store data such as images, audio, and large video files. This cannot be performed or fulfilled by the real-time database. Using Firebase SDK, you can store such objects in the cloud. Uploading and downloading such data is cost-effective. You also get the benefit of Google's scalable cloud storage. This works in poor network connections as well.

- **Hosting**: A good cloud service is never complete without a hosting facility. With Firebase, it's really easy to host on the web. With Firebase's hosting service, you automatically get free SSL certificates, and a secure, low-latency, and reliable experience.

- **Authentication**: Without a secure and simple user authentication, one cannot deliver a complete solution. Firebase offers multiple methods using email and password. It also supports third-party providers such as Google+ and Facebook. You can build your own customizable UI.

- **Cloud function**: Cloud function lets you deploy custom backend code. It contains key business logic. You can easily trigger cloud functions by various type of events, such as HTTP requests and database updates. This uses webhooks to perform such things. You can compare this with AWS's very popular Lambda functions service.

- **Cloud Firestore**: This is a new flagship database that claims to have powerful and more intuitive data models. It has richer and faster queries compared to a real-time database.

With all these services, we can think about going serverless and completely relying on Firebase.

To give you a more confident situation, here are some industry giants that are using Firebase:

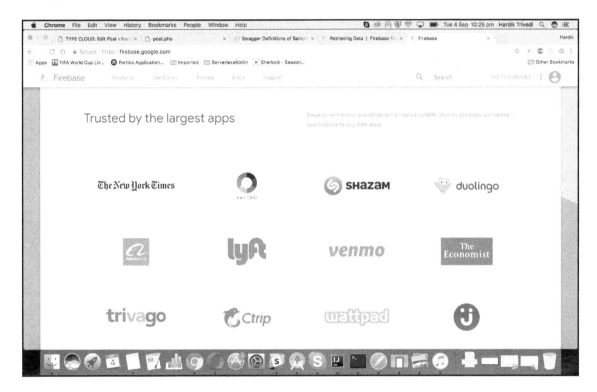

Firebase authentication

In *Chapter 4*, `Develop your Serverless Application`, we added an authentication service, integrated a simple sign up form, and had user-authentication functionality ready. Firebase also offers various authentication methods. Let's integrate them.

Configuring authentication methods

With Firebase, I found setting up configuration easier than setting up the AWS. It has a very user-friendly interface. It authenticates users with the following:

- Email/Password
- Phone
- Google+ login
- Facebook
- Twitter
- GitHub
- And even anonymously, see the following screenshot with all of the supported methods for user authentication:

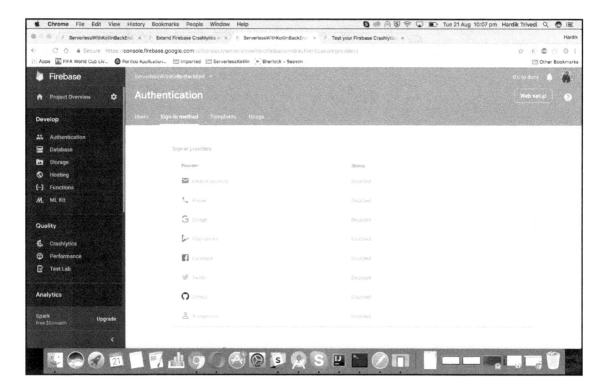

For our app, we have choose to use Email/Password to authenticate users. Let's enable it by turning the switch on:

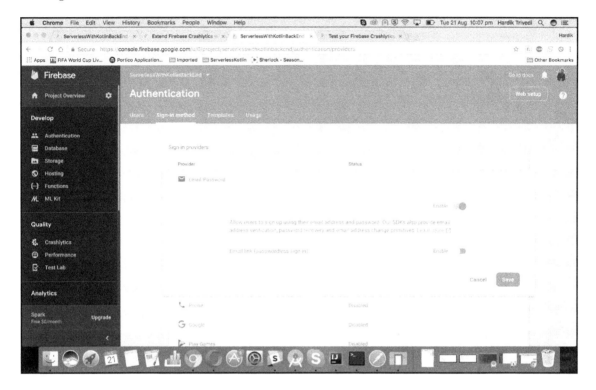

You can edit the email template for verification email/password reset/email address change, which you will send to your user when they request for sign up, password reset, or email address change. The good point is that you can also configure your own SMTP for the emails.

See the following screenshots. The full screenshot should help you navigate to the proper tabs in your project and compare them with our app:

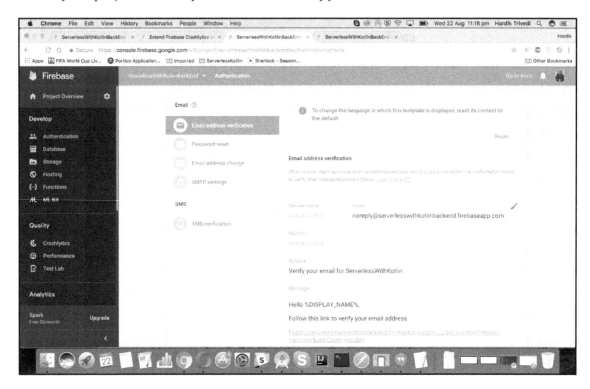

Configuring the client app to use the authentication service

Once the project is configured, go to **Project Setting** | **General** | **Your Apps**. You should see the app that you created. Download `google-services.json` and put it inside your root directory of the project. Afterwards, just run your app. If your app has launched and you can see your activity on the screen, it means Firebase is correctly configured in the app.

Now, it's time to write some Kotlin code.

If you see in the source code, we have written `FirebaseLoginActivity`. This activity has all the code that takes care of user authentication using Firebase. We are not discussing all of it here, but we will cover the important functions.

The when() expression

In the app, the Firebase login screen has multiple views, such as TextView, Button, and so on. Each button has click event to consume. In Android, we usually implement a click listener and then check which button is clicked with the help of a switch case. The following is the way we have written a case to consume a click for each respective button in Kotlin:

```
override fun onClick(v: View) {
    when (v.id) {
        R.id.emailCreateAccountButton ->
createAccount(edtEmailId.text.toString(), edtPassword.text.toString())
        R.id.emailSignInButton -> signIn(edtEmailId.text.toString(),
edtPassword.text.toString())
        R.id.signOutButton -> signOut()
        R.id.verifyEmailButton -> sendEmailVerification()
    }
}
```

Typically, this replaces the switch case of traditional programming languages, such as C and Java. A simple when block can will look something like this:

```
when (x) {
    1 -> print("x == 1")
    2 -> print("x == 2")
    else -> {
        // Note the block  print("x is neither 1 nor 2")
    }
}
```

There's no verbosity and it's simple to understand, isn't it? We have used the when block in the app in multiple places.

when() can also be used as a replacement for an if...else chain. If no argument is supplied, the branch conditions are simply Boolean expressions, and a branch is executed when its condition is true. See the following code, which explains how the if...else ladder can be replaced with the when function:

```
when {
    x.isOdd() -> print("x is odd")
    x.isEven() -> print("x is even")
else -> print("x is funny")
}
```

Improving the signIn() function using Lambda functions

Lambda functions are nothing but functions without a name. We used to call them anonymous functions. A function is basically passed into a parameter of a function call as an expression. They are very useful. They save us a lot of time by not writing specific functions in an abstract class or interface.

Lambda usage can be as simple as the following code snippet, where it seems like we are simply binding a block to some property. But that property can be invoked as a function. "hello is actually a Lambda function.":

```
fun main(args: Array<String>) {
    val hello = { println("Hello from ServerlessWithKotlin team!") }
    hello()
}
```

At the same time, the Lambda can be a bit complex, just like the following code block:

```
fun <T> lock(lock: Lock, body: () -> T): T {
    lock.lock()
    try {
        return body()
    } finally {
        lock.unlock()
    }
}
```

The following are the functions that use the Lambda as the last parameter. You can call them in different ways:

```
yourFunction({})
yourFunction("ServerlessWithKotlin",1,{})
yourFunction("ServerlessWithKotlin",1){}
yourFunction{}
```

A typical java `signIn()` function can look like this:

```
mAuth.signInWithCustomToken(mCustomToken)
        .addOnCompleteListener(this, new OnCompleteListener<AuthResult>() {
            @Override
            public void onComplete(@NonNull Task<AuthResult> task) {
                if (task.isSuccessful()) {
                    FirebaseUser user = mAuth.getCurrentUser();
                    updateUI(user);
                } else {
```

```
                            Toast.makeText(CustomAuthActivity.this, "Authentication
failed.",
                            Toast.LENGTH_SHORT).show();
                            updateUI(null);
                    }
            }
        });
```

But thanks to Kotlin's Lambda functions making code concise and readable, our `signIn` function looks as follows:

```
auth.signInWithEmailAndPassword(email, password)
        .addOnCompleteListener(this) { task ->
            if (task.isSuccessful) {
                updateUI(auth.currentUser)
                showPollListActivity()
            } else {
                Toast.makeText(this@FirebaseLoginActivity, "Authentication
failed.",
                            Toast.LENGTH_SHORT).show()
                updateUI(null)
            }
        }
```

Extension functions

If you know C#, you might be familiar with extension functions. Extension functions allow you to add new functionality to the existing class without inheriting it.

Ditching the findViewById() method

In the world of Android, `findViewById()` is a necessity, and we know how painful it is to code it every time for every view. Yes, a butter knife will give some relief, but it has its own disadvantages (we will not go into them). Since Kotlin is targeting Android app development, it has to provide the solution to this problem. And Kotlin's kotlin- Android-extensions are the solution.

If the following is your view:

```
<Button
    Android:id="@+id/emailSignInButton"
    style="@style/Widget.AppCompat.Button.Colored"
    Android:layout_width="0dp"
    Android:layout_height="wrap_content"
    Android:layout_weight="1"
    Android:text="@string/sign_in" />
```

A typical piece of Java code would look as follows:

```
Button emailSignInButton = (Button)findViewById(R.id.emailSignInButton);
emailSignInButton.setOnClickListener( new OnClickListener() {
    @Override public void onClick(View v) {
        // TODO Auto-generated method stub
    }
});
```

But with Kotlin, it's one import statement and we are done:

```
import kotlinx.Android.synthetic.main.activity_firebase_auth.*
verifyEmailButton.isEnabled = false
```

To achieve this, we need to add `apply plugin:kotlin-Android-extensions` in our app-level `build.gradle` file.

View extensions

Often, we need to play with the view's visibility. Extension functions can help us here. In the `ViewExtensions.kt` file, there are two extension functions written inside:

```
fun View.show() {
    this.visibility = View.VISIBLE
}

fun View.hide() {
    this.visibility = View.GONE
}
```

Now, suppose you want to change the visibility of any of the views; you can write the code in the following way:

```
emailPasswordButtons.hide()
emailPasswordFields.hide()
signedInButtons.show()
```

 Extension functions are visible for all child classes as well. For example, we wrote the extension function for the View class. So, we can call the visible() and gone() functions from any subclass of View, that is, EditText, TextView, Button, CardView, RecyclerView, ListView, and so on.

Firebase cloud functions

Firebase cloud functions let you run a specific piece of code whenever an event is triggered or an HTTP request comes to your Firebase server. This is the same as AWS's Lambda functions. Firebase cloud functions can respond to:

- Firebase Authentication triggers
- Google Analytics for Firebase triggers
- Crashlytics triggers
- Cloud Storage triggers
- Cloud Pub/Sub triggers
- HTTP triggers

Since here we are mainly discussing Kotlin, this section will demonstrate how to use Kotlin code to write a cloud function that ultimately serves as your business logic for the API.

Furthermore, in this section, we will also see how Kotlin code is transpiled into JavaScript. Well, Firebase only supports JavaScript code (or TypeScript code to transpile at deployment) to handle events from Firebase services. For this chapter, we chose to use JavaScript. We will look at how Kotlin code can be smoothly converted into Node.js.

Prerequisites

We assume that you have a fundamental idea of how to set up the node environment. We will cover setting up the node environment at a high level. There are various popular ways of installing node and npm on any OS. Some prefer the installer, and some prefer the geeky way of doing it through the installer. For any novice user, I would suggest using the installer.

Get the appropriate installer for your OS from `https://nodejs.org/en/download/`.

Once the node is installed, verify the installation by executing the following two commands. It should print their versions:

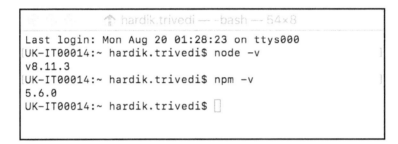

For this chapter, we will use IntelliJ Idea Community Edition as an IDE. It has the best support for Kotlin and JavaScript.

Setting up the project

Creating a Gradle project is similar to how we created the project in *Chapter 4, Developing your Serverless Application*. The following step is the only difference:

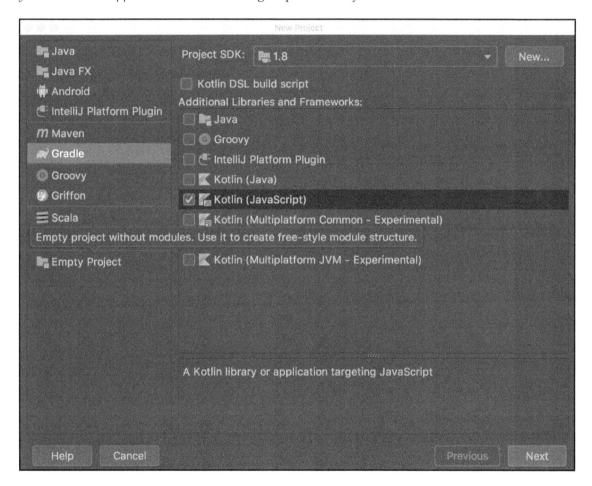

Once the Gradle project is ready, we will need Kotlin's dependency on Node.js and express.js support. From the IDE's terminal, perform the following steps:

1. Currently, the project is simple a Gradle project; it has no information regarding Node.js-related files. We need to make the project compatible with Node.js by doing the following:

   ```
   npm init
   ```

2. Install the Kotlin dependency:

   ```
   npm install kotlin --save
   ```

3. To create the API, we need ExpressJS. Add the ExpressJS library with the following code:

   ```
   npm install express --save
   ```

After this, we also need to make the project aware that it's a Kotlin + Node.js + Firebase project. Execute the following commands:

```
npm install firebase-functions@latest firebase-admin@latest --save
npm install -g firebase-tools
```

Firebase admin gives you full control over your database, which we will require in the next section. For now, it's time to initialize the Firebase SDK and cloud functions:

1. Execute `firebase login` on the terminal to the log. It will authenticate you via the browser and provide the access to the Firebase tool.
2. Jump into your Firebase project directory: `cd <your project directory>`.
3. Run `firebase init functions`. When you try executing this command, the tool will give you an option to install dependencies with npm. It's perfectly fine if you want to manage dependency in some other way and on your own.
4. Firebase supports two languages, JavaScript and TypeScript, and so it will give you these two options. Choose JavaScript.

If all four steps have been completed successfully, you should see the following directory structure in your project. It should have the `folder`, `firebase.json`, and `package.json` functions inside the `functions` directory:

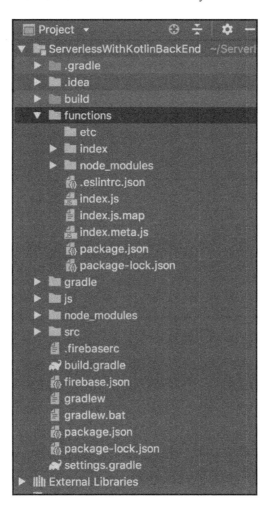

If you see this, boom! You are ready to write your first cloud function in Kotlin.

Creating a simple cloud function

Let's create a simple cloud function that accepts a string value and returns it.

Create a `Main.kt` file with the following code inside:

```
external fun require(module: String): dynamic
external val exports: dynamic

fun main(args: Array<String>) {
    val functions = require("firebase-functions")
    val admin = require("firebase-admin")
    admin.initializeApp(functions.config().firebase)

    exports.echoString = functions.https.onRequest { req, res ->
        val text = req.query.text
        res.status(200).send("Echo : $text")
    }
}
```

The dynamic keyword has a meaning. Kotlin is statically-typed, but because of interoperability features, it still has to deal with untyped or loosely-typed languages and environments. This allows you to call any property or function on any type of object. It basically turns off Kotlin's type-checker. We require an express library, so we need to use the following code:

```
require("firebase-admin")
```

The `require` function is also used to define that it's a function that takes a string parameter. It's external and dynamic, so the Kotlin compiler will skip the checks at the time of compiling the code for these functions and consider, that they are not part of Kotlin's lib and will be used by the native language for which code is converted or transpiled.

`onRequest` is nothing but a function that accepts parameters in the Lambda function style. `req` and `res` are just parameter names for the `Request` and `Response` classes, respectively.

Deploying the cloud function

We need to make a small change to our `build.gradle` file to specify the output file:

```
ompileKotlin2Js {
    kotlinOptions.moduleKind = "commonjs"
    kotlinOptions.outputFile = "functions/index.js"
    kotlinOptions.sourceMap = true
}
```

To deploy and execute `echoString`, run the following command on the terminal, building the Kotlin code:

```
./gradlew build
```

Deploy the functions:

```
firebase deploy --only functions
```

A series of a few more internal commands will be triggered and you can see what's happening on the terminal. Once the cloud function is deployed, you will see the URL displayed on the terminal itself. See the following image:

```
                                                    ServerlessWithKotlinBackEnd — -bash — 191×38
UK-IT00014:ServerlessWithKotlinBackEnd hardik.trivedi$ firebase deploy --only functions

    Deploying to 'serverlesswithkotlinbackend'...

  deploying functions
Running command: npm --prefix "$RESOURCE_DIR" run lint

> functions@ lint /Users/hardik.trivedi/ServerlessWithKotlin/Projects/ServerlessWithKotlinBackEnd/functions
> eslint .

  functions: Finished running predeploy script.
  functions: ensuring necessary APIs are enabled...
  functions: all necessary APIs are enabled
  functions: preparing functions directory for uploading...
  functions: packaged functions (55.7 KB) for uploading
  functions: functions folder uploaded successfully
  functions: creating Node.js 6 function echoString(us-central1)...
  functions: updating Node.js 6 function saveString(us-central1)...
  functions: updating Node.js 6 function getStrings(us-central1)...
  functions: updating Node.js 6 function createPoll(us-central1)...
  functions[echoString(us-central1)]: Successful create operation.
Function URL (echoString): https://us-central1-serverlesswithkotlinbackend.cloudfunctions.net/echoString
  functions[saveString(us-central1)]: Successful update operation.
  functions[createPoll(us-central1)]: Successful update operation.
  functions[getStrings(us-central1)]: Successful update operation.

  Deploy complete!

Project Console: https://console.firebase.google.com/project/serverlesswithkotlinbackend/overview
UK-IT00014:ServerlessWithKotlinBackEnd hardik.trivedi$
```

Now, try hitting the URL in the browser example: `https://us-central1-serverlesswithkotlinbackend.cloudfunctions.net/echoString?text=Hello.`

You should be able to see the output of this text displayed on a page.

Saving data into the real-time database

The Firebase real-time database is a cloud-hosted database. Data is stored as JSON and synchronized in real-time to every connected client. When you build cross-platform apps with our iOS, Android, and JavaScript SDKs, all of your clients share one real-time database instance and automatically receive updates with the newest data.

Real-time databases offer support for Android, iOS, Web, and Admin. The Firebase real-time database admin is very interesting. With the Admin SDK, you can read and write real-time database data with full admin privileges, or with finer-grained limited privileges. In this section, we'll guide you through adding the Firebase Admin SDK to your project to access the Firebase real-time database.

It is also interesting to know how we can structure data. Read more at `https://firebase.google.com/docs/database/admin/structure-data`.

Like AWS's Lambda functions, you can write and deploy as many cloud functions as you require in Firebase, doing variety of things. But we will only cover one function here. This cloud function will save data to Firebase's real-time database.

The task is very small, but it has a few steps involved. Let's break it down and get each of them done.

Structuring the request model

The client app passes the raw JSON in the body to the post request. All modern client apps use the object mapper libs, which convert the model to JSON.

Our request model should look like this:

```
data class RequestPoll(
        val pollQuestion: String,
        val pollOptions: Array<String>
)
```

For now, we are avoiding other member data, such as the user ID; you can find this in the main source code.

Let's assume that the request is coming as a raw JSON in the body of a post request. We will read that body content from the request and convert it back to the model.

We will also generate one ID, which we store on our side as a unique key to that poll.

A function for generating a random ID can look as the following:

```
fun getRandomPollId() = Math.floor(Math.random() * Int.MAX_VALUE) + 1 *
1000
```

Structuring and saving the database object

Once we have the request model and the function for generating a random ID, we will create a new object that we will store in the database. The code for that will look like this:

```
exports.createPoll = functions.https.onRequest { req, res ->
    val reqBody = req.rawBody
    val poll = JSON.parse<RequestPoll>(reqBody)
    val newPoll = ResponsePoll(getRandomPollId().toString(),
poll.pollQuestion, poll.pollOptions)
}
```

The final `onRequest` function will look like this:

```
exports.createPoll = functions.https.onRequest { req, res ->
    val reqBody = req.rawBody
    val poll = JSON.parse<RequestPoll>(reqBody)
    val newPoll = ResponsePoll(getRandomPollId().toString(),
poll.pollQuestion, poll.pollOptions)

    res.status(200).send(JSON.stringify(newPoll))
    val ref = admin.database().ref("/poll")

    ref.push(newPoll).then {
        res.status(200).send(JSON.stringify(newPoll))
    }
}
```

We are using a push function to set the data in the Firebase database.

Firebase mainly offers the following four-ways to save the data:

- **Set:** This writes or replaces data to a given path, such as `polls/users/<userName>`.
- **Update:** This updates some of the keys for a defined path without replacing all of the data.
- **Push:** This adds a list of data in the database. Whenever you push a new node onto a list, a database generates a unique key, such as `polls/users/<userId>/<username>`.
- **Transaction:** Whenever there is complex data and the possibility of concurrent updates, use transaction .

On a successful push, we send a new object as a JSON bundled as a 200 response.

Getting the list of polls

Firebase also offers two ways to retrieve the data:

- **Asynchronous listeners**: Datastore is fetched in an asynchronous fashion. Sometimes, your code has to execute so much business logic to respond to the request. You just can't afford to do it synchronously. It's like watching water boiling on the stove, while you could do much more work in parallel. Similar is the concept of asynchronous listeners. This listener triggers the first time with the initial state of the data, and then it triggers when the record is changed every time. The event is always attached to the database reference. It supports the Java, Node.js, Python, and Admin SDK languages and platforms.
- **Blocking reads**: Sometimes, it's worth waiting for the response. Let's say you cannot perform the next task until you get the status from your previous action. In such cases, you use blocking reads. Unlike asynchronous listeners, this triggers in a synchronous fashion. This also gets attached to a database reference. This returns the data stored at the reference once. Each method call is considered a one-time operation. This clearly means that after the operation is complete, you will not receive any callback if data changes. This model of data retrieval is supported in Python and Go Admin SDK only.

There are various read event types in Java and Node.js:

- `ref.on("value")`: It is used to get the static snapshot of the data at any given point of time. It is triggered only once with the initial data, and again when any data is changed. An event is passed with the snapshot with all the data contained at that location.
- `ref.on("child_added")`: Whenever you retrieve a list type of data, this is the most commonly used event type. Unlike value, which returns the entire content of the location, this is triggered for each child item. It also triggers whenever a new item is added.
- `ref.on("child_changed")`: This event is triggered any time a child node is modified. The snapshot passed to the event callback contains the updated data for the child.
- `ref.on("child_removed")`: This event is triggered when an immediate child is removed. The snapshot passed to the event callback contains the data for the removed child.
- `ref.on("child_moved")`: This event is used when working with ordered data.

Our `getAllPolls` function written in Kotlin will look as follows:

```
exports.getAllPoll = functions.https.onRequest { req, res ->
    val result = mutableListOf<String>()

    val ref = admin.database().ref("/poll")

    ref.on("child_added") { snapShot, prevChildKey ->
        result.add(js("snapShot.val()"))
    }

    res.status(200).send(JSON.stringify(result))
}
```

Interoperability with JavaScript

After all the hard work we did to develop Kotlin code, what if we have a very crucial piece of code that is well-written and well-tested, but written in JavaScript. Are we going to convert it into Kotlin? No. The way Kotlin code can interoperate with Java is the same way *Kotlin for JavaScript* is also interoperable with JavaScript. This means that JavaScript can call Kotlin code and Kotlin can call JavaScript code.

Each function is giving a call to a JavaScript function using a `js("...")` function.

You might have noticed this function's call in our code snippet. Why did we use this? In Node.js, `snapShot.val()` gives you the actual data. But val is the keyword in Kotlin, so we do not have a way to call the `val()` function from Kotlin. We have to think about interoperability. This leads us to write a line such as the following:

```
result.add(js("snapShot.val()"))
```

Monitoring crashes

When you create your application with your dedicated time and effort, you will obviously make sure that it's treated with love when it reaches the end user. Your user hates crashes. How do you gracefully handle them and fix them? Firebase's crashlytics is the answer.

Firebase Crashlytics (initially owned and known as Fabric) is a lightweight, real-time crash-reporter tool. This helps us to catch all the incorrect behavior in the app. We can track the issues and later prioritize and fix them. **Track | Prioritise | Fix this cycle** will help your app gain stability. With the facility to track the events and behavior with custom keys, it saves time in troubleshooting the crash. You don't need to debug the app to find the crash. The unique key in the code will tell you where it's coming from.

Its key capabilities are as follows:

- Well-designed crash reports
- By default, it finds crashlytics common crashes
- Integrated with analytics
- Real-time notifications

You can configure crashlytics on your Android. Here is the step-by-step tutorial on the official website: `https://firebase.google.com/docs/crashlytics/get-started#Android`.

Wouldn't it be a cool if when app is crashes, it automatically creates a Jira ticket, sends an email to the lead developer, or posts on your slack group? Well, with crashlytics, all this is possible. Crashlytics can be extended to Firebase cloud functions.

Firebase will trigger a cloud function if any new issue is reported on crashlytics.

The following code shows the Kotlin function:

```
exports.postOnNewIssue = functions.crashlytics.issue().onNew { issue ->
    val issueId = issue.issueId
    val issueTitle = issue.issueTitle
    val appName = issue.appInfo.appName
    val appPlatform = issue.appInfo.appPlatform
    val latestAppVersion = issue.appInfo.latestAppVersion

    val slackMessage = "<!here|here> A new issue is reported – $issueTitle
($issueId) in $appName, version $latestAppVersion on $appPlatform"

    //notifySlack(slackMessage)
    console.log("Posted new issue $issueId successfully to Slack")
}
```

We couldn't test it end to end, but this should give you a good idea of how it works.

Customizing the crash reports

Firebase collects the crashes by default. But if you care about your user's privacy and data and want your user to know before collecting anything from their device. You need to prevent automatic initialization, you can do this by adding the following line in the `AndroidManifest.xml` file:

```
<meta-data
    Android:name="firebase_crashlytics_collection_enabled"
    Android:value="false" />
```

You can design a nice interface where you take permission from your user to collect the data. If the user allows you, then you initialize the Firebase SDK, which is as follows:

```
Fabric.with(this, Crashlytics())
```

You can't stop Crashlytics detailing once you've started it in an app session. To opt out of outlining after you've started Crashlytics, users have to start your app again.

A typical crash report will look something like following:

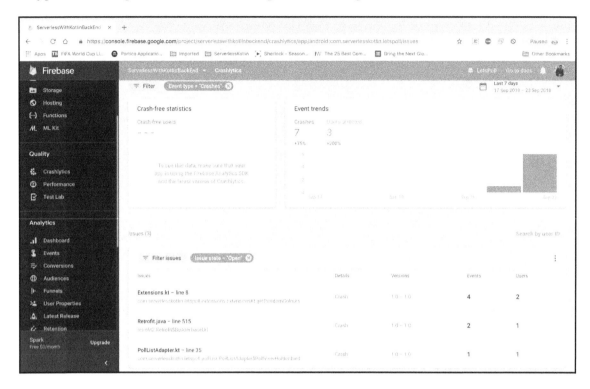

Adding custom logs and keys

Adding custom logs is super easy. It's one line of code, giving and submitting all of the information to the Firebase server about all the wrong things happening in your app.

On Android, use `Crashlytics.log` to help pinpoint issues.

Use the following code to perform a crash report and `Log.println`:

```
Crashlytics.log(Log.DEBUG, "YourTagGoesHere", "YourMessageGoesHere")
```

Use the following code to perform a crash report only:

```
Crashlytics.log("YourMessageGoesHere")
```

You can also add your own keys. Custom keys help you get the specific state of your app leading up to a crash. You can associate arbitrary key/value pairs with your crash reports, and see them in the Firebase console.

There are five methods to set keys. Each handles a different data type:

```
Crashlytics.setString(key, "foo" /* string value */)

Crashlytics.setBool(key, true /* boolean value */)

Crashlytics.setDouble(key, 1.0 /* double value */)

Crashlytics.setFloat(key, 1.0f /* float value */)

Crashlytics.setInt(key, 1 /* int value */)
```

Crashlytics supports a maximum of 64 key/value pairs. Once you reach this threshold, additional values are not saved. Each key/value pair can be up to 1 KB in size.

Monitoring the application's performance

As a developer, you would love to have the statistics about your application's performance. For example, how much time it takes to load the poll. You wouldn't like it if your user waits more than 5-6 seconds for the data. 70% of users usually leave the app if it takes more than 10-15 seconds to load. For such a use case, Firebase's performance monitoring can be a very useful service.

How does it work?

Basically, it's a game of capturing the time taken and evaluating against the benchmarked execution time of various kinds of event. For example, if your app is not responding to any keypress events or touch events, Android will throw the `Application Not Responding (ANR)` error. And it will show a popup to the user stating that error. For example, within five seconds, the touch event has to be responded to and the UI thread should be free. A broadcast receiver must finish within 10 seconds.

Having said that, data is captured between two points in time in your app:

- Whenever the app is launched, SDK will automatically capture app-launch traces. Your application's `onCreate()` function does this internally. This is done even if you do not extend the `Application` class.
- It automatically tracks when the app comes to the foreground or goes to the background. Your activity class's `onStart()` and `onStop()` events does this.

Monitoring HTTP/s network requests

By default, a performance-monitoring SDK monitors the traces for any HTTP/s or network requests in your app. Currently, the SDK is available for Android and iOS.

You can also configure *custom traces*. A custom trace is nothing but the performance data report of the code that is part of your app. You define the beginning and end of a custom trace using the APIs provided by the Performance-Monitoring SDK.

An HTTP/s network trace starts tracing when the app issues any such request, and stops the tracing when a response arrives and the request is completed. For any request going out from your application, a trace considers the following data:

- **Response time**: This is the time between when the request is made and the response is received
- **Payload size**: The byte size of the network payload downloaded and uploaded by the app
- **Success rate**: The percentage of successful responses compared to total responses (to measure network or server failures)

Using the SDK

While you are reading this section, one thing is certain: you don't need to configure the firebase SDK anymore, because we have already configured it in the previous section. We simply need to add the dependency now.

In the project-level `build.gradle`, inside `buildscripts | dependencies`, add the following line:

```
classpath 'com.google.firebase:firebase-plugins:1.1.5'
```

Now, open the app-level build.gradle and insert the following line:

```
apply plugin: 'com.google.firebase.firebase-perf'
```

After the plugin is configured, add the following line in the app-level `build.gradle` dependencies block:

```
implementation 'com.google.firebase:firebase-perf:16.1.0'
```

Recompile your app. Automatic traces and HTTP/S network requests are now monitored.

 It takes 12 hours to reflect the data on the Firebase performance portal.

Looking at the dashboard, it shows the following data:

- SplashActivity has a slower rendering
- All HTTP/HTTPs calls are successful so far

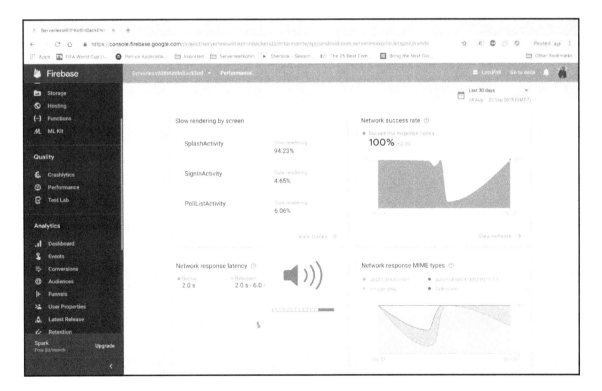

- Most of the requests are coming from the UK region
- Your request is serving an application/JSON type of data:

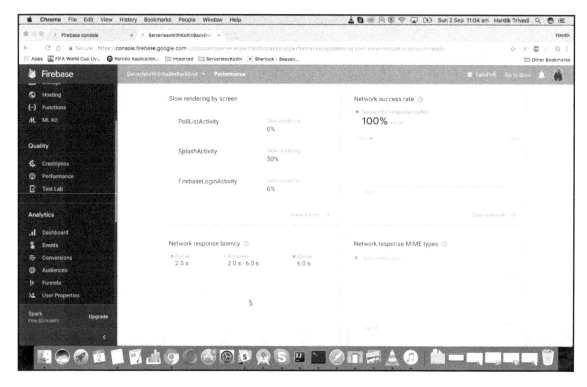

I ran the app a couple of times and could produce the following data

You can also get per-device information. There are good enough filters (device-wise, country-wise, OS-wise, and so on) available, as shown in the following screenshot:

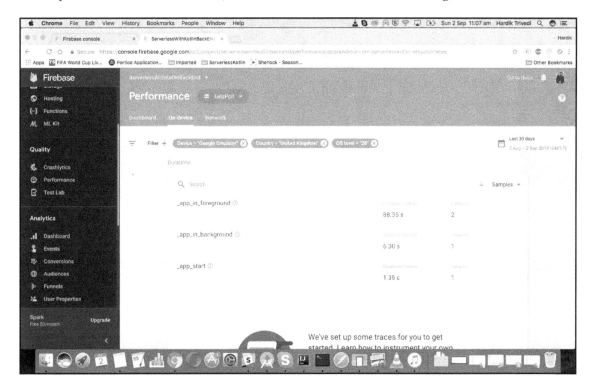

You can also specifically monitor network-request performance.

You can see that those URLs are from our app, which are hit twice, and the success rate is 100%:

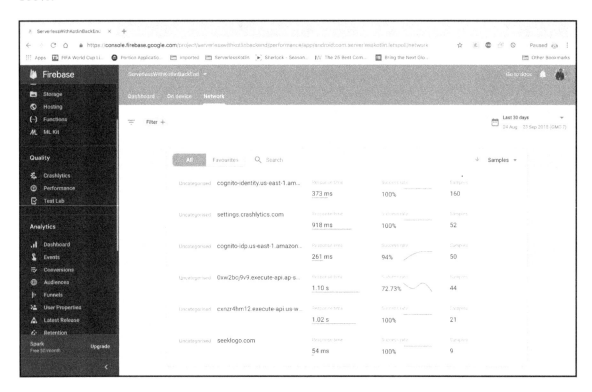

Firebase allows you to have custom traces. You can also have custom traces in the app. A custom trace is data that is part of your app. You can define some custom keys and start tracing the flow, as in the following code. There might be a situation where you want to trace multiple things at any given point in time. Well, it's possible. The trace object is a singleton object, but the `newTrace` method of it can be called from multiple places, and that returns your new object:

```
val trace = FirebasePerformance.getInstance().newTrace("poll_trace")
trace.start()
```

Let's say you want to fetch some items from your cache, and you want to track how many times loading from the cache fails. Whenever you want to count such events to trace the performance, you can add code, which can look something like this:

```
val item = cache.fetch("your_cache_key")
item?.let{
    myTrace.incrementMetric("found_in_cache", 1)
}?:myTrace.incrementMetric("not_found_in_cache", 1)
```

You can stop the tracing at any time. Just write the following code where you want to stop your trace:

```
trace.stop()
```

Summary

We have come to the end of another amazing chapter. In this chapter, we saw the capability of Firebase doing a lot of things as a backend. We also saw how easy it is to write cloud functions in Kotlin. Most of the things are taken care of by Firebase only, such as load balancing, SSL connections, server maintenance, and so on. We simply focus on our tiny cloud function in isolation. After deployment, that function becomes part of the entire Firebase infrastructure ocean.

Dealing with the Firebase real-time database is also very easy. This could get a bit complex and interesting. It depends upon the structure of your data.

Firebase's two other services, Crashlytics and Performance-monitoring, are the cherry on the cake. These are very small utilities, but make your cake – I mean app – look delicious. Unlike the humongous AWS infrastructure, Firebase is a small yet powerful platform. I like it.

Since we have now evaluated both the service providers i.e. AWS and Firebase. We wrote cloud functions/lambda functions. We saw how easy it to write and deploy the. But they are still not secure. In next chapter we will learn how to secure out lambda functions.

Analyzing Your Application

6

In the last few chapters, we designed and developed our serverless application. Up to this point, we have been implementing the functional features of the app. In the next few chapters, we will explore how to implement the non-functional requirements of a production-grade system.

In this chapter, we will cover the following topics:

- An introduction to non-functional requirements, like monitoring and log aggregation
- An introduction to CloudTrail
- An introduction to CloudWatch
- Creating a dashboard in CloudWatch
- Integrating CloudTrail in CloudWatch

By the end of this chapter, the reader should be familiar with the building blocks of application performance management, as architected on AWS.

What are non-functional requirements?

The non-functional requirements of a system are the critical components of the system that are not actively seen by the end user. Some examples of non-functional requirements are as follows:

- **Logging**: Every production system needs to have a robust logging solution backing it up. It provides insight on the status of the system and helps to track down production bugs when they occur.

- **Auditing**: Compliance is fast becoming a non-negotiable requirement. Companies that are driving traffic online are aware of the requirements of laws and regulations like GDPR, PCI, DSS, HIPAA, and so on. One of the primary requirements of such compliance is to maintain an audit trail that provides insight into who changed the state of the system or the underlying infrastructure, and when and why it changed. It is crucial that systems have a non-invasive audit trail.
- **Security**: Security is on two levels. Application security is a clear-cut functional requirement, as it has to be handled via the code. The second level of security is infrastructure security, which clamps down on unfettered access to the infrastructure resources and prevents misuse.

AWS provides turnkey solutions for implementing the preceding non-functional requirements.

AWS CloudTrail

AWS CloudTrail is an AWS offering that enables one to roll out a solution for their infrastructure's auditing and compliance needs. The minutest changes to the infrastructure configurations are logged. The source of these changes can be anything, including the console, the CLI, SDKs, and APIs that provide interactions with the AWS world. The subject of these changes (in other words, the initiator) can be a user logged in to the console or a service account with programmatic access via the CLI and SDKs.

CloudTrail works on the concept of events. Every atomic interaction with the AWS APIs is an event that gets logged, and makes up a trail. One can search, filter, and download events that make up a particular trail in a CSV or JSON format. Since these events make up sensitive data, CloudTrail provides the option of encrypting the trail.

CloudTrail is enabled by default when an AWS account is created. On the landing page of the service, one can search the master data of all events emitted, corresponding to the actions performed in the AWS infrastructure over the last 90 days. For more focused use cases, it is recommended to create a trail that encompasses the desired services and APIs.

AWS CloudWatch

Every production-grade system requires a monitoring service that gives administrators a bird's-eye view of the health of the system. The health of the system can be gauged by operational parameters, like memory utilization, CPU utilization, network throughput, and more. Any deviation from the normal values of these parameters needs to be caught and reported, as it has the potential to cause a massive disruption to the system.

For example, a spike in the memory utilization of a computer resource needs to be reported promptly, as its prolonged persistence can severely impair the system.

Monitoring a production system is a critical non-functional requirement that cannot be ignored.

In a non-serverless, partially managed infrastructure world, rolling out this solution would mean implementing tools like `Nagios` and a complementary alert system, like Pagerduty. Although these are mature tools, they come with their own share of management overhead. It is infinitely better to have a turnkey solution for this aspect, working out of the box, without a lot of effort.

AWS CloudWatch is an infrastructure monitoring service. It allows for integration with almost all AWS services, which means that it has the ability to report usage metrics for all possible parameters of all services offered by AWS.

There is an allied service of CloudWatch, called CloudWatch Logs, which is basically a log aggregation service that collects logs from various AWS infrastructure components.

AWS CloudTrail

We have already briefly introduced CloudTrail. Let's dive a bit deeper into its mechanics and create a sample audit trail.

Concepts

Let's take a look at the concepts and building blocks of AWS CloudTrail.

Overview

CloudTrail is an auditing service that logs events corresponding to atomic interactions with the AWS infrastructure. A trail can be created to log all events across all regions in your AWS infrastructure, or to log events corresponding to only a single region. This service is enabled by default, and it stores events for the last 90 days.

For a longer persistence of the events comprising a trail, they can be funneled into a log file and stored in an AWS S3 bucket. Each log file is a chunk of events that have taken place over the past five minutes. An event gets emitted approximately 15 minutes after it has occurred.

The log files are stored in an encrypted manner in S3, and can be encrypted in a more extensible fashion by using AWS **Key Managed Service** (**KMS**).

The events that are logged by CloudWatch are of the two following types:

- **Management events**: These are the default events that are logged by CloudWatch. Management events correspond to actions that access or alter the AWS infrastructure components; for example, a `ConsoleLogin` event gets logged when a user logs in to the console.
- **Data events**: These events provide insights into the resource operations performed on, or within, a resource; for example, a `GetObject` event gets logged when an object from an S3 is accessed.

Event packet structure

The following code block shows a sample event structure. This is an element in an array of records that make up a log file:

```
{
    "eventVersion":"1.05",
    "userIdentity":{
        "type":"someUserType",
        "principalId":"1234567891011",
        "arn":"arn:aws:iam::1234567891011:someUser",
        "accountId":"1234567891011",
        "accessKeyId":"SOMEACCESSKEY",
        "sessionContext":{
            "attributes":{
                "mfaAuthenticated":"false",
                "creationDate":"2018-08-15T13:02:03Z"
            }
        }
```

```
    },
    "eventTime":"2018-08-15T13:03:58Z",
    "eventSource":"config.amazonaws.com",
    "eventName":"DescribeConfigurationRecorders",
    "awsRegion":"us-west-1",
    "sourceIPAddress":"117.195.29.211",
    "userAgent":"AWSCloudTrail, aws-internal/3 aws-sdk-java/1.11.367
Linux/4.4.83-0.1.fm.327.54.326.metal1.x86_64 OpenJDK_64-
Bit_Server_VM/25.172-b11 java/1.8.0_172",
    "requestParameters":null,
    "responseElements":null,
    "requestID":"ac3ac175-a08b-11e8-b404-2bf9058b2d03",
    "eventID":"bd02a5b7-8ee2-4137-b58d-6defa0650b44",
    "eventType":"AwsApiCall",
    "recipientAccountId":"1234567891011"
}
```

Integrations

Traditionally, AWS provides deep and turnkey integrations with its offerings. CloudTrail is no different. The next sections will provide details about these integrations. Because CloudTrail is a service that can be integrated at any point of the application architecture , each AWS service that is supported has its own configuration and integration with CloudTrail. This is not meant to be an exhaustive list, but is meant to be a handy list of all integrations of CloudTrail with other AWS Services

AWS services supported for CloudTrail auditing

The following are the services that have integrations for auditing with CloudTrail:

- Alexa for Business
- Amazon API Gateway
- Application Auto Scaling
- AWS Application Discovery Service
- AWS AppSync
- Amazon Athena
- Amazon EC2 Auto Scaling
- AWS Batch
- AWS Billing and Cost Management
- AWS Certificate Manager

- Amazon Chime
- Amazon Cloud Directory
- AWS CloudFormation
- Amazon CloudFront
- AWS CloudHSM
- Amazon CloudSearch
- AWS CloudTrail
- Amazon CloudWatch
- CloudWatch Events
- CloudWatch Logs
- AWS CodeBuild
- AWS CodeCommit
- AWS CodeDeploy
- AWS CodePipeline
- AWS CodeStar
- Amazon Cognito
- AWS Config
- Amazon Data Lifecycle Manager
- AWS Data Pipeline
- AWS Database Migration Service (AWS DMS)
- AWS Device Farm
- AWS Direct Connect
- AWS Directory Service
- Amazon DynamoDB
- Amazon Elastic Container Registry (Amazon ECR)
- Amazon Elastic Container Service (Amazon ECS)
- AWS Elastic Beanstalk (Elastic Beanstalk)
- Amazon Elastic Block Store (Amazon EBS)
- Amazon Elastic Compute Cloud (Amazon EC2)
- Amazon Elastic File System (Amazon EFS)
- Amazon Elastic Container Service for Kubernetes (Amazon EKS)
- Elastic Load Balancing
- Amazon Elastic Transcoder
- Amazon ElastiCache

- Amazon Elasticsearch Service
- AWS Elemental MediaConvert
- AWS Elemental MediaStore
- Amazon EMR
- AWS Firewall Manager
- Amazon GameLift
- Amazon Glacier
- AWS Glue
- Amazon GuardDuty
- AWS Health
- AWS Identity and Access Management (IAM)
- Amazon Inspector
- AWS IoT
- AWS IoT Analytics
- AWS Key Management Service (AWS KMS)
- Amazon Kinesis Data Firehose
- Amazon Kinesis Data Streams
- AWS Lambda
- Amazon Lex
- Amazon Lightsail
- Amazon Machine Learning
- AWS Managed Services
- AWS Marketplace
- AWS Migration Hub
- AWS Mobile Hub
- Amazon MQ
- Amazon Neptune
- AWS OpsWorks
- AWS OpsWorks for Chef Automate
- AWS OpsWorks Stacks
- AWS Organizations
- AWS Personal Health Dashboard
- Amazon Pinpoint
- Amazon Polly

- AWS Private Certificate Authority (PCA)
- Amazon QuickSight
- Amazon Redshift
- Amazon Rekognition
- Amazon Relational Database Service (Amazon RDS)
- Amazon RDS Performance Insights
- AWS Resource Groups
- Route 53
- Amazon SageMaker
- AWS Secrets Manager
- AWS Security Token Service (AWS STS)
- AWS Server Migration Service
- AWS Serverless Application Repository
- AWS Service Catalog
- AWS Shield
- Amazon Simple Email Service (Amazon SES)
- Amazon Simple Notification Service (Amazon SNS)
- Amazon Simple Queue Service (Amazon SQS)
- Amazon Simple Storage Service
- Amazon Simple Workflow Service (Amazon SWF)
- AWS Single Sign-On (AWS SSO)
- AWS Step Functions
- AWS Storage Gateway
- AWS Support
- AWS Systems Manager (Systems Manager)
- Amazon Transcribe
- Amazon Virtual Private Cloud (Amazon VPC)
- AWS Web Application Firewall (WAF)
- Amazon WorkDocs
- Amazon WorkMail
- Amazon WorkSpaces
- AWS X-Ray

AWS services not supported for CloudTrail auditing

The following are the services that are not yet supported to be audited by CloudTrail, because they are either recent developments or do not expose a public API:

- Amazon AppStream 2.0
- Amazon FreeRTOS
- Amazon Kinesis
- Amazon Mobile
- Amazon Sumerian
- Amazon Translate
- AWS Cloud9
- AWS DeepLens
- AWS Snowball
- AWS Trusted Advisor
- AWS Elemental MediaLive
- AWS Elemental MediaPackage
- AWS Elemental MediaTailor
- Amazon Macie
- Amazon WorkSpaces Application Manager
- AWS Artifact

Example

Now that we have covered the basic concepts of AWS CloudTrail, let's take a look at the sample recipes that we will need to use to implement auditing and logging in our application.

Creating a simple audit trail for auditing Lambda configurations

Let's create an audit trail for the Greeter function that we created back in `Chapter 3`, *Designing a Kotlin Serverless Application*. This can easily be extended to all of the Lambda functions that we developed in `Chapter 5`, *Improve your App with Firebase Service* but for the sake of comprehension, let's keep it simple and implement an audit trail for a single function.

In the web console of AWS, navigate to the CloudTrail dashboard and click on **Create a Trail**. The process detailed in the following sections describes the configuration.

Creating a trail

1. Navigate to the CloudTrail dashboard and click on **Create a Trail**.
2. Select only the events from the current region by selecting **No** for **Apply trail to all regions**.
3. Select **All Read/Write events** to be captured.
4. In the **Data events** section, select the Lambda function **Greeter** as the resource to audit. You can select as many resources as you want to audit:

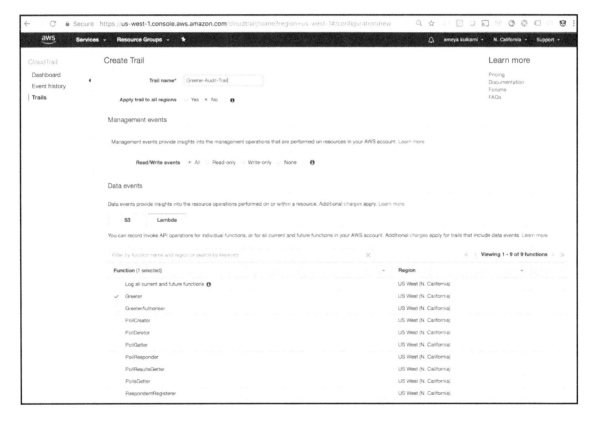

The first step in creating a trail and configuring it to record the data events for the Greeter Lambda function

Advanced configuration of the trail

1. Create a new S3 bucket for storing the log files: `greeter-audit-trail-bucket`.
2. Leave the **prefix** field blank. Applying a prefix just prepends the value supplied to each log file.
3. Choose to proceed with S3 **Server-Side Encryption (SSE)**, which is the default.
4. Choose to validate every log file when it is delivered, to detect tampering.
5. Choose a **Simple Notification Service** (**SNS**) notification, to be triggered upon every log file delivery. For this, choose to create a new topic named `greeter-audit-trail-notification-topic`, to have the message published to.
6. Do not choose to integrate CloudWatch just yet.

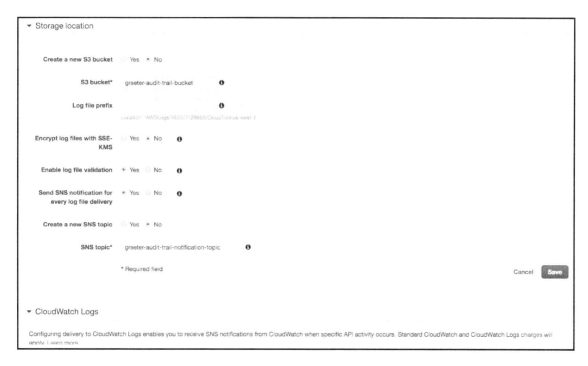

Configuring the Trail

The created trail

Clicking on the **Trails** dashboard, you can see the trail that you created, along with its details, as shown in the following screenshot:

Details of the Audit Trail that was created

Trail repository

As we discussed, the trail consists of a discrete input of event packets. AWS stores them in a bucket, which we specify while creating the trail. The bucket for this exercise is `greeter-audit-trail`.

The event packets are pushed in a discrete/batched manner, as opposed to a continuous/streamed fashion. The discrete event payload is pushed in a tarred and gzipped bundle.

The following screenshot shows the bucket location where the discrete event packets are pushed:

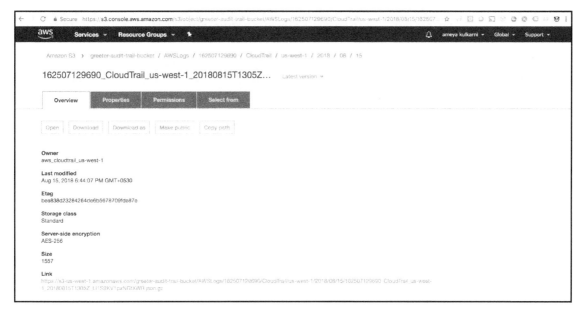

Bucket location of discrete event packets

Now that we have created an audit trail for logging the changes made to our Greeter Lambda function, let's see whether the changes are picked up by CloudTrail.

Navigate to the configuration tab of the Greeter Lambda function and update the memory allocated from 512 MB to 1,024 MB, as shown in the following screenshot:

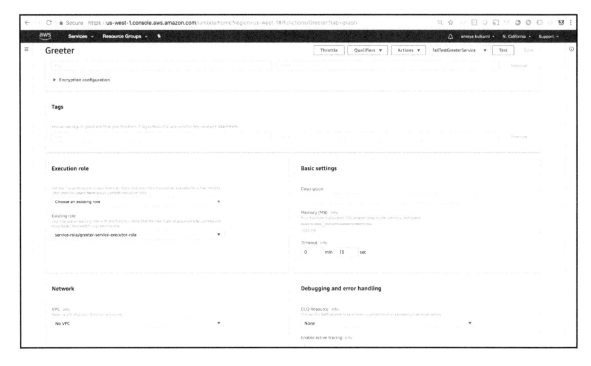

Updating the memory of the Greeter Lambda function

For the preceding exercise, one can find the event in the **Event history** section of the CloudTrail dashboard, or in the file that is synced to the S3 bucket:

The data-generated event, updateFunctionConfiguration, corresponding to changes in the Greeter Lambda function

If you click on the **View event** button, a popup is shown, including the details of the event. The details of the event are encapsulated in the following code block:

```
{
    "eventVersion":"1.05",
    "userIdentity":{
        "type":"Root",
        "principalId":"162507129690",
        "arn":"arn:aws:iam::162507129690:root",
        "accountId":"162507129690",
        "accessKeyId":"ASIASLVROANNDSFKAR5G",
        "sessionContext":{
            "attributes":{
                "mfaAuthenticated":"false",
                "creationDate":"2018-08-15T13:02:03Z"
            }
        }
    },
    "eventTime":"2018-08-15T18:56:18Z",
    "eventSource":"lambda.amazonaws.com",
    "eventName":"UpdateFunctionConfiguration20150331v2",
    "awsRegion":"us-west-1",
    "sourceIPAddress":"117.195.26.22",
    "userAgent":"aws-internal/3 aws-sdk-java/1.11.354
```

```
Linux/4.9.110-0.1.ac.201.71.329.metal1.x86_64 Java_HotSpot(TM)_64-
Bit_Server_VM/25.172-b31 java/1.8.0_172, AWSLambdaConsole/1.1",
    "requestParameters":{
        "deadLetterConfig":{
            "targetArn":""
        },
        "functionName":"Greeter",
        "memorySize":1024,
        "kMSKeyArn":"",
        "tracingConfig":{
            "mode":"PassThrough"
        },
        "environment":{

        },
        "description":"",
        "timeout":15,
        "role":"arn:aws:iam::162507129690:role/service-role/greeter-service-
executor-role",
        "handler":"com.example.Greeter::handleRequest",
        "vpcConfig":{
            "securityGroupIds":[

            ],
            "subnetIds":[

            ]
        },
        "runtime":"java8"
    },
    "responseElements":{
        "role":"arn:aws:iam::162507129690:role/service-role/greeter-service-
executor-role",
        "revisionId":"57c9203f-9d5f-4bba-83db-1e60567cbd4b",
        "handler":"com.example.Greeter::handleRequest",
        "memorySize":1024,
        "vpcConfig":{
            "vpcId":"",
            "subnetIds":[

            ],
            "securityGroupIds":[

            ]
        },
        "runtime":"java8",
        "functionArn":"arn:aws:lambda:us-
west-1:162507129690:function:Greeter",
```

```
        "functionName":"Greeter",
        "codeSize":4704410,
        "version":"$LATEST",
        "tracingConfig":{
            "mode":"PassThrough"
        },
        "description":"",
        "lastModified":"2018-08-15T18:56:18.748+0000",
        "codeSha256":"h2WlgmNZqnWkZOlgNS6HZImsGMgYGPv+eFEhssN3+G0=",
        "environment":{

        },
        "timeout":15
    },
    "requestID":"e4c8067c-a0bc-11e8-b7cc-d3bd603bbb76",
    "eventID":"1d99078c-f6eb-4d5c-8d5e-cd49046175bd",
    "eventType":"AwsApiCall",
    "recipientAccountId":"162507129690"
}
```

As you can see, the value for `requestParameters.memorySize` has changed to `1024` MB.

This exercise illustrated that even the smallest changes to the infrastructure and resources are logged by CloudTrail. One can extend this simple example to a vast serverless infrastructure. You will see this in detail in later chapters, where we explore tooling.

AWS CloudWatch

In the following sections, we'll dive deeper into the details of AWS CloudWatch.

Concepts

In the following sections, we'll take a at the building blocks of CloudWatch.

Metrics

AWS CloudWatch works on the concept of metrics. A metric is a measurable value of an infrastructure component, sampled over a period of time. AWS provides predefined metrics, but you can choose to publish your own custom metrics.

For example, CPU utilization is a metric of an EC2 instance. The number of invocations is a metric of a Lambda function. These are predefined metrics provided by AWS. An example of a custom metric might be a stream of page loads done on an application's home page. These can be ingested by CloudWatch, as well.

Namespaces

Namespaces help to group together sets of metrics for logical separation. AWS has predefined namespaces that gather sets of metrics corresponding to particular services.

Logs

CloudWatch Logs are the log aggregation components of the CloudWatch suite. Each logical log unit is called a log group. Every log group has a collection of events that are emitted by the service that generates them. Each log group can be filtered to search for a particular line item. This is especially useful for tracking down production bugs.

A Lambda function's execution output captured via the `context.getLogger().log()` method is pushed to the log group of that function. You can check the invocation state by searching and filtering in the log group.

Alarms

CloudWatch alarms aggregate metrics over a period of time and automatically initiate actions (typically, notifications). The aggregate value needs to consistently breach a predefined threshold and be sustained over a period of time for an alarm to be triggered. This filters out the false positives and temporary glitches in the metric values and ensures that the alarms are strictly actionable.

Some examples of alarms are as follows:

- One can configure an alarm to activate when the memory utilization of a computer resource stays consistently over a safe value (say, 75%)
- One can create billing alarms for when the charges for resource utilization go over a particular value (the budget set for IT)

Dashboards

CloudWatch metrics are collected in vast quantities. Analyzing such big data is futile without an elegant visualization tool. CloudWatch has a dashboard that is easily configurable from the web console.

Each dashboard has a widget that shows statistics in one of the following forms:

- **Line graph**: In these graphs, the *x*-axis consists of the time period and the *y*-axis shows the values of the mapped metrics. There is a single plotted line, and each metric is represented on the graph with a legend.

- **Stacked area graph**: In these graphs, the *x*-axis consists of the time period and the *y*-axis shows the values of the mapped metrics. Multiple line graphs are mapped and overlayed for each metric's value, as a function of time.

- **Numbers**: Metrics are mapped as pure numbers that represent the cumulative times that the metric has been captured.

- **Free text with markdown formatting**: This is used to create a custom widget with markdown formatting, often linking to external systems.

The ability to create a dashboard is invaluable, as it provides a simple way to visualize a large quantity of data. Administrators and DevOps will definitely love this.

A practical walk-through

In this section, we'll walk through some simple recipes, to put CloudWatch to good use. This is meant to be a primer on CloudWatch's practical usage. With the vast amount of metrics available for each AWS service, there is a huge number of metric visualization techniques.

Visualization using CloudWatch dashboards

In the first part of the walk-through, we'll explore how to create a CloudWatch dashboard to visualize metrics for the Greeter Lambda function.

Creating a dashboard for Greeter metrics

In this section, we'll create a dashboard for the metrics of the Greeter function, proxied by the API Gateway that we created in Chapter 3, *Designing a Kotlin Serverless Application*. This can easily be extended to the other Lambda functions created in Chapter 5, *Improve your App with Firebase Service* but for the sake of comprehension, let's keep it simple.

The following metrics are available for each Lambda function:

- ConcurrentExecutions
- Duration
- Errors
- Invocations
- Throttles
- UnreservedConcurrentExecutions

These can be applied across as many Lambda functions in the region as possible. So, a maximum total of six, multiplied by the number of functions, can be mapped on the number graph.

The following metrics are available for the API Gateway:

- Latency
- Count
- IntegrationLatency
- 4XXError
- 5XXError

These metrics can be applied by the API name and stage. So, a maximum of five, multiplied by the number of APIs, plus five, multiplied by the number of stages for each API, can be mapped on the graph.

For this exercise, we'll map two widgets, as follows:

- All of the metrics for the API Gateway for the test stage
- All of the metrics for the Greeter Lambda function

The following screenshots will show the process of creating a dashboard for visualizing the metrics of the `Greeter` function.

Creating a dashboard

To create a dashboard, navigate to the CloudWatch service, click on **Dashboards** in the navigation panel, and then click on **Create Dashboard**. A prompt will be displayed, where you can provide the dashboard with a name. The following screenshot shows this process:

Entering the dashboard's name

Adding widgets

The second step in this process is to add a widget to the dashboard. A widget is a component that encapsulates the metrics pertaining to a particular service.

In this exercise, we will create a number widget that provides a cross-sectional and instantaneous view of all of the metrics. For a more historical and perennial visualization, it is recommended to use line or stacked area widgets. The following screenshot shows the details of this process:

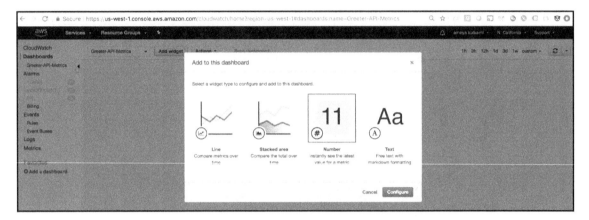

Configuring a number widget to be added to the dashboard

Metrics selection for Lambda

The third step for configuring the dashboard is selecting the metrics that will be shown on the number widget for the Lambda function.

The metrics can be selected by selecting the AWS service name (**Lambda**), then selecting the metrics by the function name (**Greeter**), then selecting all of the metrics for that particular function.

The following screenshot shows the configuration of the metrics (**Errors**, **Duration**, **Invocations**, and **Throttles**) for the Greeter Lambda function that will be added to the number widget:

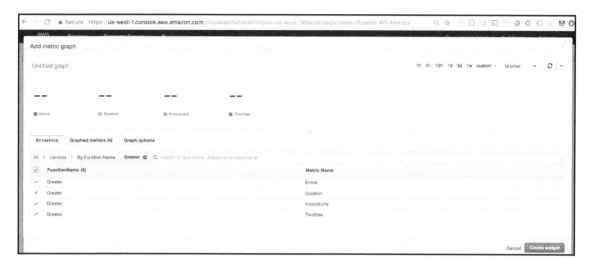

Selecting the Lambda metrics, filtered by function name, that are added to the number widget

Creating a widget for the API Gateway metrics

The next step in the process is to configure a number widget for metrics of the API Gateway that will be shown on the dashboard.

We will follow the same steps for the previous addition of a number widget, and we will filter the metric selection by the **ApiGateway** service.

The metrics for the **ApiGateway** can be selected by the stage that it is deployed to, and we plot the metrics of the **Test** stage. The metrics that are selected for the **ApiGateway** are **Latency**, **Count**, **IntegrationLatency**, **4xxErrors**, and **5xxErrors**. The following screenshot shows the details:

Selecting the ApiGateway metrics, filtered by the stage name test, that are added to the number widget

Dashboard preview

After the widgets for the Lambda metrics and API Gateway are configured, you can preview the dashboard, before saving it.

The following screenshot shows that the number metrics widget for Lambda and the API Gateway are configured in the preview. Clicking on **Save Dashboard** will create the dashboard, as follows:

Preview of the dashboard, with the two number widgets that we have configured so far

Test run

Now that the dashboard has been created, let's see the number graph in action.

Let's invoke our Greeter test stage with the correct authentication token and data, which will return a proper response, as follows:

```
$curl -X POST -H 'x-api-key:1fmETyfh8x7OazCD4nPvd9WkUPM0An953mkmpmoN'
https://8uf5e3eccd.execute-api.us-west-1.amazonaws.com/test/greeter -d
'"Ameya"'
"Hello from Kotlin to , Ameya on Fri Aug 17 15:26:38 UTC 2018"
```

Navigating to the dashboard will result in the following:

The dashboard in action

As the preceding screenshot shows, it is evident that our API Gateway's stage, named **Test**, was called once, which passed the request back to the Greeter Lambda function, which got invoked once, with no errors.

The duration of the Lambda function was **25.3 ms**, with the API Gateway's latency being **693 ms** and the integration latency being **683 ms**.

This was a simple example of how to create a visualization dashboard backed by a monitoring service like CloudWatch, for a simple Gateway to Lambda integration. This can easily be leveraged in the Lambda functions and other components that were created in Chapter 4, *Developing your Serverless Application*. We will orchestrate them by using automated tools in Chapter 8, *Scale your Application*.

Integration of CloudTrail and CloudWatch

CloudTrail and CloudWatch can be integrated together, so that the CloudWatch group will become the central repository for all events generated by the system.

Configuring CloudWatch with CloudTrail

To integrate CloudWatch with CloudTrail, we have to edit Greeter-Audit-Trail that we created in the previous section.

Navigate to the trail details by clicking on the respective trail in the **Trails** section of the CloudTrail dashboard, and edit the **CloudWatch Logs** section. We can specify a log group by either creating a new one or adding an existing one. The following screenshot shows this part of the process:

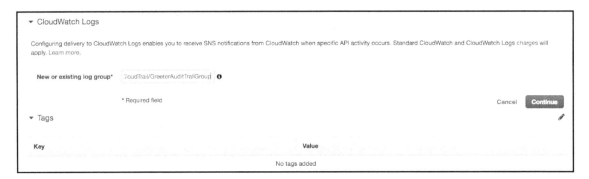

Creating **New or existing log group** in **CloudWatch Logs**

Creating an IAM role

After clicking on **Continue**, you will be redirected to the IAM console, to create an IAM role to grant the principal (in this case, `Greeter-Audit-Trail`, to assume permission to push events to the log group named `CloudTrail/GreeterAuditTrailGroup`).

This linking is done by AWS, to aid in the seamless integration of CloudTrail with CloudWatch.

After clicking on **Allow**, you will be redirected to the CloudTrail dashboard, and the integration will be complete. The following screenshot illustrates this step:

CloudTrail dashboard completing integration

The policy document for the IAM role can be viewed by clicking on **View Policy Document**. The contents are shown as follows:

```
{
  "Version": "2012-10-17",
  "Statement": [
    {
      "Sid": "AWSCloudTrailCreateLogStream20141101",
      "Effect": "Allow",
      "Action": [
        "logs:CreateLogStream"
      ],
      "Resource": [
        "arn:aws:logs:us-west-1:162507129690:log-
```

```
    group:CloudTrail/GreeterAuditTrailGroup:log-
    stream:162507129690_CloudTrail_us-west-1*"
        ]
    },
    {
      "Sid": "AWSCloudTrailPutLogEvents20141101",
      "Effect": "Allow",
      "Action": [
        "logs:PutLogEvents"
      ],
      "Resource": [
        "arn:aws:logs:us-west-1:162507129690:log-
    group:CloudTrail/GreeterAuditTrailGroup:log-
    stream:162507129690_CloudTrail_us-west-1*"
        ]
      }
    ]
}
```

The preceding policy allows for the following actions:

1. The action `logs:CreateLogStream`, to the resource `arn:aws:logs:us-west-1:162507129690:log-group:CloudTrail/GreeterAuditTrailGroup:log-stream:162507129690_CloudTrail_us-west-1*`. This is for creating a log group, if none exist.
2. The action `logsLPutLogEvents`, to the resource `arn:aws:logs:us-west-1:162507129690:log-group:CloudTrail/GreeterAuditTrailGroup:log-stream:162507129690_CloudTrail_us-west-1*`. This allows for pushing events to the log group.

Verifying the integration

The integration of CloudTrail and CloudWatch can be verified by navigating to the CloudWatch dashboard and checking the entries **CloudTrail** and **GreeterAuditTrailGroup**.

One of the entries that that constitutes a CloudTrail's event packet is pushed to the log group. The following screenshot illustrates this:

CloudTrail event entry pushed to the CloudWatch log group that was configured for Greeter-Audit-Trail

Summary

In this chapter, we explored the basic concepts of CloudTrail and CloudWatch. You saw how CloudTrail aids auditing and compliance by recording all access and interactions with the AWS world. We also covered how a CloudWatch dashboard can be configured to visualize metrics across AWS services. There are virtually limitless permutations and combinations of visualizations that can be created using CloudWatch. Finally, we covered how CloudTrail can play nicely with CloudWatch, making it a mature and one-stop solution for application performance monitoring in the cloud.

Secure Your Application

7

The security of a system is a critical requirement. It would be naive to assume that the systems deployed to production will be used as they were intended to when implementing them. Security is a cross-cutting concern encompassing all aspects of the system, including the infrastructure it is hosted on, the code that powers the business logic, and the operational aspects such as the administrators of the system. It is imperative that developers pay close attention to details when implementing an app.

In this chapter, we will explore how you can design a Serverless app for security and harden it while implementing it.

This chapter will cover the following topics:

- Security concepts pertaining to AWS and their constructs, such as IAM users, roles, and policies
- Recommended practices for securing AWS access
- Mechanisms to harden the infrastructure components that we used for our application

AWS security concepts

AWS states in their official literature that "Security is a shared responsibility of AWS and the Customer."

AWS is responsible for maintaining the security of the cloud, which includes datacentres, hardware, facilities, and enabling services. It also provides added Data Encryption at rest, **Distributed Denial of Services** (**DDOS**) mitigation, an Automated Security recommendation engine, and a robust Identity and Access-Management solution for helping the customer to harden their environments further.

The customer is responsible for maintaining security in the cloud. It basically depends on the service of AWS that is being used. The customer is typically responsible for hardening the access controls to the resources, encryption, and managing firewall settings to control the traffic to the cloud.

Some of the shared responsibilities include patch management, training and awareness, and configuration management. These need to be done at both the infrastructure/bare-metal level as well as at the customer/VM level.

In the next section, we will have a look at some of best practices for security and hardening at the AWS account level.

Account access

There are two ways to interact with the AWS services:

- **Programmatic Access via SDKs, the CLI, and APIs**: These are suitable for tools and frameworks
- **Console Access**: Useful for users logging into the console – these can be found at `https://aws.amazon.com`.

We will see how programmatic access can be secured in the next section, but there are a few things that need to be done to secure access by the user to the Web console.

Root credentials

Root credentials are the email and password pair that you register to AWS with. Whenever an account is created, a set of key/pair values (Access Key and Secret Key) is generated. AWS recommends you delete them as they grant unfettered access to the AWS account. If a miscreant gets a hold of these keys, they can use them to wreak havoc on the environment.

Enabling Multifactor authentication

AWS recommends that every user that is created who can access the AWS console needs to be authenticated via **Multifactor authentication** (**MFA**).

This means that along with an email and password pair, a user needs to supply another piece of evidence, typically a six-digit code delivered via a trusted medium, proving their identity beyond reasonable doubt. AWS currently supports the following MFA mechanisms:

- Virtual MFA device
- Hardware Key Fob MFA
- Device hardware Display Card MFA Device
- SMS MFA Device (Preview)
- Hardware Key Fob MFA Device for AWS GovCloud (US)

These are a variety of mechanisms for adopting MFA. The difference between them is to do with form factor (Physical/Virtual), target audience (SME/Enterprise,Govermental), cost (free/subscription/one-time), and the level of anti-tampering.

For all practical purposes, a Virtual MFA enabled by an app such as Google Authenticator provides strong enough security for a small-to-medium business.

Need based account creation

AWS recommends that every account that is created should have a fixed and often narrow permissions scope. An account should not have proliferation of accounts with administrative.

IAM groups

Instead of granting permissions to each user/account created at the granular level, it is a good practice to centralize the permissions into a concept of groups and attach a group to a user. It is a corollary of the DRY (Don't Repeat Yourself) principle.

Password policy

It is highly recommended that the password policy be set centrally so that every account with Web console access has got the equivalent password strength and password age.

IAM roles and policies

AWS **Identity and access management** (**IAM**) is a service of AWS that deals with the authentication and authorization of AWS account and resources. Let's have a look at these concepts in brief.

Subject/principal

The subject or principal is an entity in the system to which access controls and permissions are granted for the perusal of the resources in the system.

For example, a user logging into the Web console is a principal or a subject. A service account consuming AWS SDK to interact with AWS resources is a principal.

Resources

Resources are the object of the subject's actions. They are typically infrastructure or architectural components hosted in the AWS account.

For example, a lambda function is a resource.

Permissions

The permission is the entity on which access of a principal to a particular resource is granted or denied.

Policies

AWS Policies tie together the concept of principal, permissions, actions, and resources. They define what action is allowed to be performed by a principal on resources. They are typically JSON objects.

Groups

Groups are a logical set of subjects with common permissions. Groups can be used to centralize access-control policies for a user.

Roles

Roles are a logical group of permissions that can be assigned to different AWS resources to perform actions on a user's behalf.

Identities

Identity is when a person/entity is who/what they claim to be. In the IAM world, these are nothing but authentication enablers.

Users

Users are the entities that use the AWS services. Users can interact with the AWS world either via programmatic access (via the SDK, CLI, and API) or by the Web console. Users are of three types:

- **First-Time Access User**: This is the root user who signs up and creates an AWS account. The identity of this user has unfettered access.
- **IAM Users**: These are the users in a particular AWS account that can be created and granted roles and permissions.
- **Federated Users**: These are users that have identities in the outside world, such as Active Directory or any other standard **Identity Provider** (**IdP**) such as Facebook or Twitter. The process of leveraging those identities and granting them access and permissions to AWS resources is called federation.

Best practices for creating IAM users

In this section, we'll take a look at the best practices for creating IAM users who have permissions to access the resources in an AWS account. This is critical to do. Failure to harden access to the AWS world might result in an unintended increase in costs and misuse of resources.

Creating individual users

It is recommended that no two users with accounts in AWS (or any cloud provider for that matter) share credentials. Distinct users in the physical world should have distinct identities in the virtual world.

The principle of least privilege

Identities and Accesses should be granted to users/processes based on the Principle of Least Privilege.

This means that access should be granted with only bare-minimum permissions in order for the subject to carry out the interaction with the cloud legitimately. Additional permissions can be granted as and when the needs and requirements evolve.

Leveraging predefined policies

AWS has created predefined policies with sane defaults to allow most of the commonly used services. It is recommended to use them as a starting point for granting permissions to new or existing users. The advantage is that they are penetration tested and are maintained in a central place maintained by AWS, so the possibility of bit rot is eliminated.

Rotating passwords and keys

IAM users are supplied with a password and a pair of keys called Access Keys and Secret Access Keys. The IAM user needs to supply both of them together to be authenticated. It is recommended that these keys and credentials are rotated frequently so that any compromised credential becomes ineffective after that time frame.

Using temporary credentials

The process that requires access to AWS services across the board needs to be granted permissions by using temporary credentials instead of hardcoding fixed credentials in the process memory space. AWS Cognito's Identity Pool and Amazon STS are a few options for implementing a mechanism where services can request temporary credentials that are scoped to the narrowest possible permissions and are valid for a short period of time (typically an hour).

Adopting this approach, the scope of misuse of compromised credentials is reduced in time and space.

IAM policy conditions

IAM policies have a concept of conditions where extra security can be implemented. They further restrict the scope of the permissions that are granted to a subject. This is particularly useful in enforcing geo restrictions, temporal restrictions to services.

Continuous and exhaustive monitoring

Services such as AWS CloudWatch, AWS CloudTrail, AWS Inspector, and AWS GuardDuty provide insights into the security aspects of a system. It is recommended to leverage them to achieve an optimum level of security.

AWS Virtual Private Cloud

The AWS **Virtual Private Cloud** (**VPC**) is AWS's take on traditional Virtual Networking. VPC is a logical group of connected computing devices that are isolated from other virtual networks and their components.

Subnets

Subnets are logically-grouped networked elements inside a virtual network.

Private subnets

A private subnet is the logical group of resources that don't have direct network access (inbound or outbound) to the outside world.

For example, API Servers, Web servers, and Database Servers are typical components in the private subnet.

Public subnets

A public subnet is the logical group of resources that have direct network access (inbound or outbound) to the outside world.

Security groups

Security Groups are AWS's take on traditional firewalls. They consist of a set of network rules that dictate whether network traffic (inbound or outbound) to/from a particular IP, CIDR subnet, or another security group should be allowed or denied to be passed through.

Inbound

Inbound security groups dictate the conditions under which incoming traffic to a resource should be allowed.

For example, a web server needs to accept inbound traffic on ports 443 and 80 from the entire internet. A MySQL server, on the other hand, should only be allowed traffic only on port 3306 (default) from a subnet consisting of the application servers.

Outbound

Outbound security groups dictate the conditions under which outgoing traffic from a resource should be allowed.

It is a good practice to clamp down on outgoing traffic as well as it severely reduces the risk of a resource being used as a hop in a Denial of Service attack.

For example, a web server should have outgoing access only on port 443 to a third-party API service that it consumes.

Infrastructure hardening

In this section, we'll take a look at how we can harden the infrastructural components of our system. The following components need to be hardened:

- AWS Cognito
- AWS API Gateway
- AWS Lambda
- AWS RDS

Hardening AWS Cognito

AWS Cognito is pretty secure by itself, but the following are the additional and advanced security features that can be applied to harden it further.

Security measures for users

This section will define the security mechanism that Cognito provides for securing user identities.

Allowing user signup

While creating a user pool for backing a system, one can choose to allow or deny users to sign up. If user signup is blocked, only administrator entities can create users, thereby regulating the users that are on boarded to the system. This is extremely useful in an MVP state where the early adopters of the system have to be seeded by a trusted source.

Expiring unused accounts

An account created by the administrator and unused by the intended user can be made to expire after a certain period of time.

Setting password policies

When creating a Cognito user pool where a user can sign up, we can specify password policies so that the user-supplied password conforms to a well-accepted password policy. With this, administrators can choose a particular length of password and composition of the string.

Enabling MFA

When creating a Cognito user pool that allows users to sign up, we can enforce the users to comply with **Multifactor Authentication** (**MFA**) for an added layer of security.

The second factor can be either of the following two mechanisms:

- SMS Message
- One-Time Password

User verification

AWS Cognito has a mechanism with which we can enforce user email/phone number verification to prove their identity when logging in for the first time or when doing a password reset.

Hardening AWS API Gateway

API Gateway is the first interaction of the outside world with the system. The security of this piece is crucial and needs to be configured properly. Let's take a look at the security best practices for an API Gateway.

SSL/HTTPS

API Gateway, when deployed, comes with a default SSL certificate configured. This is provided out of the box.

API key and usage plans

An API hosted using API gateway needs to be configured with an API Key and a Usage plan. The API key is associated with a usage plan, which in turn is associated with a stage. This ensures that the API is called only by trusted clients who have a valid API key.

Resource policies

We can provide resource policies with extra conditions to restrict or allow traffic when particular conditions are met. This is helpful when we want to allow access to the API from another AWS account, whitelist access from a VPC, or deny access from a particular range of IP addresses.

Authorizers

There is a nifty concept called Lambda authorizers, where access to an API can be controlled by using either a Cognito user Pool or a lambda function.

For an API protected by Cognito User Pool Authorizers, a token passed in a request header of choice is validated against a pool of tokens issued by Cognito.

For an API protected by a Lambda authorizer, a token passed in the request header or a query parameter or a stage context is passed to a lambda function that's executed when the aforementioned request is received by the API gateway. The token-validation logic contained in the lambda can be as complex and flexible as desired.

The `official documentation` describes it in more detail.

CORS support

Cross-origin resource sharing (**CORS**) is a protocol that allows resources across distinct origins (servers) to be shared across boundaries.

Clients send an **OPTIONS** pre-flight request and expect the API to respond with the following mandatory headers in the response:

- **Access-Control-Allow-Methods**
- **Access-Control-Allow-Headers**
- **Access-Control-Allow-Origin**

Enabling CORS on API Gateway sets up a mock integration for each HTTP method that responds with the preceding headers, their values, and a 200 code to the Options pre-flight request that is made.

By enabling CORS, we can further restrict the accesses to the API.

Throttling

Once an API is deployed to a stage, we can enable throttling, which restricts the number of times the API can be called. This can be configured as a blanket rule that applies to all the requests made to the API or by allocating a quota of requests that a client can be allowed to make. Client-specific throttling is configured through a usage plan.

We created a Greeter-Usage-Plan in `Chapter 3`, *Designing a Kotlin Serverless Application*. Let's extend that to introduce throttling.

In the details tab of the Greeter-Usage plan, we show a list of associated API stages.

Clicking on the **Configure Method Throttling** option yields a popup where we can enter the **Rate (requests per second)** and the burst for a particular method:

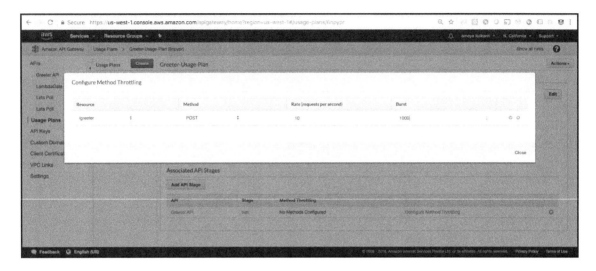

Specify a request rate of 10 per second and a burst of 1000. This amounts to the fact that clients with the API keys associated with this usage plan are allowed to make, at most, 2 requests per second, limited to a ceiling of 1,000.

Hardening AWS Lambda

The following are the pointers for hardening AWS Lambda.

Using KMS to encrypt sensitive information

The AWS **Key Managed Service** (**KMS**) can be used to encrypt sensitive information that is passed to the lambda function, which it can decrypt and use. We will see a practical example in the next section.

Execution role

It is recommended to create an execution role for lambda that can be easily controlled. This is an assumed role, and the permissions added to this role are inherited by the lambda function that this role is assigned to. We must be careful as this role transcends service boundaries and can introduce security loopholes.

Hardening AWS RDS

The following are the practices for securing RDS.

Moving RDS into a VPC's private subnet

We have seen the concepts of a VPC and a private subnet. An RDS instance is recommended to be launched into a private subnet of a VPC so that it is not publicly accessible.

Do not use master credentials

The username and password supplied when creating the RDS cluster have the role of `rds_superuser`, which grants permissions to the user for doing advanced database management activities. It is recommended that a service user can be created whose credentials can be distributed to clients accessing the database (for example, a lambda function).

This makes credential-rotation easy and prevents the proliferation of master credentials.

Practical walk–through

Now that we have seen the best practices and pointers for covering the security aspects of a system, let's do a hands-on exercise to implement the security in the Greeter API that we created in `Chapter 2`, *AWS Serverless Offerings*.

To do this, we need to create a test bed by extending the current scope of the Greeter lambda function to talk to the RDS instance and execute a simple database query. With this set up, we have a simplified version of the actual LetsPoll APIs that can be looked at cross-sectionally.

The setup is as follows:

- API Gateway calls out to the Greeter lambda function
- The Greeter lambda function makes a DB call
- The database credentials are hardcoded in the lambda function
- The PostgresDB has a master user
- The Postgres RDS DB is in a public subnet

Setting up the test bed

In this section, we'll set up a testbed. The test will consist of greeting the user and fetching the time either from the database by firing a `select * from now()` query or as a fallback to supply the default time of the lambda function.

We will use the Postgres database that we set up in *Chapter 4, Developing your Serverless Application*. Please note that the database is publicly accessible. Let's revise the database parameters as follows:

- **URL**: `letspolldb.c9mlwulrnppz.us-west-1.rds.amazonaws.com`
- **Port**: 5432
- **Username**: letspollDB_master
- **Master Password**: obfuscated
- **Database Name**: letsPoll

To query the database, we will use a nifty tool called JOOQ.

Database access using JOOQ

So far, our Greeter Lambda function does not have a database connection. We need to change the code to be able to query to the database.

The build.gradle file

First, modify the contents of the build.gradle file as follows:

```
buildscript {
    repositories {
        jcenter()
        mavenCentral()
    }
    dependencies {
        classpath 'com.github.jengelman.gradle.plugins:shadow:2.0.1'
    }
}



apply plugin: 'java'
apply plugin: 'idea'
apply plugin: 'com.github.johnrengelman.shadow'



repositories {
    jcenter()
    mavenCentral()
}

// In this section you declare the dependencies for your production and
test code
dependencies {
    compile 'org.slf4j:slf4j-api:1.7.7'
    compile group: 'com.amazonaws', name: 'aws-lambda-java-core', version:
'1.2.0'
    compile group: 'com.amazonaws', name: 'aws-lambda-java-events',
version: '2.1.0'
    compile 'org.jooq:jooq:3.8.2'
    compile 'org.jooq:jooq-meta:3.8.2'
    runtime group: 'org.postgresql', name: 'postgresql', version:
'9.4-1201-jdbc41'

    testCompile 'junit:junit:4.12'
}
```

A few points to note:

- We need the Lambda package to be built with dependencies, especially with "org.postgresql:postgresql:9.4-1201-jdbc41". The driver required to connect to the database is present in this jar.
- We added the Gradle Shadow Plugin. This is needed to create a jar with dependencies, as the postgres driver is required during runtime.

Handler

Then, modify the handler code to be as follows:

```
@Override
    public String handleRequest(String greetee, Context context) {
    LambdaLogger logger = context.getLogger();
    logger.log("Lets greet "+ greetee);


    String userName = "letspollDB_master";
    String password = ".......";
    String url = "jdbc:postgresql://letspolldb.c9mlwulrnppz.us-
west-1.rds.amazonaws.com:5432/letsPoll";
    try {
        Connection conn = DriverManager.getConnection(url, userName,
password);
        DSLContext dslContext = DSL.using(conn, SQLDialect.POSTGRES);
        Record result = dslContext.fetchOne("SELECT * FROM now()");
        Timestamp ts = (java.sql.Timestamp) result.get("now");
        return "Hello, " + greetee + " on "+ts.toString() +" as per the
time on database server";

    }
    catch (Exception e) {
     e.printStackTrace();
    }

    return "Hello, " + greetee + " on "+new Date().toString() +" as per the
default time on lambda";
    }
```

A few points to note in the preceding code block are as follows:

- The password for the database is obfuscated
- The code queries the database to get the timestamp on the server by using the Postgres now() function
- If the database call succeeds, the time on the database is returned as the greeting
- If the database call fails, the time on the lambda is returned

Once this is set up, deploy the package via the console and proceed to the next step.

Invocation

Invoke the API by using the curl command:

```
Ameyas-MacBook-Pro:greeter-service Webonise$ curl -X POST -H 'x-api-
key:1fmETyfh8x7OazCD4nPvd9WkUPM0An953mkmpmoN'
https://8uf5e3eccd.execute-api.us-west-1.amazonaws.com/test/greeter -d
'"ameya"'
"Hello, ameya on 2018-08-29 12:48:54.947853 as per the time on database
server"
```

As you can see, the output has the time sourced from the database server.

Now that our test bed is set up, let's proceed with hardening this setup.

Database configuration as environment variables

The test bed code has the database configuration parameters hardcoded into the code. What happens when the credentials have to be changed as part of regular rotation, or due to unforeseen reasons the URL of the database changes?

One way is to edit and deploy a new copy of the function each time, but that becomes cumbersome and unscalable. It also quickly becomes unwieldy and difficult to manage as the number of such configuration parameters grows.

Another way to solve this problem is to inject the parameters as an environment configuration.

Defining environment variables

The first step is to define the parameters that can change over a period of time as environment variables in the AWS Lambda Configuration Tab in the console:

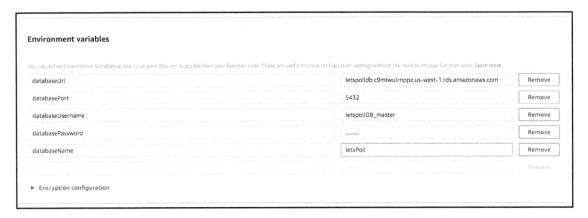

As shown in the preceding screenshot, we define the following environment variables and supply their respective values:

- databaseUrl
- databasePort
- databaseUsername
- databasePassword
- databaseName

 The value for databasePassword is obfuscated.

Modifying the handler to source these environment variables

Now, the handler needs to be modified to source the configuration from the environment variables by using "System.getEnv(String variableName)".

The modified code looks as follows:

```
@Override
    public String handleRequest(String greetee, Context context) {
    LambdaLogger logger = context.getLogger();
    logger.log("Lets greet "+ greetee);

    String userName = System.getenv("databaseUsername");
    String password =  System.getenv("databasePassword");
    String databaseUrl = System.getenv("databaseUrl");
    String databasePort = System.getenv("databasePort");
    String databaseName = System.getenv("databaseName");


    StringBuilder sb = new StringBuilder();
    sb.append("jdbc:postgresql://");
    sb.append(databaseUrl);
    sb.append(":");
    sb.append(databasePort);
    sb.append("/");
    sb.append(databaseName);

    String url = sb.toString();

    try  {
        Connection conn = DriverManager.getConnection(url, userName,
password);
        DSLContext dslContext = DSL.using(conn, SQLDialect.POSTGRES);
        Record result = dslContext.fetchOne("SELECT * FROM now()");
        Timestamp ts = (java.sql.Timestamp) result.get("now");
        return "Hello, " + greetee + " on "+ts.toString() +" as per the
time on database server";

    }
    catch (Exception e) {
     e.printStackTrace();
    }

    return "Hello, " + greetee + " on "+new Date().toString() +" as per the
default time on lambda";
}
```

Building and deploying

To build the package, use the following command from the root directory of the project:

```
./gradlew clean shadowJar
```

It yields greeter-service-all.jar in the "build/libs" directory. Upload this jar as the function package via the console.

Invoking the API

Now that the package is uploaded and deployed, invoke the API as follows:

```
Ameyas-MacBook-Pro:greeter-service Webonise$ curl -X POST -H 'x-api-
key:1fmETyfh8x7OazCD4nPvd9WkUPM0An953mkmpmoN'
https://8uf5e3eccd.execute-api.us-west-1.amazonaws.com/test/greeter -d
'"ameya"'
"Hello, ameya on 2018-08-29 14:11:48.280327 as per the time on database
server"
```

As the output can attest, the database configurations are supplied as environment variables and are picked up by the handler.

Encrypting the environment variables

Now that we have injected configuration parameters as environment variables, the next step is to encrypt them so that they don't exist in the plaintext format.

To achieve this, we will use the AWS KMS (Key Managed Service) mechanism to encrypt data in transit to mask the environment variable values that are entered.

AWS Lambda and KMS have a default integration that allows the data to be encrypted at rest. To mask the environment variables that we defined, we need to go a step further and enable the "encryption in transit". The following sections show how to achieve this.

Configuring KMS

This section shows how to create and manage a key for encrypting the environment variables by using KMS so that they are masked and not comprehensible.

Creating a Key

The first step is to configure KMS via the AWS Dashboard. Navigate to the IAM service and click on the **Encryption Key** section in the sidebar and click on **Create Key**:

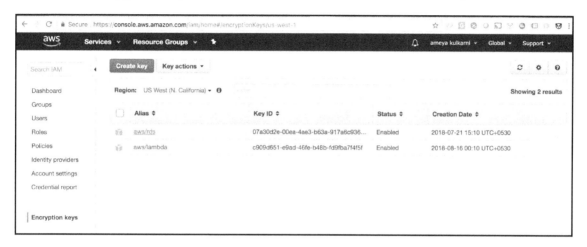

Supplying key details

Provide the alias for the key named **Greeter-Service-Key**:

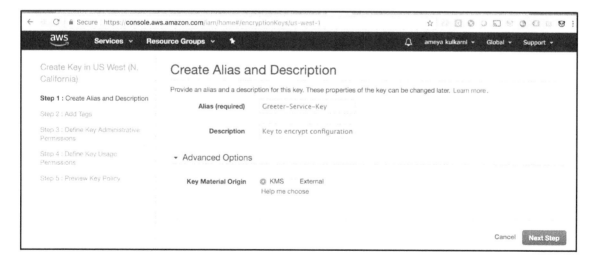

Defining administrative permissions

We grant the **ameyak** IAM user the administrative access to manage this key:

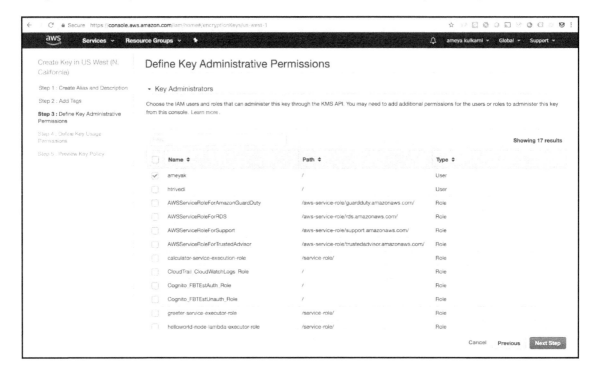

Defining usage permissions

This is an important step where we grant **greeter-service-executor-role ,** which is the IAM role that we created for the execution of the Greeter lambda function. This includes the permissions to use for KMS decryption

This allows the resource that assumes the **greeter-service-executor-role** role to access the cryptographic metadata to attempt to decrypt the masked key:

Key created

The newly created **Greeter-Service-Encryption-Key** is available in the dashboard:

Configuring Lambda with KMS

Now that we have created a key from KMS and given the usage permissions, let's configure this key so that it can be used with the Greeter lambda function.

Enabling encryption in transit

In the configuration section of the **Greeter** lambda function, check the box for enabling helpers for encryption in transit and select the key that was just created, **Greeter-Service-Encryption-Key**.

Selecting that puts the ARN in the text box and enables an **Encrypt** button next to each environment variable row.

Clicking on that button masks the value of that variable:

Decrypting in the handler

Now that we have masked the sensitive environment variables by encrypting them with the key, we need to change the handler code to decrypt them for use.

Boilerplate decryption

In the preceding screenshot, we can get the boilerplate code that aids us with this decryption. The following code block shows it adapted for our use case:

```
private String decryptKey(String keyName) {
        System.out.println("Decrypting key");
        byte[] encryptedKey = Base64.decode(System.getenv(keyName));

        AWSKMS client = AWSKMSClientBuilder.defaultClient();
```

```
DecryptRequest request = new DecryptRequest()
        .withCiphertextBlob(ByteBuffer.wrap(encryptedKey));

ByteBuffer plainTextKey = client.decrypt(request).getPlaintext();
return new String(plainTextKey.array(), Charset.forName("UTF-8"));
}
```

The handler class

The final handler class looks as follows:

```
public class Greeter implements RequestHandler<String,String> {

    @Override
    public String handleRequest(String greetee, Context context) {
    LambdaLogger logger = context.getLogger();
    logger.log("Lets greet "+ greetee);

    String userName = decryptKey("databaseUsername");
    String password =  decryptKey("databasePassword");
    String databaseUrl = decryptKey("databaseUrl");
    String databasePort = decryptKey("databasePort");
    String databaseName = decryptKey("databaseName");


    StringBuilder sb = new StringBuilder();
    sb.append("jdbc:postgresql://");
    sb.append(databaseUrl);
    sb.append(":");
    sb.append(databasePort);
    sb.append("/");
    sb.append(databaseName);

    String url = sb.toString();

    try {
        Connection conn = DriverManager.getConnection(url, userName,
password);
        DSLContext dslContext = DSL.using(conn, SQLDialect.POSTGRES);
        Record result = dslContext.fetchOne("SELECT * FROM now()");
        Timestamp ts = (java.sql.Timestamp) result.get("now");
        return "Hello, " + greetee + " on "+ts.toString() +" as per the
time on database server";

    }
    catch (Exception e) {
     e.printStackTrace();
    }
```

```
        return "Hello, " + greetee + " on "+new Date().toString() +" as per
    the default time on lambda";
        }

    private String decryptKey(String environmentKeyName) {
        System.out.println("Decrypting key");
        byte[] encryptedKey =
    Base64.decode(System.getenv(environmentKeyName));

        AWSKMS client = AWSKMSClientBuilder.defaultClient();

        DecryptRequest request = new DecryptRequest()
            .withCiphertextBlob(ByteBuffer.wrap(encryptedKey));

        ByteBuffer plainTextKey = client.decrypt(request).getPlaintext();
        return new String(plainTextKey.array(), Charset.forName("UTF-8"));
    }
}
```

The build.gradle file

The dependency for KMS needs to be added in the `build.gradle` file:

```
compile group: 'com.amazonaws', name: 'aws-java-sdk-kms', version:
'1.11.397'
```

Deploying and testing

Now, we build and deploy the package in the usual way via the console, and test it using the curl command. The output is as follows:

```
Ameyas-MacBook-Pro:greeter-service Webonise$ curl -X POST -H 'x-api-
key:1fmETyfh8x7OazCD4nPvd9WkUPM0An953mkmpmoN'
https://8uf5e3eccd.execute-api.us-west-1.amazonaws.com/test/greeter -d
'"ameya"'
"Hello, ameya on 2018-08-29 16:30:46.515508 as per the time on database
server"
```

As we can verify the output is the same as was expected, this shows how we can use AWS KMS to encrypt environment variables supplied to a lambda function and decrypt them during its execution.

This is a very elegant way of designing lambda functions inline with the 12-Factor App philosophy. With this approach, one can design functions that are environment-agnostic and free of any information-security violations.

Creating an RDS user

As described previously, we are using the using the RDS instance that was set up in Chapter 4, *Developing your Serverless Application*. So far, the database access is done using the master user and password. This has to change as the master user has access to all privileges to do with database administration.

Let's create a service user that can be used for our application purposes.

Creating a user

First, let's create a user named letsPollUser:

```
CREATE USER letsPollUser WITH PASSWORD 'someSecurePassword';
```

Granting privileges

Grant privileges to the newly created user:

```
GRANT ALL PRIVILEGES ON DATABASE "letsPoll" to letsPollUser;
```

This user can be used for database access, thereby eliminating the need to distribute and manage the master username and password that are created when creating the database.

VPC changes

In this section, we will explore how the resources Lambda and RDS created can be moved into a **Virtual Private Cloud** (**VPC**). This is necessary in order to ensure the ingress and egress traffic that the resources generate is controlled and no entity from the outside of the VPC can have a handle on it.

Current setup

When we created the RDS instance, it was done using the defaults provided by AWS. This meant that it was created in the default VPC with public access and a default security group that allowed traffic from `0.0.0.0/0` to port `5432`.

Also, the **Greeter** lambda was created with defaults, which means that it wasn't launched in a VPC. We need to move it to the default VPC that was created.

 It is recommended that for a production system, a VPC apart from the default one has to be created. This VPC has public and private subnets along with a NAT server. We will see this being set up in `Chapter 9`, *Advanced AWS Services* when we orchestrate the system with a tooling framework.

Creating the VPC

To clamp down the network access, the first thing that needs to be done is to create an Amazon VPC. This requires a fair bit of understanding of networking concepts, which are beyond the scope of this book. Long story short: we will provide an infrastructure as described here, that is, a VPC with two subnets, public and private, with a NAT Gateway.

 Creating and setting up a VPC in the proper way is an elaborate task better done by an orchestration tool. We will have a look at how it is done in `Chapter 8`, *Scale Your Application*.

Creating security groups

Security groups are AWS's concept of firewalls. They define what conditions network traffic is allowed from and the resource to which a security group is attached to.

Security groups for Lambda

We will create a security group for RDS called `greeter-security-group`. It is created in the default VPC, `vpc-f1c5ab96`. We allow outgoing traffic on port `5432` to the security group named `letspoll-database-security-group`, which was created in the *Security Group For RDS* section.

The following screenshot shows the details of `greeter-security-group`:

Security groups for RDS

We will create a security group for RDS called `letspoll-database-security-group`. It is created in the default VPC, `vpc-f1c5ab96`. We allow traffic on port `5432` from the security group named `greeter-security-group` with ID, which was created in the previous section.

The following screenshot shows the details of `letspoll-database-security-group`:

Modification of RDS

Now that we have created the security groups, we need to modify the RDS instance to attach these security groups.

From the dashboard of RDS, navigate to **letspolldb** and click on **modify**. We can then modify the instance details. The following things needs to be done:

1. Attach the security group named `letspoll-database-security-group` that we created in the previous section
2. Disable the public accessibility of the instance by selecting the **No** radio button
3. Click on **Continue**
4. Select **Apply immediately**
5. Click on **Modify**

The following screenshot shows these details:

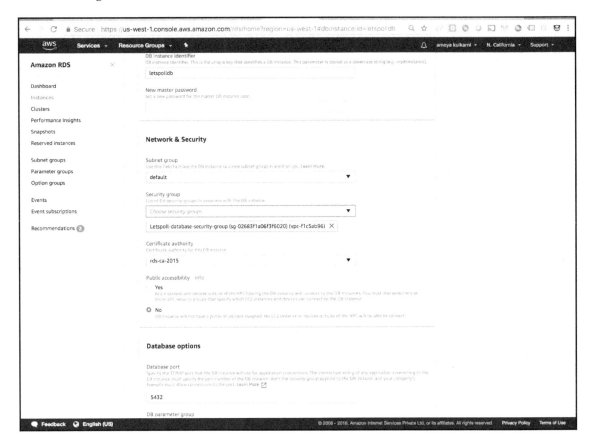

It is recommended that modification of an RDS instance should be done very rarely, if at all, and should be managed by AWS to do in the scheduled maintenance window. Otherwise, a production system may encounter unexpected downtime.

Modification of Lambda

Some modifications do need to be made to the Greeter Lambda function to ensure that it can access the RDS server in the VPC.

Attaching security groups and specifying subnets

For Lambda functions to access resources in a VPC, they need to be moved to the same VPC. This can be done from the **Configuration** tab of the Lambda function. There are few caveats to this:

- Lambdas can exist only in private subnets of the VPC.
- It is recommended that the Lambda runs in at least two or more availability zones for fault-tolerance.
- The VPC where the lambda functions are executed should have enough ENI pool size to cater to the ramped-up concurrent execution of the lambda.
- In our case, lambda should be able to call out to the KMS to be able to decode the environment variables. This traffic has to be routed over the internet and therefore there has to be a NAT gateway in the VPC.

 AWS recently introduced the AWS PrivateLink service, which exposes endpoints of other AWS Services into a VPC. If we had implemented the KMS VPC endpoint in this case, we would not have had to allow internet access from the Lambda function. This would have required a code change in the Lambda function.

The following screenshot shows the details of editing the Lambda function after a proper setup of VPC:

Modifying permissions of the IAM role

`greeter-service-executor-role`, which is the IAM role assigned to lambda, needs to be modified to add an `AWSLambdaVPCAccessExecutionRole` policy. This allows the lambda to access resources inside a VPC. This role provides the Lambda service with the ability to scale ENI as per demands:

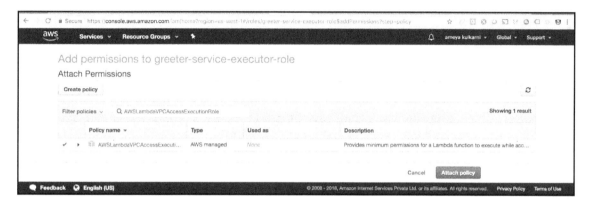

Conclusion of the walk–through

At the end of this exercise, we have achieved the following:

- Set up a VPC with public and private subnets, NAT Gateway, and appropriate security groups
- Moved RDS to the private subnet
- Moved Lambda to the private subnet
- Enabled Lambda to access the internet
- Connected Lambda to RDS through security groups
- Modified Lambda to source configuration parameters from environment variables
- Used KMS to encrypt the environment variables and decoded them in lambda
- Throttled the API Gateway usage through API Key and Usage plans

The treatment in this walkthrough that was applied to the Greeter lambda function can be easily extended to the other lambda functions that make up our LetsPoll Serverless App. We will see how this can be done by using an orchestration tool in the next chapter.

Summary

In this chapter, we looked at best practices for securing a Serverless app. We also looked at the security model recommended by AWS, and the basic constructs provided for securing accesses and infrastructure resources in an AWS account. We also underwent a practical walkthrough of securing the application that we created by launching resources in a VPC and encrypting the environment variables supplied to Lambda. This chapter can be treated as a primer in securing the Serverless system and its components on AWS. Security is ever-changing, and it is recommended that the reader keeps abreast of the different innovations that happen in this field.

Scale Your Application

8

So far, we have seen how Serverless systems are designed, implemented, monitored, and secured. In this chapter, we will look at how Serverless systems can be scaled. Scalability is often associated with the ability of a system to withstand a high load seamlessly. While this is true, the scalability of Serverless systems often encompasses a lot more.

Serverless systems typically consist of ephemeral functions and third-party services. The notion of **state** is almost nonexistent and hence statelessness is a key attribute of constituent functions of a Serverless system. The surface area and the responsibility of these functions are very minimal and should strictly adhere to the single-responsibility principle. Systems powered by serverless architectures consist of hundreds of nanoservices (typically an ephemeral function), each doing one job and doing it well, coming together at scale to solve a common problem. Each of these functions/nanoservices has fixed execution boundaries and communicates with each other by using events or message brokers. Thus, Serverless systems are inherently very similar to distributed systems. There needs to be a different approach taken for understanding how these components can function cohesively and tolerate failures across potential multiple execution boundaries. Business growth puts a high pressure on the correctness and robustness of these systems. Being able to withstand high sporadic demand and yet process correctly is another indicator of the scalability of a Serverless system.

The extensibility of the system as a result of quick prototypical cycles is also a key indicator of the scalability of the system. The promise of Serverless Architecture is that a Serverless system in production must be able to be iterated and quickly prototyped on. This vastly reduces the time to market of the feature and enables us to gauge feedback earlier in the product-development life cycle. This can only be possible if the cloud-native nature of Serverless architecture is embraced and not fought against.

Cloud providers have enabled the scaling of such systems to some extent. Inherently, these systems have a low cost associated with initial scaling as compared to systems running on traditional self-managed infrastructures. But, these scaling enablers are often dictated by their own internal capacity and business decisions. Adopters of Serverless systems are subject to a Fair Usage Policy, which is normal in a shared-infrastructure multitenant world. These often get manifested in the form of `Service Limits` in the case of AWS.

But, the adopters of Serverless architectures need to re-evaluate and adapt the way they have hitherto been thinking about architecting, developing, deploying, and versioning their code to be able to scale systems above and beyond the limits provided by the cloud providers.

In this chapter, we will have a look at the following:

- Serverless Tooling
- Challenges of Scaling Serverless Systems
- Solutions to these challenges

Infrastructure as code

Due to the microservice/nanoservice architecture of the component functions, the code for a Serverless system is very modular. These modular components need to be decoupled from the environments they run on so that they can be deployed on demand. Further, these environments also need to be created, scaled up and out, and disposed of on demand. This dynamic cloud-native nature is impossible to manage by hand. Automation has to be the name of the game.

Infrastructure as Code (IaC) is a technique that is used to model, provision, and manage the infrastructure of cloud systems with code. With automated infrastructure management, human intervention is reduced almost entirely. So, IaC provides speed, security, precision, and most importantly reproducibility while managing environments.

As we saw in `Chapter 1`, *Basics of Serverless*, there are multiple tooling options that provide IaC for the serverless world. For the purpose of this exercise, we will explore one of the fastest-growing tools, which is called Serverless Platform. It is not to be confused with the actual Serverless Architectural paradigm that we are exploring in this book.

Serverless Platform itself has three components:

- Serverless Framework
- Serverless Event Gateway

- Serverless Dashboard

In the remaining part of this chapter, we will focus on the Serverless framework, which is an open source CLI that is used to build and manage Serverless Architectures.

Serverless Framework

Serverless Framework is a **command-line interface** (**CLI**) component of the Serverless platform that is used for building and deploying Serverless applications. In the next few sections, we will have a look at the basic concepts of the framework, and then undergo a practical walkthrough for retrofitting Serverless Framework in the LetsPollAPI configuration.

Concepts

In this section, let's explore the basic building blocks of the Serverless Frameworks.

Providers

Providers are the Serverless compute providers, such as AWS, Google, and Azure. They expose APIs and SDKs to interact and avail their services. Serverless framework encapsulates those APIs and tries to abstract them under the concept of providers. Serverless supports the following providers:

- AWS
- Azure
- Cloudflare Workers
- Fn
- Google
- Kubeless
- OpenWhisk
- Spotinst
- AuthO webtasks

Serverless Framework is growing at a very fast pace and the reader should stay updated about the `providers` as and when they are added.

Services

A service is a basic building block of a system. A service can perform any number of tasks that make up the business logic of a system. Each service can have any number of functions that are executed under the function as a service paradigm and infrastructural resources such as databases, networking rules, and other services that are needed for the functions to do their job.

Resources

Resources are infrastructural components and other services that the cloud provider offers that aid in the functioning of the Serverless system. The concept of Resources holds ground in Serverless when it is used to build systems, assuming AWS as the provider. Any AWS service can be thought of as a Resource. Serverless uses CloudFormation under the hood to provision and configure AWS resources, and hence all AWS services that can be orchestrated using CloudFormation can be managed using Serverless.

Functions

Functions are what is said on the tin. They are the **F** in FaaS. When Serverless Framework is used with AWS as a provider, functions correspond to lambda functions.

Events

Events are the triggers that cause the functions to get executed. We saw the concepts of events in Chapter 2, *AWS Serverless Offerings*, and these are nothing different. The current set of events that are supported by serverless framework for AWS as a provider are as follows:

- API gateway
- Kinesis & DynamoDB
- S3
- Schedule
- SNS
- SQS
- Alexa Skill
- IoT
- CloudWatch Events

- CloudWatch Logs
- Cognito User Pool
- Alexa Smart Home

In this chapter, we will explore how API gateway can be be used as a trigger for the functions to run via Lambda Proxy Integration. Currently, every service gets deployed to a single API gateway. So, it will deploy a single service package with a single API gateway stage as the upstream and trigger execution of different functions depending on the paths of the API.

The more complex but flexible method of using API gateway as the event source to the lambda gateway is the lambda integration. The official documentation has got good pointers on how to implement this.

Practical walk-through

In this section, we will have a look at provisioning our system through the Serverless Framework. We will achieve the following:

- Organize the code base as per modern software-development practices.
- Provision infrastructure components using the Serverless Resources:
    - Provision VPC
    - Provision RDS
    - Provision Lambda functions and API gateway
    - Provision KMS
    - Provision the Cognito User pool
- Implement, test, and deploy the Lambda functions that make up the business logic for the LetsPoll app.

Getting started

In `Chapter 3`, *Designing a Kotlin Serverless Application*, we saw the code for the lambda functions in pieces, but did not look at how it looked together holistically. The focus there was more to familiarize you with the code and the workings of Lambda and other services. The orchestration and application of modern software practices was left until we were to use a third-party orchestration tool.

In this section, we will have a look at how the code for both infrastructure and business logic for our Serverless system is structured. This involves creating a new structure of the code base, porting the functions, and modifying them if needed to be better organized in a logically grouped project structure.

Installation

Lets have a look at installing the Serverless framework. It is shipped as an npm package, and once installed can be used as a simple command through the CLI.

Prerequisites for installation

The prerequisites for installing the serverless platform are as follows:

- An AWS account
- Administrative IAM Keys
- Node Package Manager (npm) installed

Installing the framework

Once the prerequisites are met, installing the framework is as simple as firing this command via the CLI:

```
npm install serverless
```

Once this is installed, you can verify the installation by doing serverless -v.

The sample output is as follows:

```
Ameyas-MacBook-Pro:letspoll Webonise$ serverless -v
1.30.3
```

Configuring the CLI tool

Now that the CLI is installed, we need to configure it with the administrative IAM user that we created for the purpose of this framework. The creation of this user is via the IAM Web console.

Once the keys are handy, use serverless config credentials to configure the CLI agent.

Sample usage is as follows:

```
serverless config credentials --provider aws --key AWS_ACCESS_KEY --secret
AWS_SECRET_KEY --profile lets-poll-default
```

 This creates an entry in the `~/.aws/`credentials file on unix-based systems with the `lets-poll-default` profile. Since this is the only authentication that is required by the serverless framework to interact with your AWS account, ample caution should be exercised in ensuring that the current setup of the existing keys is not disturbed. There can be unintended consequences if this step is not executed properly. Read more at the `official documentation`.

Bootstrapping the project

We will now bootstrap the project using the Serverless CLI. As we have seen, a service is considered as the building block of the infrastructure. Each service has got infrastructural components and the code for function(s). Serverless doesn't enforce any opinions on how to the structure constituent services together apart from it having a `serverless.yaml` file in the root of the service. Developers are free to structure the project in any way they see fit, as per their use cases and their preference of granularity. Please note that every service that is created corresponds to a single API gateway in the AWS Infrastructure. This means that in a nanoservice infrastructure, each function becomes a service that is deployed to a single API gateway. For example, a system with five APIs composed of five services will yield five API gateways at the very least.

While this is desirable in many cases, this approach requires us to exercise caution and matured tooling primarily because of the proliferation of API gateway and their stages. The reuse strategy for infrastructural components and code has to be defined and strictly stuck to. This proliferation is often hard to manage for people coming from a traditional background. Currently, Serverless doesn't support multiple services deployed to a Single API gateway, but this feature is a `top priority` and is under development. For our APIs, we will adopt a hybrid structure where we have a single Service with different functions. This means that our service is deployed to a single API gateway on the requested stage. The endpoints of this API gateway are pointed to different functions that can be modified and shipped independently. This approach, though not a true nanoservices style, promotes package cohesion, code reusability, and decoupled deployments.

In any case, nanoservices/microservices have to be extracted and not written.

Creating a service

Serverless Framework provides a nifty way to get started with a service using the `serverless create` command. They also provide a wide variety of `templates` so as to skip writing boilerplate code every time a service has to be created. If one needs to create a service powered by Kotlin and Gradle, the following command can be used:

```
serverless create --template aws-kotlin-jvm-gradle  --path letsPollApi
```

The Output is as follows:

```
/letsPollApi        #project root directory
-build.gradle       #build file
-setting.gradle     #settings file
-gradle/            #gradle file
-gradlew            #gradle wrapper shell script for Unix
-gradlew.bat        #gradle wrapper batch file for Windows
-serverless.yml     #overarching serverless.yaml file
-resources/         #fragrments of the serverless.yaml file
-src/               #typical JVM project structure supplied by Serverless
```

But, since we already have our Lambda handlers written in Chapter 4, *Developing Your Serverless Application*, let's try to retrofit that code into a package that can be managed by serverless.

Code organization and boilerplate

In this section, let's briefly look at the code organization and the workspace structure.

Workspace structure

Since we have our lambda handlers and the code ready, to get it running with the serverless framework, we need to do the following:

- Create a `serverless.yaml` file in the root directory.
- Create a `resources/` folder in the root directory. This will be used to put individual `.yml` files that will be included in the parent `serverless.yaml` file.

This aids in code organization:

```
/letsPollApi               #project root directory
  -build.gradle            #build file
  -setting.gradle          #settings file
  -gradle/                 #gradle directory
```

```
-gradlew                        #gradle wrapper shell script for Unix
-gradlew.bat                    #gradle wrapper batch file for Windows
-serverless.yml                 #overarching serverless.yaml file
-resources/                     #fragments of the serverless.yaml file
 -functions/
  -pollGetter.yml
  -pollCreator.yml
  -pollsGetter.yml
  -#other_functions.yml
 -api/
   -api.yml                     #API Models documentation
-src/main/                      #typical JVM project structure
```

The build.gradle file

As explained, we are creating a single service that corresponds to single distribution (either
`.jar` or `.zip`) that is deployed. This single function will have different lambda functions
for distinct business flows. To build and package it together, we are using Gradle and the
`build.gradle` file of our service, which looks as follows:

```
apply plugin: 'java'
apply plugin: 'maven'
apply plugin: 'idea'
group = 'com.packt.serverless.kotlin.letspoll'
version = '1.0.0'

description = """Lets Poll API"""


sourceCompatibility = 1.8
targetCompatibility = 1.8
tasks.withType(JavaCompile) {
  options.encoding = 'UTF-8'
}

buildscript {
  repositories {
    mavenCentral()
    maven { url "https://plugins.gradle.org/m2/" }
  }
  dependencies {
    classpath "org.jetbrains.kotlin:kotlin-gradle-plugin:1.1.51"
    classpath "io.spring.gradle:dependency-management-plugin:1.0.3.RELEASE"
    classpath "com.github.jengelman.gradle.plugins:shadow:2.0.1"
    classpath "de.sebastianboegl.gradle.plugins:shadow-log4j-
transformer:2.1.1"
  }
```

```
}

apply plugin: 'kotlin'
apply plugin: "io.spring.dependency-management"
apply plugin: 'com.github.johnrengelman.shadow'
apply plugin: "de.sebastianboegl.shadow.transformer.log4j"

repositories {
  maven { url "http://repo.maven.apache.org/maven2" }
}

dependencies {
  compile group: 'org.jetbrains.kotlin', name: 'kotlin-stdlib', version:
'1.1.51'

  compile group: 'com.amazonaws', name: 'aws-lambda-java-core',
version:'1.1.0'
  compile group: 'cóm.amazonaws', name: 'aws-lambda-java-log4j2',
version:'1.0.0'
  compile group: 'com.amazonaws', name: 'aws-lambda-java-events',
version:'2.0.1'

  compile group: 'com.fasterxml.jackson.core', name: 'jackson-core',
version:'2.8.5'
  compile group: 'com.fasterxml.jackson.core', name: 'jackson-databind',
version:'2.8.5'
  compile group: 'com.fasterxml.jackson.core', name: 'jackson-annotations',
version:'2.8.5'
  compile group: 'com.fasterxml.jackson.module', name:'jackson-module-
kotlin',version :'2.9.+'

  compile group: 'org.jooq', name: 'jooq', version:'3.11.4'
  compile group: 'org.jooq', name: 'jooq-meta', version:'3.11.4'
  compile group: 'org.liquibase', name: 'liquibase-core', version:'3.4.1'
  runtime group: 'org.postgresql',name:'postgresql',version:'9.4-1201-
jdbc41'

}

shadowJar{
    mergeServiceFiles('META-INF/spring.*')
    exclude "META-INF/*.SF"
    exclude "META-INF/*.DSA"
    exclude "META-INF/*.RSA"
    exclude "META-INF/LICENSE"
    archiveName = "lets-poll-${version}.${extension}"
}
```

The build file is configured such that the `/gradlew clean shadow` command will yield a uber JAR of all the dependencies and the handler JAR at the `/build/libs/lets-poll-1.0.0.jar`.

The serverless.yaml file

Usually, a greenfield Serverless system should be created on these lines from the get-go. We will start with a barebones `serverless.yaml` and keep adding to it as we create the infrastructure. The base template is as follows:

```
service: lets-poll-api-with-serverless-fw

custom:
  accountId: AWS::AccountId
  documentation: ${file(./resources/api/api.yml)}



frameworkVersion: ">=1.0.0 <2.0.0"



plugins:
- serverless-cf-vars
- serverless-aws-documentation
-  serverless-reqvalidator-plugin

provider:
  name: aws
  runtime: java8
  stage: ${opt:stage,'beta'}
  region: ${opt:region,'ap-south-1'}
  profile: ${opt:profile,'lets-poll-default'}
  apiKeys:
     - letspoll-${self:provider.stage}-api-key
  usagePlan:
    quota:
      limit: 5000
      offset: 2
     period: MONTH
    throttle:
      burstLimit: 200
     rateLimit: 100
  vpc:
    securityGroupIds:
    - { Fn::GetAtt: [ "lambdaSecurityGroup", "GroupId" ] }
    subnetIds:
```

```
          - Ref: letsPollPrivateSubnet1
          - Ref: letsPollPrivateSubnet2

    resources:
    - ${file(./resources/vpc.yml)}
    - ${file(./resources/rds.yml)}
    - ${file(./resources/cognito.yml)}
    - ${file(./resources/lambdaExecutionRole.yml)}
    - ${file(./resources/lambdaBasicExecutionPolicy.yml)}
    - ${file(./resources/lambdaVpcPolicy.yml)}
    - ${file(./resources/kms.yml)}
    - ${file(./resources/api/apiValidator.yml)}


    package:
      artifact: build/libs/lets-poll-1.0.0.jar

    functions:
    - ${file(./resources/functions/pollsGetter.yml)}
    - ${file(./resources/functions/pollCreator.yml)}
    - ${file(./resources/functions/pollGetter.yml)}
    - ${file(./resources/functions/respondentRegistrer.yml)}
    - ${file(./resources/functions/pollResponder.yml)}
    - ${file(./resources/functions/pollDeletor.yml)}
    - ${file(./resources/functions/databaseMigrator.yml)}
    - ${file(./resources/functions/databaseMigratorFixer.yml)}
```

A few things to note:

- We create a service named `lets-poll-api-with-serverless-fw` using a framework version that is between 1 and 2.
- We are provisioning the services on AWS so we use appropriate values for the provider block. In this, we create and attach a usage plan and an API key that is sourced from the `LP_API_KEY` environment variable. The output of the deploy command will have the actual value of the key to use. This can then be distributed and used as the value of the `x-api-key` header, as we saw in Chapter 3, *Designing a Kotlin Serverless Application*.
- We also mention the subnet IDs and the Security Groups that are applicable for each function. We will explore their creation in the next section. They are defined in the `resources/vpc.yml` file.

- In the custom block, we alias the AWS CloudFormation pseudo-parameter, `AWS::AccountId`, as `accountId`. This is useful for referencing `accountId` in different files.
- We reference the contents of the `resources/api/api.yml` file under the documentation block. This is required by the serverless-aws-documentation plugin. With this, we can provision models of the API gateway using the Serverless Framework. This is similar to creating an API gateway Model by using the swagger extensions. We saw this in `Chapter 4`, *Developing Your Serverless Application*.
- Serverless 1.x has a rich plugin ecosystem that furthers the power of the framework. For the purpose of this exercise, we will include the following plugins in our project:
    - serverless-aws-documentation
    - serveless-cf-vars
    - serverless-reqvalidator-plugin
- We provide a stage named beta.
- We choose the region to provision this infrastructure as **ap-south-1**, which is AWS Mumbai's datacenter.
- We will split the resources into logical fragments for better code organization and reference them by using the `$file()` syntax.
- Currently, they are commented. We will uncomment them as we iteratively go through the next sections.
- The code for this service is found by the `artifact` value under the `package` block. It should have the path of the lambda function package that is to be deployed. Since we are using Gradle to yield a distributable zip file, we give the path accordingly.
- Each of the functions is defined in their own file under the `functions` block. We will uncomment the files as we deploy those functions.
- The `/resources/api/apiValidator.yml` file has got the request validators.

Workflow

In this section, let's have a look at some of the basic workflows that we will encounter while exploring serverless framework

Building the package

Any changes to the code of any functions need to be packaged before they can be picked up by serverless framework. The command to build a package is:

```
./gradlew clean build
```

We will run this command at the root of the directory once. This assumes that the code for the handlers is ready from Chapter 3, *Designing a Kotlin Serverless Application*. If any change is to be done to that code, the preceding command to build a new package has to be run.

Deploying the entire Service

As we saw, a service in serverless framework is a composition of Functions, Events, and Resources. To deploy the service for the first time, we use the following command:

```
sls deploy --aws-profile=lets-poll-default
```

A few things to note:

- `sls` is the shorthand for the serverless command.
- `deploy` is the command to package all the artifacts and submit it to CloudFormation to provision.
- `--aws-profile` is the flag to denote the profile that has to be used. Remember, we created a profile when configuring the serverless CLI in the previous section.
- This command is to be used when there is a configuration change that is to be deployed.

Deploying a single function

To deploy a single function, we use the following command:

```
sls deploy function --function functionName --aws-profile=lets-poll-default
```

Please note, this command is used to deploy a single function when the only code for that function has changed.

Actual workflow

As mentioned, we are going to be uncommenting the file fragments in `serverless.yaml`. After every uncomment activity, the following command needs to be run. This command will deploy the changes to the AWS infrastucture.

Since we already have the functions ready from `Chapter 3`, *Designing a Kotlin Serverless Application*, we don't need to rebuild the package:

```
sls deploy --aws-profile=lets-poll-default
```

Environment variables

As we have seen in the boilerplate, we require a few environment variables to be set that will be supplied to the AWS resources:

- `LP_DATABASE_USERNAME`: This will store the database username
- `LP_DATABASE_PASSWORD`: This will store the database password
- `LP_DATABASE_PORT`: This will store the database port
- `LP_DATABASE_NAME`: This will store the database name

The readers are expected to set them to values at their discretion via an appropriate `mechanism` pertaining to their OS.

Provisioning the VPC

The first step in this exercise is to provision the VPC. For this, we will create a file named `/resources/vpc.yml` and refer to it in the parent `serverless.yaml`. The code in the next section is all part of the `/resources/vpc.yml` file.We will be seeing each logical components in the VPC in a single section.After we familiarise ourselves with the contents of the VPC,we will provision it by firing a single command.

Creating a VPC

To create the VPC, we will use the `Resources` block of the `vpc.yml` file. The following code block shows the definition of the VPC:

```
Resources:
  letsPollVPC:
    Type: AWS::EC2::VPC
    Properties:
      CidrBlock: 172.31.0.0/16
      EnableDnsSupport: true
      EnableDnsHostnames: true
      InstanceTenancy: default
      Tags:
          - Key: Name
            Value: Lets Poll VPC
```

A few things to note in the preceding code block:

- The `resources` block takes in a raw CloudFormation stack reference. We will use this to define the resources by using the CloudFormation syntax.
- We create a `letsPollVPC` of the `AWS::EC2::VPC` type (this is the CloudFormation syntax to define a VPC).
- We specify a CIDR and other defaults.

Creating and attaching the internet gateway

For the Lambdas that have to exist in a private subnet of the VPC, an internet gateway has to be created. The following code block has to be added under the `Resources` section of the `vpc.yml` file, at the same level as the `letsPollVPC` element. The following code block shows the way it is done:

```
letsPollIGW:
    Type: AWS::EC2::InternetGateway

letsPollVPCGatewayAttachment:
    Type: AWS::EC2::VPCGatewayAttachment
    Properties:
      VpcId:
        Ref: letsPollVPC
      InternetGatewayId:
        Ref: letsPollIGW
```

A few points to note for the preceding code:

- We created an Internet Gateway using the `AWS::EC2::InternetGateway` CloudFormation type.
- We attached the newly created gateway to the `letsPollVPC` using the `AWS::EC2::VPCGatewayAttachment` CloudFormation type.
- To Attach the VPC to the Gateway, we need to specify two properties of the `VPCGatewayAttachement` block, such as `VpcId` and `InternetGatewayId`. We use CloudFormation's `Ref` function to get a handle on the previously created elements by specifying the logical names of the VPC and the Internet Gateway in the stack.

To deploy this change, run the following command:

```
sls deploy --aws-profile=lets-poll-default
```

Public subnet

Let's have a look at creating the public subnet. The following code block shows the mechanism:

```
letsPollPublicSubnet:
  Type: AWS::EC2::Subnet
  Properties:
    VpcId:
      Ref: letsPollVPC
    AvailabilityZone: ${self:provider.region}a
    CidrBlock: 10.0.0.0/24
    MapPublicIpOnLaunch: true
    Tags:
       - Key: Name
         Value: Lets Poll VPC Public Subnet 1
```

A few things to note about the code:

- We specify the VPC for this subnet by using the `Ref` function as before.
- We allocate a `CidrBlock` for it.
- We specify the availability zones for this subnet.
- We set `MapPublicIpOnLaunch` to be `true`. This will ensure that any resource launched in this subnet will have a public IP and hence internet access.
- We specify the tags for easy handling.

Private subnet

Let's provision/create two private subnets for High Availability of Lambda, the Lambda functions are as recommended:

```
letsPollPrivateSubnet1:
  Type: AWS::EC2::Subnet
  Properties:
    VpcId:
      Ref: letsPollVPC
    CidrBlock: 10.0.1.0/24
    AvailabilityZone: ${self:provider.region}a
    MapPublicIpOnLaunch: false
    Tags:
       - Key: Name
         Value: Lets Poll VPC Private Subnet 1

letsPollPrivateSubnet2:
  Type: AWS::EC2::Subnet
```

```
      Properties:
        VpcId:
            Ref: letsPollVPC
        CidrBlock: 10.0.2.0/24
        AvailabilityZone: ${self:provider.region}b
        MapPublicIpOnLaunch: false
        Tags:
            - Key: Name
              Value: Lets Poll VPC Private Subnet 2
```

NAT gateway

Now that we have created public and private subnets, let's associate a NAT gateway to it. There are two steps to do so:

1. Creation of Elastic IPs
2. Creation of Nat Gateway and association of the EIPs to it

Because we have only a single public Subnet, it is sufficient to create only one EIP and associate it with one NAT gateway.

Elastic IP allocation

We first need to allocate an EIP for our NAT gateway. The following code block shows how an EIP can be requested:

```
letsPollVPCNatGateway1EIP:
    Type: AWS::EC2::EIP
    DependsOn: InternetGatewayAttachment
    Properties:
        Domain: vpc
```

Creation of NAT gateway and EIP Association

Now that we have EIP allocated, let's create NAT gateways and associate them with the EIPs. The following code block shows how the allocated EIP can be associated with the NAT gateway:

```
letsPollVPCNatGateway:
    Type: AWS::EC2::NatGateway
    DependsOn: letsPollVPCNatGatewayEIP
    Properties:
        AllocationId: { Fn::GetAtt: [ "letsPollVPCNatGatewayEIP",
"AllocationId" ] }
```

```
SubnetId:
  Ref: letsPollPublicSubnet
Tags:
    - Key: Name
      Value: Lets Poll VPC NAT Gateway 1
```

Route association

Now that a NAT gateway is created, we need to specify the route mapping for dictating the hops of the traffic.

Creating a Route Table for the Public Subnet

The following code block shows how to create a public route table:

```
letsPollVPCPublicRouteTable:
    Type: AWS::EC2::RouteTable
    Properties:
        VpcId:
          Ref: letsPollVPC
        Tags:
            - Key: Name
              Value: Lets Poll Public Subnet Route Table
```

Default Public Route

First, we need to specify a default public route. The following code block shows us how:

```
letsPollVPCDefaultPublicRoute:
  Type: AWS::EC2::Route
  Properties:
    RouteTableId:
      Ref: letsPollVPCPublicRouteTable
    DestinationCidrBlock: 0.0.0.0/0
    GatewayId:
      Ref: letsPollIGW
```

Association of a Public Route Table to a Public Subnet

Now that we have created a Route Table and a Default Route, let's associate it with the public subnet. The following code block shows us how:

```
letsPollPublicSubnet1RouteTableAssociation:
  Type: AWS::EC2::SubnetRouteTableAssociation
  Properties:
    RouteTableId:
      Ref: letsPollVPCPublicRouteTable
    SubnetId:
      Ref: letsPollPublicSubnet
```

Routing in the Private Subnet

The following code block shows how we can create route tables in each of the two private subnets, and add routing rules to route all traffic to the NAT gateway that we created in the public subnet:

```
letsPollPrivateRouteTable1:
  Type: AWS::EC2::RouteTable
  Properties:
    VpcId:
      Ref: letsPollVPC


letsPollDefaultPrivateRoute1:
  Type: AWS::EC2::Route
  Properties:
    RouteTableId:
      Ref: letsPollPrivateRouteTable1
    DestinationCidrBlock: 0.0.0.0/0
    NatGatewayId:
      Ref: letsPollVPCNatGateway


letsPollPrivateSubnet1RouteTableAssociation:
  Type: AWS::EC2::SubnetRouteTableAssociation
  Properties:
    RouteTableId:
      Ref: letsPollPrivateRouteTable1
    SubnetId:
      Ref: letsPollPrivateSubnet1

letsPollPrivateSubnet2RouteTableAssociation:
  Type: AWS::EC2::SubnetRouteTableAssociation
  Properties:
```

```
RouteTableId:
  Ref: letsPollPrivateRouteTable1
SubnetId:
  Ref: letsPollPrivateSubnet2
```

A few points to note:

- We created two route tables: `letsPollPrivateRouteTable1` and `letsPollPrivateRouteTable2`
- We associated the two route tables to each of the private subnets we created
- We added two default routes in each of the route tables, enabling internet access from each of the private subnets

Security groups

Now that we have created the basic VPC structure, let's go ahead and create security groups. We need the following security groups:

- `lambdaSecurityGroup`: It should allow all outgoing traffic. This is to be attached to the lambda functions.
- `databaseSecurityGroup`: It should allow incoming traffic on port 5432 only from the `lambdaSecurityGroup` previously created.

Following code snippet shows the creation of the security groups:

```
lambdaSecurityGroup:
  Type: AWS::EC2::SecurityGroup
  Properties:
    GroupDescription: Security Group for Lambda
    VpcId:
      Ref: letsPollVPC
    Tags:
        - Key: Name
          Value: Lambda Security group


databaseSecurityGroup:
  Type: AWS::EC2::SecurityGroup
  Properties:
    GroupDescription: Security Group for database
    VpcId:
      Ref: letsPollVPC
    SecurityGroupIngress:
    - IpProtocol: tcp
      FromPort: 5432
```

```
            ToPort: 5432
            SourceSecurityGroupId:
              Ref: lambdaSecurityGroup
          Tags:
            - Key: Name
              Value: Database Security group
```

Now that we have seen how a VPC can be created using serverless framework, uncomment the reference to `/resource/vpc.yml` in the parent `serverless.yml` file and run the following command:

```
sls deploy --aws-profile=lets-poll-default
```

At this point of time, let's navigate to the console and check whether the resources we created from the serverless CLI are created. The following screenshot shows that the VPC and the public and private subnets are created properly, and hence we can deduce that the resources in `vpc.yml` are created successfully:

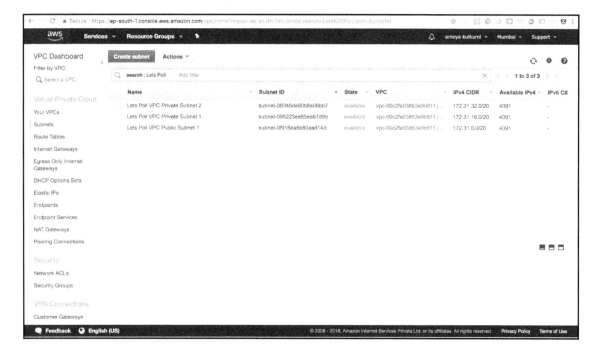

Provisioning IAM policies and roles for Lambda execution

In this section, let's provision the IAM policies and roles that are required to be assumed by Lambda for execution.

Execution role creation

The following are the contents of the `/resources/lambdaExectionRole.yml` file:

```
Resources:
  letsPollLambdaExecutionRole:
    Type: "AWS::IAM::Role"
    Properties:
      AssumeRolePolicyDocument:
        Version: "2012-10-17"
        Statement:
          -
            Effect: "Allow"
            Principal:
              Service:
                - "lambda.amazonaws.com"
            Action:
              - "sts:AssumeRole"
```

Please note, we create an execution role that allows the holder to assume the role to execute the `lambda.amazonaws.com` service.

Basic execution policy

The following are the contents of the `/resources/lambdaBasicExectionPolicy.yml` file:

```
Resources:
  letsPollLambdaBasicExecutionPolicy:
    Type: AWS::IAM::Policy
    Properties:
      PolicyName: "LetsPollLambdaBasicExecutionPolicy"
      PolicyDocument:
          Version: '2012-10-17'
          Statement:
          - Effect: Allow
            Action: logs:CreateLogGroup
            Resource:
```

```
arn:aws:logs:${self:provider.region}:#{AWS::AccountId}::*
            - Effect: Allow
              Action:
              - logs:CreateLogStream
              - logs:PutLogEvents
              Resource:
              - arn:aws:logs:162507129690:log-
group:/aws/lambda/${self:service.name}-${self:provider.stage}-logGroup:*
        Roles:
            -
              Ref: letsPollLambdaExecutionRole
```

A few things to note in the preceding code block:

- We created a policy that allows the basic actions that are required by a lambda function to run properly
- We referenced the AWS accountId by using the `#{AWS::AccountId}` syntax, which is made possible by the `serverless-cf-vars` plugin

VPC execution policy

The following are the contents of the `/resources/lambdaVpcPolicy.yml` file:

```
Resources:
  LambdaInVPCExecutionPolicy:
    Type: AWS::IAM::Policy
    Properties:
      PolicyName: "LambdaInVPCExecutionPolicy"
      PolicyDocument:
        Version: '2012-10-17'
        Statement:
        - Effect: Allow
          Action:
          - ec2:CreateNetworkInterface
          - ec2:DescribeNetworkInterfaces
          - ec2:DeleteNetworkInterface
          Resource: "*"
        Roles:
            -
              Ref: letsPollLambdaExecutionRole
```

Provisioning a Cognito user pool

In this section, let's have a look at how to provision a Cognito user pool. The code blocks in this section will reside in a file called `cognito.yml`, which will be referenced in the `serverless.yml` file:

```
Resources:
  CognitoUserPoolUserPool:
    Type: "AWS::Cognito::UserPool"
    Properties:
      UserPoolName: ${self:service}-user-pool-${self:provider.stage}-1
      AutoVerifiedAttributes:
        - email
```

Provisioning the KMS key

In this section, let's provision a key that will be used to encrypt environment variables supplied to Lambda. We have seen this in Chapter 7, *Secure Your Application*, where we created a key from the web console. The following code block shows us how to provision a KMS key using the serverless framework. The following are the contents of the `/resources/kms.yml` file:

```
Resources:
  letsPollKMSKey:
    Type: AWS::KMS::Key
    Properties:
      Description: "Key to aid in masking of environment variables used by
AWS Lambda Env Var"
      Tags:
        - Key: Name
          Value: Lets Poll CMK
      KeyPolicy:
        Version: "2012-10-17"
        Id: "Administrator Access to manage the key"
        Statement:
          -
            Sid: "Allow administration of the key"
            Effect: "Allow"
            Principal:
              AWS :
                Fn::Join:
                  - ""
                  - - "arn:aws:iam::"
                    - Ref: AWS::AccountId
                    - ":root"
```

```
Action:
  - "kms:Create*"
  - "kms:Describe*"
  - "kms:Enable*"
  - "kms:List*"
  - "kms:Put*"
  - "kms:Update*"
  - "kms:Revoke*"
  - "kms:Disable*"
  - "kms:Get*"
  - "kms:Delete*"
  - "kms:ScheduleKeyDeletion"
  - "kms:CancelKeyDeletion"
Resource: "*"


Sid: "Allow use of the key"
Effect: "Allow"
Principal:
  AWS :
    Fn::Join:
      - ""
      - - "arn:aws:iam::"
        - Ref: AWS::AccountId
        - ":role/"
        - Ref: letsPollLambdaExecutionRole
Action:
  - "kms:Encrypt"
  - "kms:Decrypt"
  - "kms:ReEncrypt*"
  - "kms:GenerateDataKey*"
  - "kms:DescribeKey"
Resource: "*"
```

There are a few points to note in the preceding code:

- We used `Fn::join` to derive the principle `arn:aws:iam::AccountId:root`. This way, we don't need to hardcode any accountId in the code. This policy grants administrative privilege to the root user to manage this key.
- Similarly, we used CloudFormation's `Fn::join` to derive the principal `arn:aws:iam::AccountId:role/<Arn_of_letsPollLambdaExecutionRole >`, which we provisioned in the `lambdaBasicExecutionRole.yml` file. This is a trick to reference ARNs of previously created resources. We gave this role access to the created key for using it to encrypt and decrypt the environment variables. This way, our lambda functions can access and use KMS.

The serverless framework doesn't support encrypting values encrypted by provisioning a key in the `sls deploy` life cycle. To achieve supplying encrypted environment variables to lambda, which can then be decrypted, we need to use the serverless-kms-secrets plugin. Using this plugin, we can encrypt values outside of the `sls deploy` life cycle, and they are available to supply to environment variables of lambda in the custom block of `serverless.yaml`.

Please refer to the documentation of the plugin for more details.

> In this exercise, we are not encrypting the environment variables. We are hiding them in environment variables of the machine where we are running the `sls deploy` command.

Provisioning RDS

Now that we have provisioned the VPC and the security groups, let's proceed to provision the RDS Cluster. The following code block goes in a new file, named `rds.yml`, which is in `resources/` of the root directory:

```
Resources:
 letsPollDBSubnetGroup:
 Type: AWS::RDS::DBSubnetGroup
 Properties:
 DBSubnetGroupDescription: "RDS Subnet Group"
 SubnetIds:
 - Ref: letsPollPrivateSubnet1
 - Ref: letsPollPrivateSubnet2
 letsPollDatabase:
 Type: "AWS::RDS::DBInstance"
 Properties:
 DBName: ${env:LP_DATABASE_NAME}"
 AllocatedStorage: 5
 DBInstanceClass: "db.t2.micro"
 Engine: "postgres"
 EngineVersion: "9.5.4"
 MasterUsername: ${env:LP_DATABASE_USERNAME}
 MasterUserPassword: ${env:LP_DATABASE_PASSWORD}
 VPCSecurityGroups:
 - "Fn::GetAtt": databaseSecurityGroup.GroupId
 DBSubnetGroupName:
 Ref: letsPollDBSubnetGroup
 Tags:
 -
```

```
Key: "Name"
Value: "LetsPollAPI"
DeletionPolicy: "Snapshot"
```

A few things to note in the preceding code base:

- We created `AWS::RDS::DBSubnetGroup` with the two private subnets that we had created in `vpc.yml`.
- We created `AWS::RDS::DBInstance` with the required configuration.
- We supplied `MasterUsername`, `MasterUserPassword`, and `DBName` as environment variables using the `${env:}` syntax. This is used to reference any environment variables as a serverless framework variable.

After this RDS is provisioned, it is launched in the private `letsPollPrivateSubnet1` and `letsPollPrivateSubnet2`, and hence it will not have any public accessibility. Also, note that this is a pristine instance so it doesn't have the schema structure that our application requires. The DDL commands have to be run either by a lambda function using a programmatic tool, such as Liquibase, or temporary enabling access for your network and running the DDL queries listed in `Chapter 3`, *Designing a Kotlin Serverless Application*, by hand. Please be sure to revert any networking tweaks that are done outside of the `sls deploy` life cycle.

Provisioning lambda functions

In this section, let's provision the lambda functions. Since we are deploying multiple lambda functions inside a single service, the functions have to be properly wired up by the handler property and the HTTP path property. Also, note that we are using the Lambda-Proxy integration of the API gateway.

Model definitions

First, let's define the models that we require the API gateway to receive. The following contents go in the `/resources/api/api.yml` file. With this, the serverless-aws-documentation plugin generates the models for use in the API gateway:

```
api:
  info:
    version: '2'
    title: Lets Poll API Documentation
    description: Documentation to support the Lets Poll API and
generate its models.
```

```
    tags:
      -
        name: Name
        description: Lets Poll API
# Now we describe all the models that we use
models:
  -
    name: Poll
    contentType: "application/json"
    schema :
        type: "object"
        required:
        - "pollOptions"
        - "pollQuestion"
        - "pollTitle"
        properties:
          pollId:
            type: "string"
          pollTitle:
            type: "string"
          pollQuestion:
            type: "string"
          pollOptions:
            type: "array"
            items:
                type: "string"


  -

    name: Polls
    contentType: "application/json"
    schema:
      type: "object"
      properties:
        polls:
          type: "array"
          items:
            $ref: "{{model: Poll}}"
  -
    name: PollCreationRequest
    contentType: "application/json"
    schema:
      type: "object"
      required:
      - "createdBy"
      - "pollQuestion"
      - "pollTitle"
      properties:
        pollTitle:
```

```
            type: "string"
          pollQuestion:
            type: "string"
          createdBy:
            type: "string"
  -
    name: PollResponseRequest
    contentType: "application/json"
    schema:
      type: "object"
      required:
      - "pollResponse"
      - "pollId"
      - "respondentId"
      properties:
        pollId:
          type: "string"
        pollResponse:
          type: "string"
        respondentId:
          type: "string"
  -
    name: PollResponseResponse
    contentType: "application/json"
    schema:
      type: "object"
      properties:
        message:
          type: "string"

  -
    name: PollResponseStatistics
    contentType: "application/json"
    schema:
      type: "object"
      properties:
        response:
          type: "string"
        count:
          type: "integer"
        percentage:
          type: "number"
  -
    name: PollResponsesResultResponse
    contentType: "application/json"
    schema:
      type: "object"
      properties:
```

```
          pollId:
            type: "string"
          pollTitle:
            type: "string"
          pollQuestion:
            type: "string"
          responses:
            type: "array"
            items:
              #$ref: "#/definitions/PollResponseStatistics"
              $ref: "{{model: PollResponseStatistics}}"


  name: Polls
  contentType: "application/json"
  schema:
    type: "object"
    properties:
      polls:
        type: "array"
        items:
          $ref: "{{model: Poll}}"


  name: RespondentRegistrationRequest
  contentType: "application/json"
  schema:
    type: "object"
    required:
      - "token"
      - "emailId"
      - "displayName"
    properties:
      token:
        type: "string"
      emailId:
        type: "string"
      displayName:
        type: "string"

  name: RespondentRegistrationResponse
  contentType: "application/json"
  schema:
    type: "object"
    properties:
      letsPollRespondentId:
        type: "string"
```

```
  -
    name: RespondentDetails
    contentType: "application/json"
    schema:
      type: "object"
      properties:
        respondentDisplayName:
          type: "string"
        respondentEmail:
          type: "string"

  -
    name: PollDetails
    contentType: "application/json"
    schema:
      type: "object"
      properties:
        createdBy:
          type: "object"
          $ref: "{{model: RespondentDetails}}"
        poll:
          type: "object"
          $ref: "{{model: Poll}}"
        statistics:
          type: "array"
          $ref: "{{model: PollResponseStatistics}}"
```

API gateway Validation

As seen in `Chapter 3`, *Designing a Kotlin Serverless Application*, API gateway has a mechanism to wire up request validations so that an incorrect payload is not passed down to lambda. We saw then how we could wire it up with the Web console. In the serverless framework, we need to specify this programatically. For this, we will use the `serverless-req-validator` plugin.

Installing the request validator plugin

To install the request validator plugin, run the following command:

```
npm install serverless-reqvalidator-plugin
```

Usage of the plugin

The following are the contents of the resource/api/apiValidator.yml file:

```
Resources:
  requestBodyValidator:
    Type: AWS::ApiGateway::RequestValidator
    Properties:
      Name: 'lets-poll-api-request-body-validator'
      RestApiId:
        Ref: ApiGatewayRestApi
      ValidateRequestBody: true
      ValidateRequestParameters: false
  requestParmaterValidator:
    Type: AWS::ApiGateway::RequestValidator
    Properties:
      Name: 'lets-poll-api-request-parameters-validator'
      RestApiId:
        Ref: ApiGatewayRestApi
      ValidateRequestBody: false
      ValidateRequestParameters: true
```

A few things to note in the preceding code:

- We define a AWS::APIGateway::RequestValidator resource named requestBodyValidator by using CloudFormation syntax. This will be used to validate the request body for the API receiving it. The request body will have to conform to the models provisioned by the serverless-aws-documentation plugin.
- We define a AWS::APIGateway::RequestValidator resource named requestParameterValidator by using CloudFormation syntax. This will be used to validate the request parameters for the APIs who expect appropriate parameters present in the URL.
- We attach this to the APIGatewayRestApi.

Integration of the validators

The validators are integrated with APIs by supplying value to the `reqValidatorName` key in the `.yml` definitions of the functions. This will be seen when we have a look at the function definitions.

Lambda to Register a Respondent

The following are the contents of the `/resource/functions/respondentRegistrer.yml` file:

```
respondentRegistrer:
  handler:
com.packt.serverless.kotlin.letspoll.handlers.RespondentRegistrer
    environment:
      databaseUsername: ${env:LP_DATABASE_USERNAME}
      databasePassword: ${env:LP_DATABASE_PASSWORD}
      databaseUrl: { Fn::GetAtt: [ "letsPollDatabase", "Endpoint.Address" ] }
      databasePort: ${env:LP_DATABASE_PORT}
      databaseName: ${env:LP_DATABASE_NAME}
    events:
    - http:
        path: /respondent/
        method: POST
        cors: true
        private: true
        reqValidatorName: requestBodyValidator
        documentation:
          summary: Registers a respondent
          requestBody:
            description: "Request body description"
          requestModels:
            "application/json": "RespondentRegistrationRequest"
          methodResponses:
            -
              statusCode: '200'
              responseModels:
                "application/json": "RespondentRegistrationResponse"
```

A few things to note in the preceding code block:

- The handler function is called `PollGetter`, which is defined in the `com.packt.serverless.kotlin.letspoll.handlers` package.
- Environment variables supplied to the Lambda are as follows:
    - `LP_DATABASE_USERNAME`: The database username
    - `LP_DATABASE_PASSWORD`: The database password
    - `LP_DATABASE_URL`: The database URL sourced by referencing CloudFormation's `GetAtt` function of the `letsPollDatabase` resource, and getting the `Endpoint.Address` attribute
    - `LP_DATABASE_PORT`: The database port
    - `LP_DATABASE_NAME`: The database name

- The path is `/respondent/`.
- The HTTP Method is `POST`.
- CORS is enabled.
- The private is set to true so this API will be protected by the API key that we set up in the provider section.
- We attach the request validator, `requestBodyValidator`, which validates the body by supplying this value to `reqValidatorName` key.
- MethodRequest is of the `RespondentRegistrationRequest` model type, which is defined in `/resources/api/api.yml`.
- Method Response is of the `RespondentRegistrationResponse` model type, which is defined in `/resources/api/api.yml`.

Lambda to fetch all polls

Following are the contents of the `/resources/functions/pollsGetter.yml` file:

```
pollsGetter:
  handler: com.packt.serverless.kotlin.letspoll.handlers.PollsGetter
  environment:
    databaseUsername: ${env:LP_DATABASE_USERNAME}
    databasePassword: ${env:LP_DATABASE_PASSWORD}
    databaseUrl: { Fn::GetAtt: [ "letsPollDatabase", "Endpoint.Address" ] }
    databasePort: ${env:LP_DATABASE_PORT}
    databaseName: ${env:LP_DATABASE_NAME}
  events:
    - http:
```

```
path: /polls/
method: get
cors: true
private: true
documentation:
  summary: Gets all Polls
  tags:
    - Tag1
  description: >
    Gets a List of All polls
  methodResponses:
    - statusCode: '200'
      responseModels:
        "application/json": "Polls"
    - statusCode: '404'
      responseModels:
        "application/json": "APIErrorResponseWithMessage"
```

A few things to note in the preceding code block:

- The handler function is called `PollGetter`, which is defined in the `com.packt.serverless.kotlin.letspoll.handlers` package.
- Environment variables supplied to Lambda are as follows:
  - `LP_DATABASE_USERNAME`: The database username
  - `LP_DATABASE_PASSWORD`: The database password
  - `LP_DATABASE_URL`: The database URL sourced by referencing CloudFormation's GetAtt function of the `letsPollDatabase` resource, and getting the `Endpoint.Address` attribute
  - `LP_DATABASE_PORT`: The database port
  - `LP_DATABASE_NAME`: The database name
- The path is `/polls`.
- The HTTP Method is `GET`.
- CORS is enabled.
- The private is set to true, so this API will be protected by the API key that we set up in the provider section.
- Method Response is of the `Polls` model type, which is defined in `/resources/api/api.yml`.

Lambda to create polls

Following are the contents of `/resources/functions/pollCreator.yml` file:

```
pollCreator:
  handler: com.packt.serverless.kotlin.letspoll.handlers.PollCreator
  environment:
    databaseUsername: ${env:LP_DATABASE_USERNAME}
    databasePassword: ${env:LP_DATABASE_PASSWORD}
    databaseUrl: { Fn::GetAtt: [ "letsPollDatabase", "Endpoint.Address" ] }
    databasePort: ${env:LP_DATABASE_PORT}
    databaseName: ${env:LP_DATABASE_NAME}
  events:
    - http:
        path: /polls/
        method: POST
        cors: true
        private: true
        reqValidatorName: requestBodyValidator
        documentation:
          summary: Creates a Poll
          tags:
            - Name
          description: >
            Creates a Poll

          requestBody:
            description: "Request body description"
          requestModels:
            "application/json": "PollCreationRequest"

          methodResponses:
          - statusCode: '200'
            responseModels:
              "application/json": "Polls"

          - statusCode: '409'
            responseModels:
              "application/json": "APIErrorResponseWithMessage"
```

A few things to note in the preceding code block:

- The handler function is called `PollCreator`, which is defined in the `com.packt.serverless.kotlin.letspoll.handlers` package.
  - Environment variables supplied to the Lambda are as follows:
    - `LP_DATABASE_USERNAME`: The database username
    - `LP_DATABASE_PASSWORD`:The database password

- **LP_DATABASE_URL**: The database URL sourced by referencing CloudFormation's `GetAtt` function of the `letsPollDatabase` resource, and getting the `Endpoint.Address` attribute
  - **LP_DATABASE_PORT**: The database port
  - **LP_DATABASE_NAME**: The database name
- Path is `/polls/`.
- The private is set to true so this API will be protected by the API key that we set up in the provider section.
- Method is `POST`.
- We attach the request validator, `requestBodyValidator`, which validates the body by supplying this value to `reqValidatorName` key.
- Method Request is of the `PollCreationRequest` model type, which is defined in `/resources/api/api.yml`.
- Method Response is of `Poll` type if the HTTP code is `200`.
- Method Response is of `APIErrorResponseWithMessage` type when the HTTP code is `409`.

Lambda to delete a poll

Following are the contents of `/resources/functions/pollDeletor.yml` file:

```
pollDeletor:
  handler: com.packt.serverless.kotlin.letspoll.handlers.PollDeletor
  environment:
    databaseUsername: ${env:LP_DATABASE_USERNAME}
    databasePassword: ${env:LP_DATABASE_PASSWORD}
    databaseUrl: { Fn::GetAtt: [ "letsPollDatabase", "Endpoint.Address" ] }
    databasePort: ${env:LP_DATABASE_PORT}
    databaseName: ${env:LP_DATABASE_NAME}
  events:
  - http:
      path: /polls/{pollId}/
      method: DELETE
      cors: true
      private: true
      request:
        parameters:
          paths:
            pollId : true
      reqValidatorName: requestParmaterValidator
```

```
documentation:
  summary: Gets a single poll by Id
  tags:
  - Name
  description: >
    Deletes a Poll
  methodResponses:
  - statusCode: '200'
    responseModels:
      "application/json": "APISuccessResponseWithMessage"
  - statusCode: '409'
    responseModels:
      "application/json": "APIErrorResponseWithMessage"
```

A few things to note in the preceding code block:

- The handler function is called `PollDeletor`, which is defined in the `com.packt.serverless.kotlin.letspoll.handlers` package.
- Environment variables supplied to the Lambda are as follows:
    - `LP_DATABASE_USERNAME`: The database username.
    - `LP_DATABASE_PASSWORD`: The database password.
    - `LP_DATABASE_URL`: The database URL sourced by referencing CloudFormation's `GetAtt` function of the `letsPollDatabase` resource, and getting the `Endpoint.Address` attribute.
    - `LP_DATABASE_PORT`: The database port.
    - `LP_DATABASE_NAME`: The database name.
- Path is `/polls`.
- Method is `GET`.
- The private is set to true so this API will be protected by the API key that we set up in the provider section.
- Method Response is of the `Polls` model type, which is defined in `/resources/api/api.yml`.
- A `Lambda Authorizer` named `PollDeletorAuthorizer` can be configured for it; currently it is not enabled, but can be easily written. This can be used to authorise the execution of the `PollDeletor` lambda function.For example - `PollDeletor` should only be invoked if the user who is requesting for the deletion of the poll is the one who created that poll in the first place.

Lambda to fetch a poll

Following are the contents of `/resources/functions/pollGetter.yml` file:

```yaml
pollGetter:
  handler: com.packt.serverless.kotlin.letspoll.handlers.PollGetter
  environment:
    databaseUsername: ${env:LP_DATABASE_USERNAME}
    databasePassword: ${env:LP_DATABASE_PASSWORD}
    databaseUrl: { Fn::GetAtt: [ "letsPollDatabase", "Endpoint.Address" ] }
    databasePort: ${env:LP_DATABASE_PORT}
    databaseName: ${env:LP_DATABASE_NAME}
  events:
    - http:
        path: /polls/{pollId}/
        method: GET
        cors: true
        private: true
        request:
          parameters:
            paths:
              pollId : true
        reqValidatorName: requestParmaterValidator
        documentation:
          summary: Gets a single poll by Id
          tags:
            - Name
          description: >
            Gets a Poll
          methodResponses:
            - statusCode: '200'
              responseModels:
                "application/json": "PollDetails"
            - statusCode: '404'
              responseModels:
                "application/json": "APIErrorResponseWithMessage"
            - statusCode: '409'
              responseModels:
                "application/json": "APIErrorResponseWithMessage"
```

A few things to note in the preceding code block:

- The handler function is called `PollGetter`, which is defined in the `com.serverless.letspoll.handlers` package

- Environment variables supplied to the Lambda are as follows:
    - `LP_DATABASE_USERNAME`: The database username
    - `LP_DATABASE_PASSWORD`: The database password
    - `LP_DATABASE_URL`: The database URL sourced by referencing CloudFormation's `GetAtt` function of the `letsPollDatabase` resource, and getting the `Endpoint.Address` attribute
    - `LP_DATABASE_PORT`: The database port
    - `LP_DATABASE_NAME`: The database name
- Path is `/polls`.
- Method is `GET`.
- CORS is enabled.
- The private is set to true so this API will be protected by the API key that we set up in the provider section.
- We attach the request validator, `requestParameterValidator`, which validates the body by supplying this value to `reqValidatorName` key.
- Method Response is of the `PollsDetails` model type if the HTTP code is 200, which is defined in `/resources/api/api.yml`.
- Lambda to register poll results.

Lambda for responding to a poll

Following are the contents of `/resources/functions/pollResponder.yml` file:

```
pollsResponder:
  handler: com.packt.serverless.kotlin.letspoll.handlers.PollResponder
  environment:
    databaseUsername: ${env:LP_DATABASE_USERNAME}
    databasePassword: ${env:LP_DATABASE_PASSWORD}
    databaseUrl: { Fn::GetAtt: [ "letsPollDatabase", "Endpoint.Address" ] }
    databasePort: ${env:LP_DATABASE_PORT}
    databaseName: ${env:LP_DATABASE_NAME}
  events:
    - http:
        path: /response/
        method: POST
        cors: true
        private: true
        reqValidatorName: requestBodyValidator
        documentation:
```

```
summary: Responds to the poll
tags:
  - Name
description: >
  Records the response for a poll

requestBody:
  description: "Request body description"
requestModels:
  "application/json": "PollResponseRequest"


methodResponses:
  - statusCode: '200'
    responseModels:
      "application/json": "APISuccessResponseWithMessage"
```

A few things to note in the preceding code block:

- The handler function is called `pollResponder`, which is defined in the `com.packt,serverless.kotlin.letspoll.handlers` package.
- Environment variables supplied to the Lambda are as follows:
    - `LP_DATABASE_USERNAME`: The database username
    - `LP_DATABASE_PASSWORD`: The database password
    - `LP_DATABASE_URL`: The database URL sourced by referencing CloudFormation's `GetAtt` function of the `letsPollDatabase` resource, and getting the `Endpoint.Address` attribute
    - `LP_DATABASE_PORT`: The database port
    - `LP_DATABASE_NAME`: The database name
- Path is `/polls`.
- Method is `GET`.
- The private is set to true so this API will be protected by the API key that we set up in the provider section.
- Method Request is `PollResponseRequest`.
- Method Response is of the `PollResponseResponse` model type, which is defined in `/resources/api/api.yml`.

Lambda to migrate the database

As we have seen in Chapter 3, *Designing a Kotlin Serverless Application*, we are using Liquibase to migrate the database. Also, note that the RDS instance that we created now is in a private subnet in a VPC, and hence does not have any public accessibility. We therefore create a lambda function that can migrate the database. Its configuration is found in /resources/functions/databaseMigrator.yml.

The contents of this are as follows:

```yaml
databaseMigrator:
  handler: com.packt.serverless.kotlin.letspoll.handlers.DatabaseMigrator
  environment:
    databaseUsername: ${env:LP_DATABASE_USERNAME}
    databasePassword: ${env:LP_DATABASE_PASSWORD}
    databaseUrl: { Fn::GetAtt: [ "letsPollDatabase", "Endpoint.Address" ] }
    databasePort: ${env:LP_DATABASE_PORT}
    databaseName: ${env:LP_DATABASE_NAME}
  events:
  - http:
      path: /migrations
      method: POST
      timeout: 60
      cors: true
      private: true
      documentation:
        summary: Migrates a database
        tags:
        - Name
        description: >
          To migrate the database running in a VPC
        methodResponses:
        - statusCode: '200'
          responseModels:
            "application/json": "APISuccessResponseWithMessage"
        - statusCode: '409'
          responseModels:
            "application/json": "APIErrorResponseWithMessage"
```

To migrate the database, the following API needs to be invoked by the HTTP method, GET:

```
curl https://API_BASE_URL/STAGE/migrations
```

Lambda to fix the database migrations

The way Liquibase works is by making an entry into the DATABASECHANGELOGLOCK table when it starts to migrate a database. If the migration fails, sometimes this lock is not released. In such a case, we need to explicitly truncate that table. We have written a lambda that does just that for you. Its configuration is found in /resources/functions/databaseMigratorFixer.yml:

```
databaseMigratorFixer:
  handler:
com.packt.serverless.kotlin.letspoll.handlers.DatabaseMigratorFixer
  environment:
    databaseUsername: ${env:LP_DATABASE_USERNAME}
    databasePassword: ${env:LP_DATABASE_PASSWORD}
    databaseUrl: { Fn::GetAtt: [ "letsPollDatabase", "Endpoint.Address" ] }
    databasePort: ${env:LP_DATABASE_PORT}
    databaseName: ${env:LP_DATABASE_NAME}
  events:
  - http:
      path: /migrations
      method: DELETE
      timeout: 60
      cors: true
      private: true
      documentation:
        summary: Migrates a database
        tags:
        - Name
        description: >
          To fix the database changelog lock
        methodResponses:
        - statusCode: '200'
          responseModels:
            "application/json": "APISuccessResponseWithMessage"
        - statusCode: '409'
          responseModels:
            "application/json": "APIErrorResponseWithMessage"
```

To fix the database if the migrations get locked, the following API needs to be invoked with the HTTP method as DELETE:

```
curl -X DELETE https://API_BASE_URL/STAGE/migrations
```

Let's verify the creation of the API by logging into the console and listing the API gateway in the **ap-south-1** region:

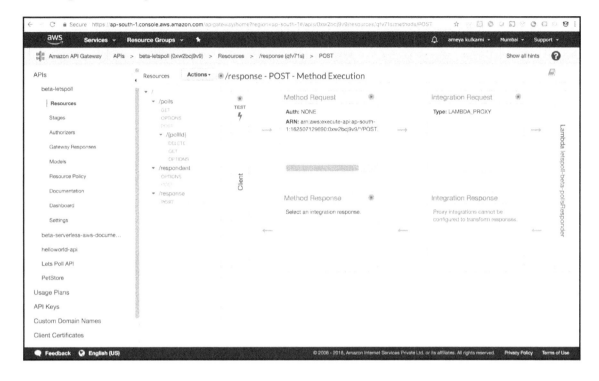

At this point, we have the Lets Poll API deployed using the serverless framework.

Caveats while scaling Serverless applications

There are a few things that need to be kept in mind when dealing with scaling Serverless applications. In this section, let's have a brief glance at some of them.

Lambda execution life cycle

In order to understand the challenges and subsequently the workaround to scale lambda functions, we need to understand how a lambda function gets executed.

As discussed in `Chapter 2`, *AWS Serverless Offerings*, an invocation of the lambda function takes place in a sandbox on an Amazon Linux AMI machine. The details on how and where this sandbox is provisioned and configured is left to Amazon's discretion. The sandbox provisioning for lambda involves the following steps:

1. Provisioning of a Sandbox
2. Copying of the distributable package to the sandbox
3. Runtime (JRE) startup and ClassLoading

The preceding steps are to be done every time a lambda function is to be invoked in a pristine Sandbox. This bootstrap of a pristine Sandbox takes anywhere between 100-200 ms. Since Lambda is an ephemeral concept, after a fixed time interval, this sandbox is reclaimed. For for the next invocation of the same function, a potential new Sandbox might get provisioned. So, potentially, if we are not cognizant of this implementation detail, we add anywhere between 100 to 200 ms to the time that is taken by the actual business logic to get executed. But, a Sandbox that is already provisioned and that has had the bootstrapping work done can be used to serve the next invocation of a function, provided the time between executions is not much. The orchestration (selection of a Sandbox) is left to AWS' discretion and there is no deterministic way to know whether a previously used Sandbox can be allocated for the second invocation of a particular function. But, empirically it has been observed that if the duration between invocations is less and if there are no code changes, then a Lambda sandbox will be reused almost always.

The Sandbox reuse is called the warm execution of a Lambda function. It means that anything that is declared outside of the handler function is available for reuse in the next invocation, should the same sandbox be chosen to fulfill the subsequent invocation. The warm execution of Lambdas gets the startup time from 100-200 ms to 10-20 ms, which is a 10x reduction.

Workarounds for scaling lambda functions

The following are the best practices while building out a Lambda function that scales well:

- Avoid cold starts by leveraging the freeze and thaw cycle of Lambda.
- Declare reusable variables outside of the handler function. We have seen this in the previous exercise, where we initialized the database connection. RDBMS connection-establishment is an expensive activity; connection pooling is a way to shave some cost off it. Freezing and Thawing RDBMS connections is a way of doing connection pooling in Lambda. Please bear in mind that this might lead to database connections being swamped if the number of warm executions equals the number of database connections available. So, there has to be a way of keeping track of connection objects and reclaiming them periodically.
- Keep Lambda functions warm by setting up a periodic invocation with dummy data. This will greatly improve the chances of container reuse.
- Rethink the Data layer.
- There are recommendations that say RDBMS is not an ideal choice for a data layer backing ephemeral Lambda functions. Their recommendations say that instead of RDS, DyanamoDB should be used as a data layer. It is a fact that DynamoDB is optimized for Lambda, but like Donald Knuth says, *Premature optimization is the root of all evil*. An informed decision has to be taken when switching out the data layer. Some of the DynamoDB caveats are its learning curve, utilization cost, vendor lock-in, and nascent state, as compared to decades-old RDBMS. If one can negotiate the caveats properly, DynamoDB is an excellent choice for the data layer.
- In the case of JVM-based lambda functions, class-loading is an expensive activity. This is acutely felt in cold starts of the Lambda function. So, the recommendation is to keep the number of dependencies in the deployment package to a minimum. A lesser number of dependencies means a lesser number of class files to load, and hence the class loading will be faster.
- Leverage AWS SQS or SNS as Dead Letter Queues in case of failures of lambda functions. In case of lambda failures, messages can be pushed to these topics to be picked up by a retrier service, typically built using AWS Step functions.

- Serverless Framework uses CloudFormation under the hood to provision AWS resources. A single service, such as the one we saw, corresponds to one CloudFormation stack. There is a hard limit for the number of resources that are present in a single stack:200. This is a limit that needs to be kept in mind because it can be hit pretty soon. To work around this, it's recommended to break down the service into sub-services, each having their own CF stack, or use different AWS account for different environments in conjunction with a multi-stack architecture.

Summary

In this chapter, we saw the basics of Infrastructure as Code and how it aids in scaling. We briefly looked at the Serverless Framework and retrofitted it in the LetsPollAPI app. With this, we saw how easy it is to provision a new environment for the code in minutes. We also looked at the caveats and challenges of scaling a serverless application, and saw some of the remediation for it.

In the next chapter, we will explore some advanced AWS Services, such as Cloud9, and write an Alexa skill that will enhance our system.

Advanced AWS Services

The last eight chapters gave us a good insight into what Serverless architectures are and how they can be designed, developed, secured, and scaled on a mature cloud provider, such as AWS. We also saw how a third-party orchestration tool such as the Serverless Framework can be used to provision these Serverless architectures. It is obvious by now that AWS is more than just a cloud provider. It offers various services that can be used by the developer to create solutions delivering newer experiences to the end user. AWS keeps on adding new offerings to their already vast repertoire, and strives not only to better the quality of the user experience but also to enrich the developer's experience when creating them.

In this chapter, we will have a look at the following:

- AWS Cloud9
- AWS Alexa

We will also walk through the creation of a simple Alexa skill that can be invoked by the user and that returns information about the stack and the technical architecture of the Lets Poll system that we created.

AWS Cloud9

In this section, let's have a look at the basics of AWS Cloud9.

Introduction to Cloud9

AWS Cloud9 is a tool chain that enables developers to develop, test, debug, and release their software in the cloud. It provides an **Integrated Development Environment** (**IDE**) that can be accessed via the web browser. The Cloud9 IDE is feature-rich and offers the same level of experience and customizability that some of the offline editors, such as Atom and Sublime Text, offer. Since the development occurs near to where it is intended to run (in the cloud), it feels like a natural fit in the developer tool chain. With Cloud9, you can compute heavy development environments and pay just a fraction of the cost. All the user needs is a local machine, which can be significantly lower in configuration than the Cloud9 environment with a good internet speed and a modern browser. In this age, this setup is easily and cheaply procured.

How does it work?

Cloud9 works on a concept of the environment as a place where you store a project's files and where the tool chain gets executed when developing the app.

Cloud9 offers two environments:

- **EC2 environment**: An EC2 instance is spun up and its life cycle is automatically managed by Cloud9. It runs on Amazon Linux, and usually comes with almost all the modern tools installed that are required to develop a modern application.
- **SSH environment**: You use an existing, or another cloud provider's, cloud instance instead of using AWS EC2. There has to be some configuration done to get Cloud9 working with this environment. The responsibility of installing the companion tool chain lies with us.

Getting started

In this section, let's have a look at creating a Cloud9 environment.

Prerequisites

The following are the prerequisites for getting started with AWS Cloud9:

- An AWS account
- IAM user with console access

Setting up an EC2 environment

To set up an EC2 environment, navigate to the AWS Cloud9 dashboard from the landing page of AWS. The following screenshot shows the landing page of Cloud9:

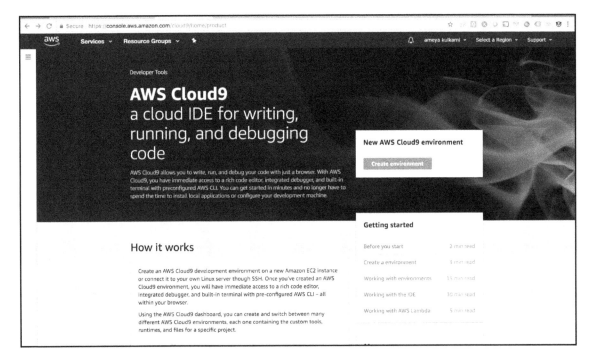

After landing on the dashboard of Cloud9, click on **Create environment**, which navigates you to the configuration screen:

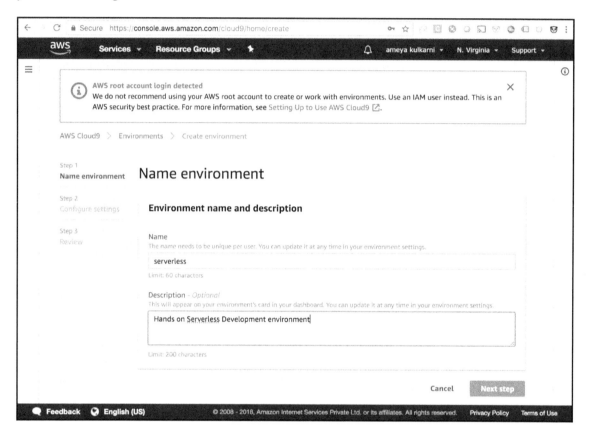

The next step of configuring the environment is to supply the details of the environment. We choose to create a new EC2 instance for this environment. Had we wanted to spin up a new SSH environment, we would have selected the **Connect** and run in remote server (SSH) option. We are also presented with an option of selecting the instance type. We select `c4.large instance type` for the purpose of this demo, but this shows the level of flexibility that we can have while configuring a development environment. Imagine the cost and the logistical steps that would have had to be taken when procuring such development environments in a physical form.

The IAM role that Cloud9 assumes is `AWSServiceRoleForAWSCloud9`. With this role, your Cloud9 development environment can call and access other AWS Services which the application requires to consume.

The following screenshot shows the details:

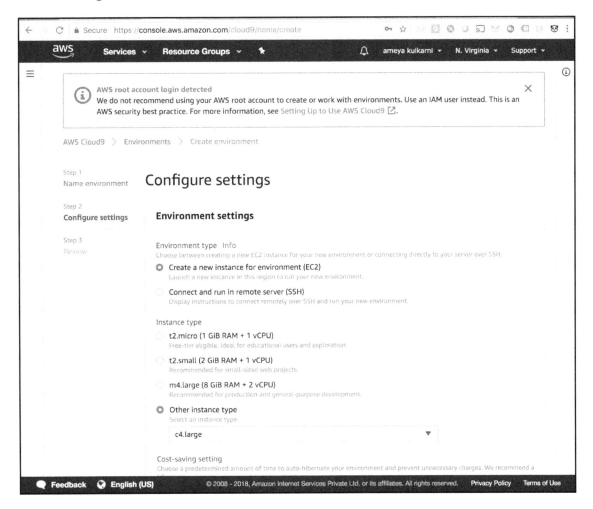

The next piece of the configuration is to select the VPC that this environment and the server will run on. We select the default for now, but you can choose the VPC that has got the proper network access configured:

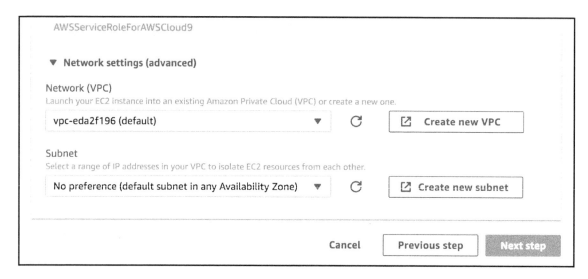

Clicking on **Next step**, we land on the review page:

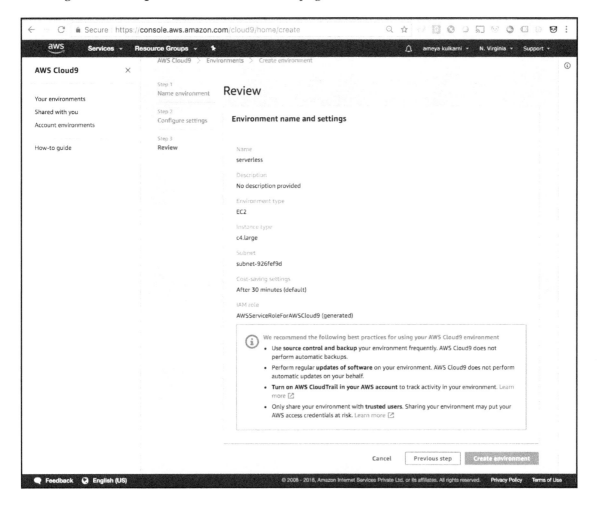

After clicking on **Create environment**, we are navigated to the loading page when the environment is being created:

And after the environment is ready, we land on the actual IDE. We also get a terminal in the bottom section of the screen, which we can use to run various commands. The environment comes bundled with commonly used developer tools and hence Git is installed. We will clone the repository for the book, which is `https://github.com/ PacktPublishing/-Hands-On-Serverless-with-Kotlin`, with the following command in the terminal:

```
$ git clone
https://github.com/PacktPublishing/-Hands-On-Serverless-with-Kotlin
```

The following screenshot shows the state after the repository is cloned:

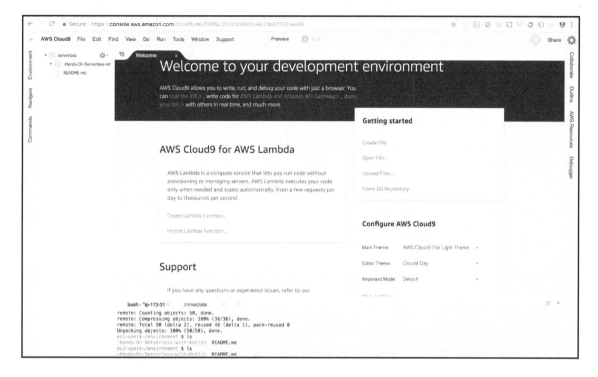

Best practices

The following are the best practices when creating and working with environments in Cloud9:

- Use source control and back up your environment frequently.
- Perform regular updates of software on your environment.
- Turn on AWS CloudTrail in your AWS account to track activity in your environment.
- Only share your environment with trusted users. Sharing your environment may put your AWS access credentials at risk.

Usage patterns

Typically the following usage patterns can be seen with Cloud9:

- Individual User
- Team setup with Blanket Access controls
- Team Setup with Granular Access controls

The source code for this can be managed by any version-control system, such as GitHub.

In a multideveloper environment, care has to be taken to set up the access controls properly in order to limit the costs incurred. The detailed steps are mentioned on the official documentation, which is linked in the preceding list of usage patterns.

There is a configurable auto-hibernate time setting, after which the EC2 instance is shut down. This is done to avoid running costs incurred when a developer is not using the environment.

Environments can be used as sandboxes or by sharing them among peer developers. The list of environments is available in the Cloud9 dashboard (`https://console.aws.amazon.com/cloud9/home`). Clicking on **Open IDE** opens up the IDE in the browser:

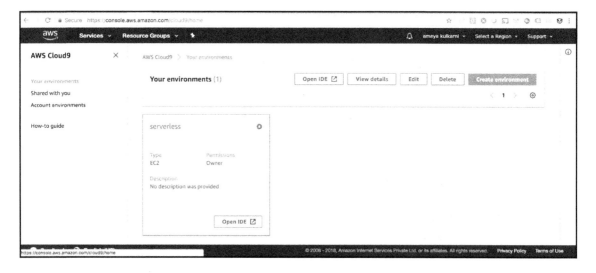

Supported languages

As explained, Cloud9 comes with an Integrated Development Environment. The languages supported here are:

- C++
- C#
- CoffeeScript
- CSS
- Dart
- Go
- Haskell
- HTML
- Java
- JavaScript
- Node.js
- PHP
- Python
- Ruby
- Shell script

Please keep an eye on the official documentation (`https://docs.aws.amazon.com/cloud9/latest/user-guide/language-support.html`) for any newly added languages.

 Unfortunately, Cloud9 currently doesn't support Kotlin in the IDE. So for the rest of the exercise, we will write code in Java that is 100% interoperable with Kotlin.

Practical walk-through of authoring the lambda function in Cloud9

In this section, let's have a practical walkthrough of creating a lambda function triggered by an API gateway in Cloud9. There are a few caveats to this:

- We will create a Node.js function using the wizard. We are not using Java/Kotlin since the main aim of this section is to get familiar with the Cloud9 environment. The wizard currently provides templates for Python and Node.js only.

- We will run the functions locally.
- We will deploy the lambda functions using the IDE and verify the companion API gateway creation.
- Developing lambda functions using Cloud9 uses the **Serverless Application Model** (**SAM**) (as opposed to the Serverless Framework that we saw in *Chapter 8, Scale Your Application*) under the hood. Readers with experience with SAM can proceed to create lambda functions in Java or any other Cloud9-supported language, and author `template.yaml` themselves and then deploy it using the IDE.

To create a lambda function from the template, the Cloud9 IDE provides a wizard that can be accessed from the toolbar on the far-right side of the IDE, named **AWS Resources**. Clicking on the tab will yield a navigation panel on the right side of the screen with the lambda functions that are present. To create a new lambda function, you have to click on the λ symbol (highlighted in orange). The following screenshot shows the details:

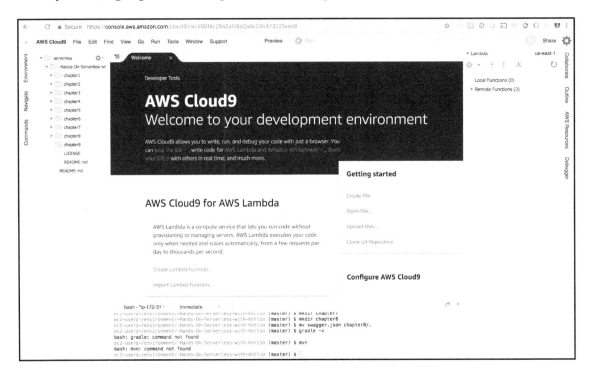

When you click on the λ, a popup is shown where you are prompted to enter the lambda function name and the application name. The application name creates a folder for the function, and the function name creates a function. As mentioned in the notes, Cloud9 uses CloudFormation under the hood to create this function:

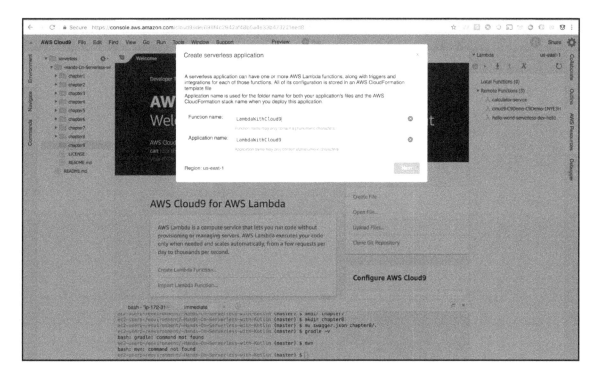

After clicking on **Next**, the wizard presents you with a list of blueprints to create the function from. We will select the **api-gateway-hello-world** template:

A Serverless application requires a trigger to invoke the lambda function on. For this exercise, we will select the API gateway as the trigger and the resource path will be /; that is, any call to this path will trigger the lambda function. We choose not to configure security for this API. Otherwise, an IAM role can be supplied to authorize this API:

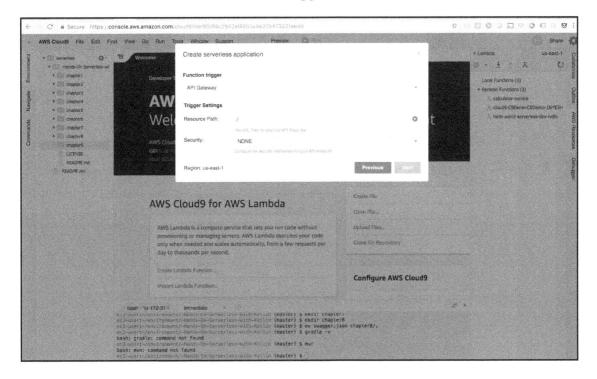

The next step in creating the Lambda function via Cloud9 is to supply the settings for the function. Cloud9 will create an IAM role automatically for us:

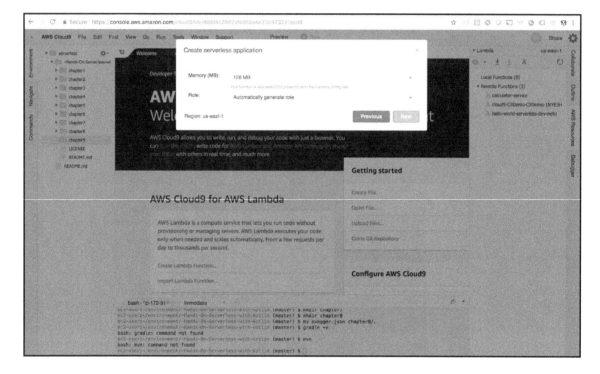

The last step before creating the function is to review the details of the function and the application:

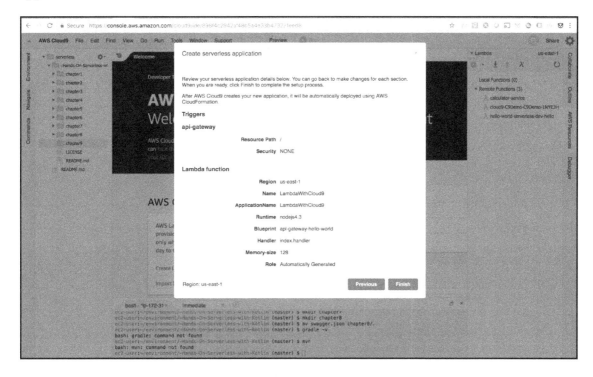

Clicking on **Finish** will yield the boilerplate code. The LambdaWithCloud9 folder has the code and a template.yaml file, which is the Serverless Application Model file:

```
AWSTemplateFormatVersion: '2010-09-09'
Transform: 'AWS::Serverless-2016-10-31'
Description: An AWS Serverless Specification template describing your
function.
Resources:
  LambdaWithCloud9:
    Type: 'AWS::Serverless::Function'
    Properties:
      Handler: LambdaWithCloud9/index.handler
      Runtime: nodejs4.3
      Description: ''
      MemorySize: 128
      Timeout: 15
      Events:
        LambdaMicroservice:
          Type: Api
```

```
        Properties:
          Path: /
          Method: ANY
  LambdaWithCloud9Permission:
    Type: 'AWS::Lambda::Permission'
    Properties:
      Action: 'lambda:InvokeFunction'
      FunctionName:
        'Fn::GetAtt':
          - LambdaWithCloud9
          - Arn
      Principal: apigateway.amazonaws.com
      SourceArn:
        'Fn::Sub': 'arn:aws:execute-
api:${AWS::Region}:${AWS::AccountId}:*/*/*/*'
```

The preceding file is the definition of a serverless application created using AWS SAM. This is another option to provision.

Also note the `LambdaWithCloud9` function gets listed under the local function in the navigation panel on the right side:

Cloud9 also gives us a mechanism to test the Lambda function locally. It is similar to configuring `Test Event` in the Lambda console and executing the function. The following screenshot shows how to set up the local testing in Cloud9:

We configure the payload that is passed to the handler. Clicking on **Run** will give the output under the **Execution Results** tab:

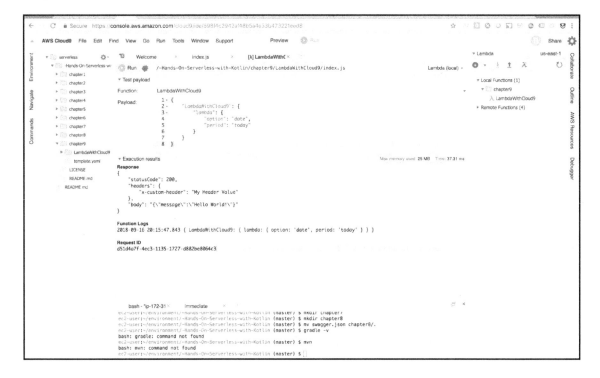

We can also deploy the lambda function and the accompanying API gateway, if there are
any changes, by right-clicking on **LambdaWithCloud9**:

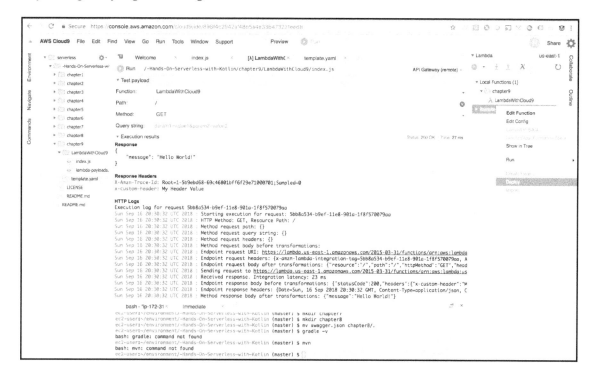

We can verify the creation of the API gateway by navigating to the API gateway console and checking that the API has indeed been created:

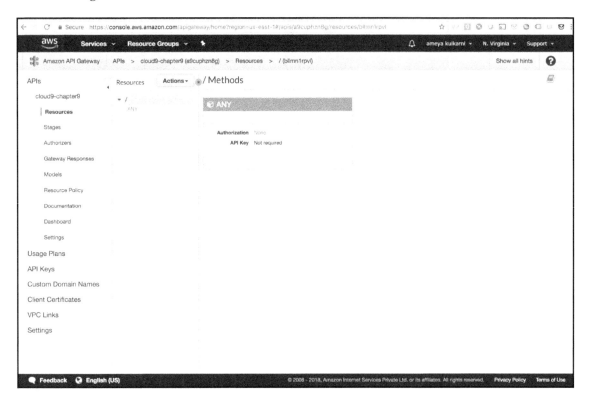

Use cases of Cloud9

Lets have a look at some of the use cases of Cloud9:

- **Develop applications in a sandboxed and securely controlled environment**: The necessary and sufficient requirement for a developer machine is a decent workstation with good internet speed and a modern browser.With Cloud9 environments, the need for the local developers to clone the code is eliminated. The source code lies in a secure and controlled environment so the possibility that fungible copies of the code are made is eliminated.

- **Faster development environment setup**: New team members can have their local development environments created in a jiffy and can be productive pretty soon. Cloud9 eliminates the need to maintain extensive documentation to set up environments and the associated tool chain.

- **Deeper integration**: Modern applications often depend on BaaS and other turnkey solutions in the cloud. Getting them to work on a local development environment is simply not possible. At times, interactions with such services often have to be mocked out, which impedes end-to-end integration testing. Because Cloud9 runs in the AWS ecosystem, it is deeply integrated with other services, enabling developers to perform the integration tests in the development cycle as opposed to in the QA or integration testing cycle.
- **Sharing of application previews**: With EC2 Cloud9 environments, developers can share their local work with other team members. This enables concurrent integration cycles as opposed to staggered integration cycles with upstream components.
- **Virtual private servers**: Cloud9 also enables developers to work with AWS LightSail, which is the virtual private server offering
- **Integration with continuous delivery pipelines**: Cloud9 enables developers to work with AWS CodeStar.

AWS Alexa

In this section, let's have a brief introduction to AWS Alexa and develop a basic skill for the LetsPoll application.

Introduction to Alexa

Alexa is the AWS service for voice processing, which allows intuitive and conversational interfaces to be built for users to interact with applications. Alexa is exposed to end users with proprietary Amazon hardware, such as Echo, Echo Dot, Sonos One, and Echo Plus, in addition to numerous partner devices. Alexa is powered by Amazon Lex, which is a service that marries **Automatic Speech Recognition** (**ASR**), which converts speech to test, and **Natural Language Understanding** (**NLU**), which detects the intent from the text that can be taken as an input to code that responds to that intent.

Building blocks

In this section, let's have a look at the building blocks for Alexa.

Skills

Alexa Skills are the functionalities or tasks that can be performed on voice commands as interpreted by Alexa. There are three types of skills:

- Flash Briefing Skill
- Custom Skill
- Smart Home Skill

Skills Kit

The Alexa Skills Kit is abbreviated and marketed as ASK—it is the tool chain consisting of APIs and boilerplate code samples that help a developer get started when creating an Alexa Skill.

Interaction model

The interaction model is the set of rules that govern how users' spoken request can be interpreted into a machine-understandable format, which then can be processed.

Invocations

Invocations are utterances that are used to invoke the skill. The invocations are typically captured by a hardware device, such as Echo Dot, and then relayed to the machinery that powers Alexa.

Intents

An intent represents a machine-understandable construct that encapsulates a user request for service, which they express via the invocation.

Slot types

Slots are the the arguments or placeholders that can optionally be present in an intent. They are used to multiplex the user's original request further.

Interfaces

Interfaces are the hardware with which Alexa Skills are exposed to the end user. In addition to Echo series there are various Alexa enabled devices that are being created and sold online.

Functional endpoints

Functional endpoints expose the business logic as an HTTP/S API. Functional endpoints consume the intents, slots that are distilled by Alexa, and output an action that can either be synthesized in speech or anything that can be piped to downstream APIs.

Account linking

For an Alexa skill to be useful, it is necessary that the functional endpoints know a bit about the end user who has invoked the skill. For example, a hypothetical food-delivery app exposing its ordering API as an Alexa skill needs to know the delivery location. For this reason, it needs to have some context of the user who is invoking it.

To solve this problem, there is the concept of account linking, where a user account is to be linked. This can be achieved in two ways by extending the OAuth2 framework's semantics of:

- Implicit grant
- Auth code grant

This requires some work to be done by the developer to expose an authorization server where a user identity can be captured while they are enabling the skill. A token that represents the user identity is issued and returned to the hardware interface that the user is using. This token is tied to that hardware and is passed down to the functional endpoint every time a skill is invoked.

Details about account linking can be found in official documentation (`https://developer.amazon.com/docs/account-linking/understand-account-linking.html`).

Walkthrough of creating a simple custom Alexa Skill

In this section, let's walk through creating a simple Alexa Skill that responds to the user intent to know more about the LetsPoll application architecture. There are two components for creating a skill:

- Defining the interaction model of the skill
- Supplying a lambda function to serve the skill

There are many aspects to designing and creating an Alexa Skill. It requires in-depth knowledge of how people speak in different parts of the world. A production-grade skill requires exhaustive study certification and compliance with respect to how the skill might be used by the users. This walkthrough only provides a starting point for developing a custom skill.

Problem statement

Create an Alexa skill that will be invoked by a user, which will give a detailed description of the LetsPoll APIs.

Sample invocations can be as follows:

- Ask LetsPoll, what its technical architecture is
- Ask LetsPoll about its technical stack
- Ask LetsPoll about its architecture

The action that is to be taken is to respond with a speech snippet that encapsulates the description of the LetsPoll architecture.

Creating a skill

In this section, let's have a look at how a custom Alexa Skill can be created.

Registration on Amazon Developer Console

The first step is to create an account on Amazon Developer Console (`https://developer.amazon.com/`).This should be created with the same root email ID that was used to set up the AWS account. Otherwise, a root user has to invite a user so that person can be added to the organization in the developer console. The sign-up is pretty straightforward. Once the account is created, signing in on the developer console lands us on the dashboard:

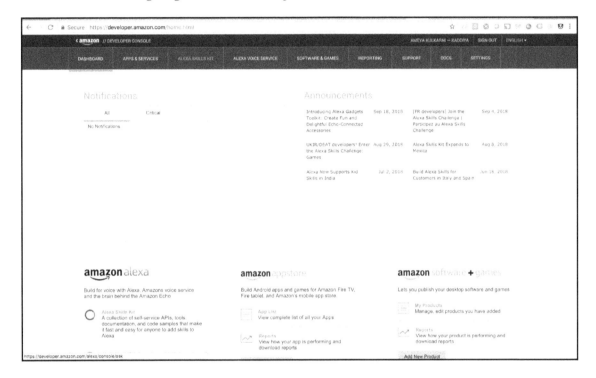

On clicking the **Alexa Skills Kit** tab, we are redirected to the skills kit dashboard:

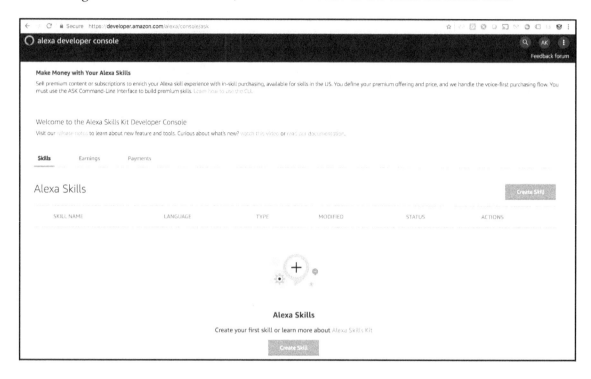

Naming a skill

On clicking **Create Skill**, we are navigated to the page where we can name and supply the basic details about the skill. We name our skill `Lets Poll` and use the template of `Custom Skill` to get started:

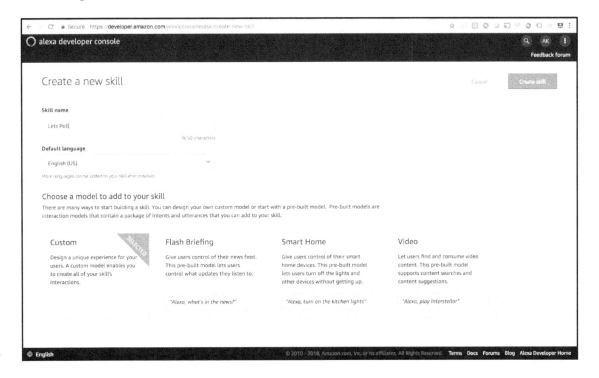

We are then presented with options to select a template to build the skill on. We choose to build the skill from scratch:

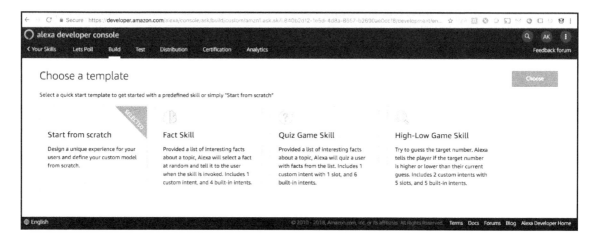

When the **Choose** button is pressed, we are navigated to the screen where we have to do the bulk of the configuration:

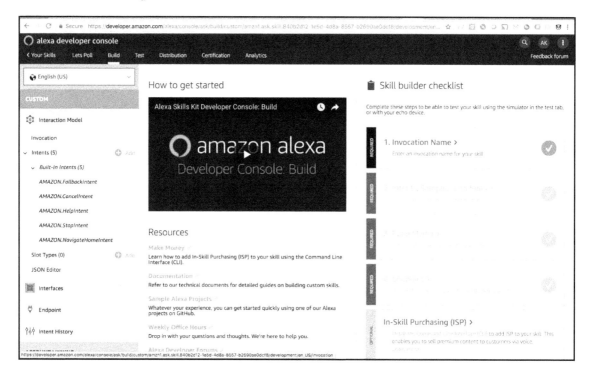

As shown in the preceding diagram, the template gives us the following things:

1. **Built-in intents:**
   - `AMAZON.FallbackIntent`: This is the intent resolved when Alexa can't match the invocation to any of the supplied intent
   - `AMAZON.CancelIntent`: This is the intent resolved when the user wants to cancel the current action requested by them
   - `AMAZON.HelpIntent`: This is the intent resolved when the user asks for help or guidance
   - `AMAZON.StopIntent`: This is the intent resolved when the user wants to stop the current action requested by them
   - `AMAZON.NavigateHomeIntent`: This is the intent resolved when the user asks for help to navigate home

2. **Checklist/wizard:**

   On the right-hand side, there is a checklist that we have to go through to create the skill. The following are the steps to do:

   - Define the invocation name
   - Define the intents, sample utterances, and slots
   - Build the model
   - Provide the functional endpoint

Optionally, we can configure an in-skill purchase mechanism that authorizes payments to be made like in-app purchases on mobile apps.

Defining invocations

The invocation of our Skill is the invocation name for our skill, which is `Lets Poll`. So the user needs to invoke this skill by saying something such as `Alexa, ask Lets Poll....`

Defining intents and utterances

Next, we need to create a custom intent. We name it `TechnicalArchitectureIntent`. This is what Alexa will map the user-spoken request to:

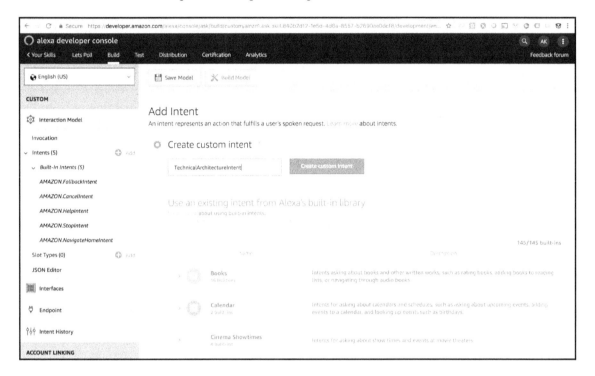

After clicking on **Create custom intent**, we need to supply the sample utterances that the user will speak that will help Alexa resolve `TechnicalArchitectureIntent`. We supply the following utterances:

- How it is built
- Technical details
- Stack
- Technical architecture

So a sample invocation that the user will have to say includes the following:

- Alexa, ask Lets Poll how it is built
- Alexa, ask Lets Poll about its technical architecture
- Alexa, ask Lets Poll about its stack
- Alexa, ask Lets Poll about its technical details

The following screenshot shows the creation of sample utterances:

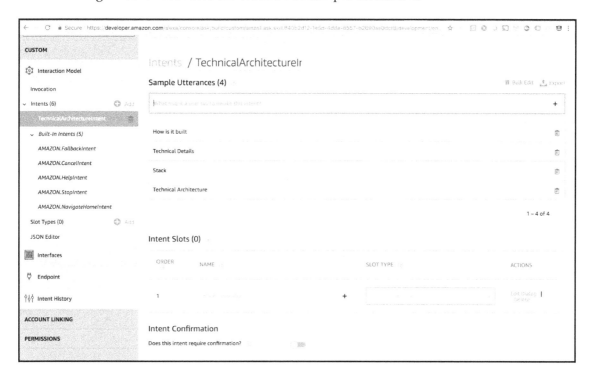

Linking the functional endpoint

Now we have to negotiate the tricky part to configure the functional endpoint. There are multiple parts to this.

First, click on **Functional Endpoint** and select the endpoint to be the **Lambda** function. We can also select an HTTPs endpoint, but that requires a fair bit of understanding of the working of Lambdas. After clicking on the Lambda radio button, we are presented with a skill ID. The **Skill ID** for this tutorial is `amzn1.ask.skill.840b2d12-1e5d-4d8a-8557-b2690ae0dcf8`. Make a note of it. Let's have a look at the following screenshot:

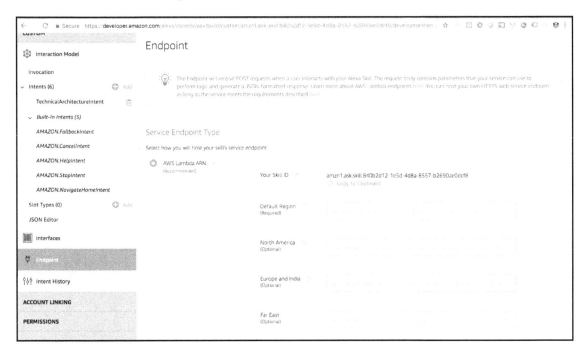

Also note that we are expected to supply a Lambda ARN. But a Lambda function doesn't exist. So we will have to create one; we will circle back to this step after we have set up a Lambda function.

Creating a Lambda function

We will be using Alexa Skills Kit SDK (`https://alexa-skills-kit-sdk-for-java.readthedocs.io/en/latest/`) for Java and we will author the skill in Java to create this functional endpoint. This has been a recent development that has made it even easier to create Alexa Skills using JVM languages. Till recently, developers had to implement the `com.amazon.speech.speechlet.SpeechletV2` interface while creating a Lambda function that became the functional endpoint for a skill. The skill's code developed in this way was pretty verbose. A sample implementation using this approach can be found `here`. Interested readers can go and check out the skill sample. After the Skill Kit SDK for Java was released, it became even easier to start creating skills in a more concise fashion. The migration guide from the previous version to the current version can be found at: `https://alexa-skills-kit-sdk-for-java.readthedocs.io/en/latest/Migrating-To-ASK-SDK-v2-For-Java.html`. One can understand the differences between the two approaches after reading the documentation.

To start with writing the skill function we need to set up a skeletal lambda function. Setting up a lambda function is fairly straightforward. In a directory run the following command:

```
sls create --template=aws-java-gradle --path  lets-poll-alexa-skill
```

With this, we will create a skeleton lambda function with Java and Gradle.

A few tweaks

The template generates a boilerplate code that needs some tweaks:

- Rename the package to
  `com.packt.serverless.kotlin.letspoll.alexaskill`
- Apart from the `Handler.java` class, delete the other classes

The build.gradle file

Following are the contents of the `build.gradle` file:

```
apply plugin: 'java'
apply plugin: 'idea'

repositories {
    mavenCentral()
}

sourceCompatibility = 1.8
targetCompatibility = 1.8
```

```
dependencies {
    compile (
        'com.amazonaws:aws-lambda-java-core:1.1.0',
        'com.amazonaws:aws-lambda-java-log4j:1.0.0',
        'com.fasterxml.jackson.core:jackson-core:2.8.5',
        'com.fasterxml.jackson.core:jackson-databind:2.8.5',
        'com.fasterxml.jackson.core:jackson-annotations:2.8.5',
        'com.amazon.alexa:ask-sdk:2.5.5'
    )
}

// Task for building the zip file for upload
task buildZip(type: Zip) {
    // Using the Zip API from gradle to build a zip file of all the
dependencies
    //
    // The path to this zip file can be set in the serverless.yml file for
the
    // package/artifact setting for deployment to the S3 bucket
    //
    // Link:
https://docs.gradle.org/current/dsl/org.gradle.api.tasks.bundling.Zip.html

    // set the base name of the zip file
    baseName = "lets-poll-alexa-skill"
    from compileJava
    from processResources
    into('lib') {
        from configurations.runtime
    }
}

build.dependsOn buildZip

task wrapper(type: Wrapper) {
    gradleVersion = '3.5'
}
```

A few points to notice about the preceding code:

- We added the dependency for the ASK SDK as `com.amazon.alexa:ask-sdk:2.5.5`
- We changed the name of the deployable package that is created as part of the build task to `lets-poll-alexa-skill`

Entrypoint handler function

First we will create the entrypoint to the Lambda function. The following are the contents of the `Handler.java` class that extends the `com.amazon.ask.SkillStreamHandler` abstract class. This class itself implements the `com.amazonaws.services.lambda.runtime.RequestStreamHandler` interface. Also notice how we supply `TechnicalArchitectureHandler` as the request handler for handling the intent. If the skill has multiple intents that require handling, the respective request handlers can be added accordingly:

```
package com.packt.serverless.kotlin.letspoll.alexaskill;


import com.amazon.ask.Skill;
import com.amazon.ask.SkillStreamHandler;
import com.amazon.ask.Skills;

public class Handler extends SkillStreamHandler {

 private static Skill getSkill() {
  return Skills.standard()
   .addRequestHandlers(new TechnicalArchitectureHandler())
   .build();
 }

 public Handler() {
  super(getSkill());
 }


}
```

Technical architecture handler

`TechnicalArchitectureHandler` is the request handler, which implements the `com.amazon.ask.dispatcher.request.handler.RequestHandler` interface. This class will handle `TechnicalArchitectureIntent` that we defined in the interaction model.

Notice the following things:

- The `canHandle()` method provides a way to let the caller know whether it can handle `TechnicalArchitectureIntent`
- The `handle()` method provides the actual request and builds out a speech response that is to be synthesized
- We registered this request handler in the `Handler` class in the previous section

Following is the relevant code -

```
package com.packt.serverless.kotlin.letspoll.alexaskill;


import com.amazon.ask.dispatcher.request.handler.HandlerInput;
import com.amazon.ask.dispatcher.request.handler.RequestHandler;
import com.amazon.ask.model.Response;


import java.util.Optional;

import static com.amazon.ask.request.Predicates.intentName;

public class TechnicalArchitectureHandler implements RequestHandler {

    @Override
    public boolean canHandle(HandlerInput input) {
        return input.matches(intentName("TechnicalArchitectureIntent"));
    }

    @Override
    public Optional<Response> handle(HandlerInput input) {
        String speechText = "Lets Poll is a serverless system powered by
AWS Lambda";
        return input.getResponseBuilder()
            .withSimpleCard("Technical Architecture", speechText)
            .withSpeech(speechText)
            .withShouldEndSession(true)
            .build();
    }

}
```

The serverless.yaml file

The following is the content of the `serverless.yaml` file:

```
service:
  name: lets-poll-alexa-skill



frameworkVersion: ">=1.0.0 <2.0.0"


provider:
  name: aws
  runtime: java8
  stage: ${opt:stage,'beta'} # Set the default stage used. Default is dev
  region: ${opt:region,'us-east-1'} # Overwrite the default region used.
Default is us-east-1
  profile: ${opt:profile,'lets-poll-default'}
package:
  artifact: build/distributions/lets-poll-alexa-skill.zip

functions:
  hello:
    handler: com.packt.serverless.kotlin.letspoll.alexaskill.Handler
    events:
    - alexaSkill: amzn1.ask.skill.840b2d12-1e5d-4d8a-8557-b2690ae0dcf8
```

There are a few points to be noted in the preceding code block:

- We supplied an Alexa Skill as `event to trigger this lambda function`. This will ensure that this lambda function will be called only by this skill ID and won't be open to the outside world. This is the skill ID that we noted in the previous sections.
- The deployable package is `lets-poll-alexa-skill.zip` that we configured in the `build.gradle`.

Building the lambda function

To build the lambda function use the following command:

```
./gradlew clean build
```

This will yield `build/distributions/lets-poll-alexa-skill.zip` as the deployment package.

Deploying the lambda function

At this point in time our Lambda handler to serve the skill is set to be deployed. We will deploy the function using the following command:

```
sls deploy --aws-profile=lets-poll-default
```

This lambda function will get deployed to the `us-east-1` region, which is a region supported for hosting Lambda functions that back Alexa Skills.

We need to find this ARN from `Lambda Console,` and now we are ready to go back to configuring the Alexa skill in the developer console.

Linking the Lambda to the Skill

Now that we have the ARN of the Lambda function to link to, let's go back to the Amazon Developer Console and finish linking the Alexa Skill.

Add the value of the ARN in the **Default Region** field. It is recommended that for fault tolerance and redundancy that we supply more than one Lambda function to serve the skill.For now we just supply the ARN of the function that we just provisioned.

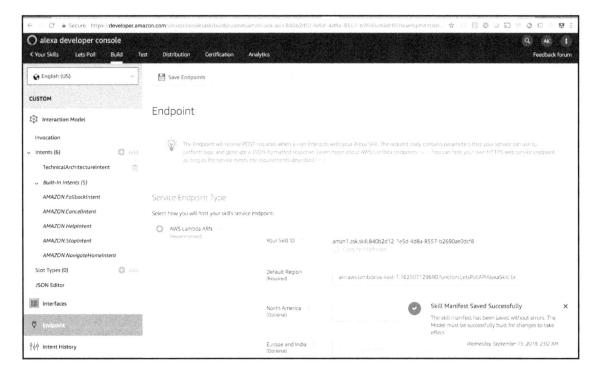

Testing

If everything was correctly deployed, we can test the skill. On the dashboard of the skill, there is a tab named **Test**. Clicking on it will navigate us to the testing screen. Note that the testing is disabled by default. The toggle has been switched to enable testing for the skill. There are various options to test the skill. The developer console provides a nifty way of simulating the Alexa companion hardware devices. It is called **Alexa Simulator**. Other options supply the JSON manually, which requires in-depth knowledge of the payload that is passed to the Alexa backend from the hardware. The following screenshot shows the details for an invocation. One needs to hold down the microphone button and utter the sample invocations.

The Alexa simulator accesses the microphone of the machine and intakes a spoken request that simulates a real-world invocation. Notice how the invocation phase, *Hey Alexa, ask letsPoll architecture* was synthesized from Speech using ASR and the `TechnicalArchitectureIntent` intent was proven to be derived from the JSON input box. Also notice the output that Alexa would have received:

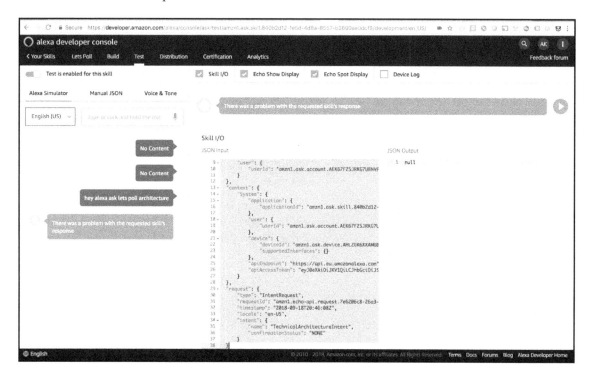

Applying the finishing touches

We now have a quick-and-dirty Alexa skill up and running. There are a few rough edges that need to be polished, which involve ensuring that the user doesn't get stuck in conversational limbo. Also, we need to pay attention to the design of the invocation and the sample utterances. When these finishing touches are done, the skill is ready to be distributed.

Distribution and certification

After the skill is tested, a distribution has to be created, and it has to undergo a strict certification that is subject to Amazon's approval. After these activities, the Skill is ready for the world to consume. The certifications and distribution activities are out of the scope of this book.

Summary

In this chapter, we saw some of the advanced AWS services, such as Cloud9 and Alexa. We saw how Cloud9 can be used to spin up a development environment on demand, and how the IDE can be used to develop and deploy Lambda functions. We also saw the basics of Alexa and how we can create a sample custom skill. Alexa skill design is a vast topic and an exhaustive study of its official developer guide is recommended. This was meant as a primer to get started with some of the advanced AWS services. The field of Serverless architectures sees innovations and improvements at a breakneck speed. Readers who have read this far are recommended to subscribe to the official announcements of the cloud providers and the frameworks to keep up to date with the developments.

Other Books You May Enjoy

If you enjoyed this book, you may be interested in these other books by Packt:

Kotlin Programming By Example
Iyanu Adelekan

ISBN: 9781-7-8847-454-2

- Learn the building blocks of the Kotlin programming language
- Develop powerful RESTful microservices for Android applications
- Create reactive Android applications efficiently
- Implement an MVC architecture pattern and dependency management using Kotlin
- Centralize, transform, and stash data with Logstash
- Secure applications using Spring Security
- Deploy Kotlin microservices to AWS and Android applications to the Play Store

Kotlin Programming Cookbook
Aanand Shekhar Roy

ISBN: 9781-7-8847-214-2

- Understand the basics and object-oriented concepts of Kotlin Programming
- Explore the full potential of collection frameworks in Kotlin
- Work with SQLite databases in Android, make network calls, and fetch data over a network
- Use Kotlin's Anko library for efficient and quick Android development
- Uncover some of the best features of Kotlin: Lambdas and Delegates
- Set up web service development environments, write servlets, and build RESTful services with Kotlin
- Learn how to write unit tests, integration tests, and instrumentation/acceptance tests.

Leave a review - let other readers know what you think

Please share your thoughts on this book with others by leaving a review on the site that you bought it from. If you purchased the book from Amazon, please leave us an honest review on this book's Amazon page. This is vital so that other potential readers can see and use your unbiased opinion to make purchasing decisions, we can understand what our customers think about our products, and our authors can see your feedback on the title that they have worked with Packt to create. It will only take a few minutes of your time, but is valuable to other potential customers, our authors, and Packt. Thank you!

Index

www.ingramcontent.com/pod-product-compliance
Lightning Source LLC
LaVergne TN
LVHW081513050326
832903LV00025B/1472